Community Living and Participation for People With Intellectual and Developmental Disabilities

Amy S. Hewitt and Kelly M. Nye-Lengerman,
Editors

Published by
American Association on Intellectual and Developmental Disabilities
www.aaidd.org

To order:
AAIDD Order Fulfillment
Phone: 202-387-1968 x 216
Email: books@aaidd.org
Online: http://aaidd.org/publications/bookstore-home

Product No. 4168
ISBN 978-0-9965068-9-2

Table of Contents

Development of this book was funded in part through Grant #90RT5019-01-01 to the Research and Training Center on Community Living and Grant #90RT5039-01-00 to the Research and Training Center on Home and Community Based Outcome Measurement by the National Institute on Disability, Independent Living, and Rehabilitation Research, U.S. Department of Health and Human Services, and through cooperative agreement #90DN0297 from the Administration on Community Living, U.S. Department of Health and Human Services. Grantees undertaking projects under government sponsorship are encouraged to express freely their findings and conclusions. Points of view or opinions do not therefore necessarily represent official NIDILRR or ACL policy.

Tables and Figures

Tables

Figures

Acknowledgments

We want to thank the individuals and families who told us their stories so that they could be included. These stories helped to ensure that the content in this book is highly connected to, and illustrative of, the lives of people with intellectual and developmental disabilities (IDD) who live in their communities. We appreciate their willingness to share.

We also want to thank the many provider, policy, and advocacy partners we have worked with over the years to better understand and promote community living for people with IDD. We know that our work is better because of our partnerships.

To the many colleagues with whom we work and to those who contributed to this book as chapter authors, thank you. We are also grateful to Jerry Smith for his work on the collection of personal illustrations found throughout the book. It was only possible to complete this undertaking because of your time and commitment to improving opportunities for community living for people with IDD.

Lastly, heartfelt thanks to our families (Brad, Amos, Jack and Dane) for their ongoing understanding and support of our careers.

Amy & Kelly

About the Authors

Brian H. Abery, PhD, is a Research Associate at the Research and Training Center on Community Living, Institute on Community Integration, University of Minnesota.

Angela N. Amado, PhD, retired, was a Research Associate at the Research and Training Center on Community Living, Institute on Community Integration, University of Minnesota.

Lynda Lahti Anderson, MA, MPH, is a Researcher at the Research and Training Center on Community Living, Institute on Community Integration, University of Minnesota.

Claire Benway, MA, is an Education Specialist at the Research and Training Center on Community Living, Institute on Community Integration, University of Minnesota.

Rebecca Dosch Brown, MFA, is an Education Specialist at the Research and Training Center on Community Living, Institute on Community Integration, University of Minnesota.

Heidi Eschenbacher, PhD, is a Research Associate at the Research and Training Center on Community Living, Institute on Community Integration, University of Minnesota.

Erin Flicker, MSW, LICSW, is a clinical trainer at the Minnesota Center for Chemical and Mental Health at the University of Minnesota.

Rachel Freeman, PhD, is a Research Associate at the Research and Training Center on Community Living, Institute on Community Integration, University of Minnesota.

Bradley Goodnight, PhD, is a Postdoctoral Fellow at the Center for Disease Control and Prevention.

Anab A. Gulaid, MPA, is an Education Specialist at the Research and Training Center on Community Living, Institute on Community Integration, University of Minnesota.

Amy Gunty, MA, is a Researcher at the Research and Training Center on Community Living, Institute on Community Integration, University of Minnesota.

Jennifer Hall-Lande, PhD, is a Research Associate at the Research and Training Center on Community Living, Institute on Community Integration, University of Minnesota.

Libby Hallas-Muchow, MS, is a Researcher at the Research and Training Center on Community Living, Institute on Community Integration, University of Minnesota.

Merrie Haskins, MS, LPCC, is a community mental health professional at MorningStar Counseling.

Amy S. Hewitt, PhD, MSW, is the Director of the Research and Training Center on Community Living and the Institute on Community Integration, University of Minnesota.

Barbara A. Kleist, MEd, JD, is an Education Program Manager at the Research and Training Center on Community Living, Institute on Community Integration, University of Minnesota.

Julie E.D. Kramme, MA, is a Researcher at the Research and Training Center on Community Living, Institute on Community Integration, University of Minnesota.

Sheryl A. Larson, PhD, is a Senior Research Associate at the Research and Training Center on Community Living, Institute on Community Integration, University of Minnesota.

Sarah E. MapelLentz, JD, MPH, is a public health professional in Minnesota.

Nancy McCulloh, MS, is an Education Specialist at the Research and Training Center on Community Living, Institute on Community Living, University of Minnesota.

Macdonald Metzger, MS, is an Education Specialist at the Research and Training Center on Community Living, Institute on Community Integration, University of Minnesota.

Kelly M. Nye-Lengerman, PhD, MSW, LGSW, is a Research Associate at the Research and Training Center on Community Living, Institute on Community Integration, University of Minnesota.

Mark R. Olson is an Education Specialist at the Research and Training Center on Community Living, Institute on Community Integration, University of Minnesota.

Susan N. O'Nell is an Education Program Manager at the Research and Training Center on Community Living, Institute on Community Integration, University of Minnesota.

Sandra L. Pettingell, PhD, is a Research Associate at the Research and Training Center on Community Living, Institute on Community Integration, University of Minnesota.

Clifford L. Poetz is the Community Liaison at the Research and Training Center on Community Living, Institute on Community Integration, University of Minnesota.

Jerry Smith, MPA, is a video and media producer at the Research and Training Center on Community Living, Institute on Community Living, University of Minnesota.

John G. Smith is the Coordinator at the Research and Training Center on Community Living, Institute on Community Integration, University of Minnesota.

Roger Stancliffe, PhD, is a Professor of Intellectual Disability at the Centre for Disability Research and Policy, The University of Sydney, Australia.

Renáta Tichá, PhD, is a Research Associate at the Research and Training Center on Community Living, Institute on Community Integration, University of Minnesota.

Joe Timmons, MSW, LGSW, is a Social Worker at the Lionsgate Academy.

Jody Van Ness, MA, is an Education Specialist at the Research and Training Center on Community Living, Institute on Community Integration, University of Minnesota.

Ellie Wilson, MA, is the Executive Director of the Autism Society of Minnesota.

SHADES OF GRAY

By Deborah "Debbi" Harris

I like this shade of gray . . .
It speaks to me in parables composed of riddles.
It sings in another language and its melody
Helps me understand the meaning of soft and cloudy words.
Oh, I like this shade of gray . . .
It reaches out to me with the boldness of a primary color.
The arms of its muted palette grab me, pulling me mightily to it,
Yet I feel nothing of its strength.
Yes, this shade of gray . . .
It reminds me of a gentle and agonizing rain.
Its streams dance joyfully upon me in great floods,
Yet I remain dry.

FOREWORD

Why it's Important That We Talk About Community Living

Today, people with disabilities and their staff go to work, doctor's appointments, and community events. Back in the early 1970s, you almost had to move mountains to do that. It's now commonplace for Direct Support Professionals (DSPs) to accompany the people they support, doing things like going to baseball games. We've certainly come a long way.

What changed to make this possible? Attitudes changed, because people with disabilities started living in their communities.

I used to live in a facility called Outreach Center in Minneapolis, a place with 200 people and very few staff. It was like a small institution, but right in the middle of the city. Every day I climbed three flights of steps, which was hard for me because of my cerebral palsy. Our director was very progressive for the time and we even had a client council, where those of us living in Outreach could set our own rules, like coming and going as we pleased. Still, it was hard to get one-on-one support with so few staff. Imagine what it was like for the people living in overcrowded institutions like Willowbrook.

When group homes began appearing in neighborhoods in the 1970s, many people were not happy. They thought crime would go up and the value of their homes would go down. This didn't happen. It took time, but our communities got to know us.

Today, people are more sensitive and better informed about people with disabilities. The supports we now receive, especially from well-trained DSPs, are person-centered and highly individualized. Living in the community means having a much higher quality of life, and it's much less expensive than living in institutions.

We've come a long way, but we need to stay strong and make sure our benefits aren't cut. Cutting Medicaid, for example, would cut necessary services, which would create chaos at the state and local levels. DSPs and self-advocates need to speak out if they see our community inclusion movement going backwards. The more we talk about it, the harder it will be to go back to the days of Willowbrook and the old ways of supporting people.

—Cliff Poetz, Minneapolis Minnesota, 2018

Cliff Poetz spoke before Congress in 1973 at the invitation of Senator Edward Kennedy. Cliff was the first person with IDD to have this distinction. He has been one of the most visible and vocal advocates for people with IDD in Minnesota for over four decades, and a pioneer in the national Self-Advocacy movement. Recognitions of his work include the Kennedy Foundation International Award in Self-Empowerment, the Founder's Award from The Arc of the Greater Twin Cities, and the Leadership in Advocacy Award from the Association of University Centers on Disabilities. As Community Liaison with the Research and Training Center on Community Living at the University of Minnesota's Institute on Community Integration, Cliff remains a champion of community inclusion and informs their work with his deep knowledge of policy and practice.

Preface

The realities and stories of community living and participation for people with IDD are as varied as the 4.3 million people living with IDD in the United States today. The question "what is community, really?" is difficult to answer. Community living and participation mean different things to different people. Community is more than just the spaces we physically occupy. It's also the relationships, activities, roles, and connectedness we share. Throughout history, people with IDD have been excluded or prevented from fully benefiting from a life in the community, but now more than ever before, people with IDD are participating in community living, taking their rightful place as active and contributing members of our community

People with IDD can and should hold valued social roles in society, but not as something special or different. Rather, people with IDD should hold valued roles as people you encounter every day—your classmates, coworkers, neighbors, and friends. It's only when all people, including those with IDD, are included, that a community can be strong and truly diverse. Disability is a natural part of the human experience, and it never means *less than*. The things that most people want out of life—happiness, love, fun, a home, a job, family, an education—are the same things that people with IDD want, too. We are not that different, and living in the community together is the vital spark that connects us all.

There has been great progress and movement toward the integration of people with IDD in the community, but there is still much that can and should be done to ensure the full inclusion of people with IDD in all aspects of community life. Many systems exist to support people with IDD, but the sole solution to increased community living and participation is not going to be found in a system. The solution is found in people—in our connectedness, in our sharing everyday spaces and places, and in seeing people with IDD as valuable contributing members of society. *Different* is not *less than,* and having raised expectations for community living and participation for all people is an agent for significant social change.

The exploration of how to create the ideal conditions to facilitate community living and participation for people with IDD is central to this book. There are many ways to "make the case" for community living. The social case for community living focuses on the rights, dignity, and value of all people. People with IDD have the right to live in the community and make choices about their own lives, bodies, and experiences. The legislative and legal case for community living highlights the many state and federal policies and litigation that mandate inclusion. Separate is not equal. The economic case for community living emphasizes the return on investment that inclusive services and supports provide. Supporting independence and integration is good for people and for taxpayers. In our continued journey toward the full inclusion of people with IDD in our communities, there are a few things to keep in mind.

Separate is Never Equal

Historically we've built segregated or separate systems for people with IDD, sometimes with the very best intentions. But what years of research and advocacy have told us is that separate is not equal. And when you *really* listen to what people with IDD say they want, it's a life and choices like everyone else has—not more than. Public systems and funding can prevent true equality and equity when they actively prioritize segregation. The negative effects of segregation and isolation for all people, including people with IDD, have been consistently demonstrated over time.

Reinvest in People and Community

People are our society's greatest resource. And DSPs are some of the service system's most valuable assets. The aspirations of the most well-written, inclusive policies for community living will remain unfilled if we do not have a workforce to support the application and execution of these policies. Workforce investment is part of critical infrastructure. In addition to investing in people within the system, we also have to invest in our communities. The solutions for full inclusion won't necessarily be provided by the system of experts; instead it can come from people and organizations who are not focused on disability. Building and showcasing the realities of what is possible for people with IDD in the community through education, advocacy, access, and raised expectations of people with IDD is critical. Reinvest in what we want to see.

Maintain Raised Expectations at all Times

Expectations are one of the powerful predictors of success in employment, school, and life for all people. When parents, teachers, professionals, policy makers, and society expect that people with IDD can live a life in the community, things will change. We must spare individuals with disabilities the soft bigotry of low expectations, and recognize and facilitate their valued social roles and contributions. Higher expectations of people with IDD can result in transformational change. People with IDD can live in the community, work, get married, pay taxes, own a home, be a friend, volunteer, coach, and so much more!

Building Capacity and System Change Take Time

To continue to move community living and participation ahead, public investments (funding) must align with public policies. Where the system invests its money matters; it matters a lot. The system responds to money, and investments in community living and participation will result in growth in those areas. These shifts can also produce significant value for both people and taxpayers, but can take time to reveal themselves in outcomes and data.

A full life in the community, with all its opportunities and challenges, should be a human experience that is available to all people.

—Kelly M. Nye-Lengerman, PhD, MSW, and Amy S. Hewitt, PhD, MSW
Minneapolis, Minnesota, 2018

Abbreviations and Acronyms

ABLE Act	Achieving a Better Life Experience Act of 2014
ACA	Affordable Care Act
ACL	Administration on Community Living
ADA	Americans with Disabilities Act
ASAN	Autistic Self Advocacy Network
ASD	Autism Spectrum Disorder
BLS	Bureau of Labor Statistics
CBT	Competency-Based Training
CDC	Centers for Disease Control and Prevention
CFC-SDPAS	Community First Choice Self-Directed Personal Assistance Services
CFR	Code of Federal Regulations
CLAS	Culturally and Linguistically Appropriate Services
CMS	Centers for Medicare and Medicaid Services
CQL	Council on Quality and Leadership
CRPD	Convention on the Rights of Persons with Disabilities
DD Act	Developmental Disabilities Assistance and Bill of Rights Act
DD Council	State Councils on Developmental Disabilities
DSP	Direct Support Professional
ESSA	Every Student Succeeds Act
FAPE	Free Appropriate Public Education
FM-CAT	Functional Model—Causal Agency Theory
HCBS	Home and Community Based Services

IDD	Intellectual and Developmental Disabilities
ICF/IID	Intermediate Care Facilities for Individuals with Intellectual Disabilities
IEP	Individualized Education Program
ILP	Independent Living Programs
ISP	Individual Support Plan or Individual Service Plan
LRE	Least Restrictive Environment
LTSS	long-term supports and services
MAPs	Making Action Plans
MCO	Managed Care Organization
MR	Mental Retardation
NCI	National Core Indicators
NCI-AD	National Core Indicators—Aging and Disability
NCLB	No Child Left Behind
NQF	National Quality Forum
OAA	Older Americans Act
P&As	Protection and Advocacy Organizations
PATH	Planning Alternative Tomorrows with Hope
PCT	person-centered thinking
PHI	Paraprofessional Healthcare Institute
PL	Public Law (e.g. *PL 132-294*)
PNS	Projects of National Significance
RJP	Realistic Job Preview
SABE	Self Advocates Becoming Empowered
SAO	Self-Advocacy Online
SDLMI	Self-Determined Learning Model of Instruction
SDM	Supported Decision Making
SE	Supported Employment
TLCPCP	The Learning Community for Person Centered Practices
UCEDDs	University Centers for Excellence in Developmental Disabilities
UGCOPAA	Uniform Guardianship, Conservatorship, and Other Protective Agreements Act
UGPPA	Uniform Guardianship and Protective Proceedings Act
VR	Vocational Rehabilitation
WIOA	Workforce Innovation and Opportunity Act

CHAPTER ONE

Community Living and Participation: A Comprehensive Framework

Kelly M. Nye-Lengerman and Amy S. Hewitt

Advance Organizers

- Community living is a complex and ever-evolving construct that is dependent on individual preferences, contexts, and cultural and linguistic lenses.
- Having a community life is a human experience that should be available to and expected of people with and without disabilities.
- Reciprocity is a critical ingredient of community living and participation.

Understanding IDD

People with IDD are friends, siblings, employees, community members, students, and parents. A person's diagnostic label does not reduce or change his or her right to have an active and engaged life in the community. The term used to define IDD in the past was *mental retardation* (MR). This term is no longer used because it is derogatory, insulting, and hurtful to many people with IDD and their allies.

There are two primary features of IDD: limitations related to intellectual functioning and deficits in adaptive behavior. As a result, someone with IDD may have challenges related to reasoning, problem solving, and learning, and may lack social and everyday skills for living (American Association on Intellectual and Developmental Disabilities, 2017; Shalock et al., 2010). In addition, the term *developmental* refers to other physical or cognitive conditions that occur during childhood but last over a lifetime. A variety of conditions fall under the IDD umbrella, including autism spectrum disorder (ASD), Down syndrome, fragile X, Rett syndrome, cerebral palsy, and others. It is important to remember that IDD affects people in varying degrees, and that it may look very different across the population. When someone has a diagnostic label of IDD, it means that they were diagnosed by a medical professional as having an intellectual and/or developmental disability before the age of 18. Diagnosing a person with IDD usually includes the use of both IQ (intelligence quotient) and adaptive behavior assessments. An IQ test score at or around 70 indicates limited intellectual functioning. Other types of adaptive behavior testing look at social skills, activities of daily living, problem solving, etc., and assist in making an IDD diagnosis (Schalock et al., 2010). Regardless of the diagnostic label that an individual with IDD has, they are still capable of learning, growing, and participating in community life.

There are an estimated 4.31 million people with IDD in the United States (Larson et al., 2017). The Centers for Disease Control and Prevention (CDC) estimate that approximately 15% of children between the ages of three and 17 have one or more developmental disabilities (Boyle et al., 2011). A developmental disability is one that is present before age 21, whereas the onset of ID is prior to age 18. Most people with IDD live in the community, go to school, and have jobs. About 1.4 million people with IDD receive or are formally waiting for services from state developmental disabilities program agencies (Anderson et al., 2016). State IDD agencies often provide funding and services related to healthcare, housing, and other supports to people with IDD.

In the United States, a number of projects of national significance collect information about people with IDD who receive formal services through state IDD agencies. Here are a few things we know about people who use these supports:

- Most people with IDD live with a family member (57%); however, 5% live with a host/foster family, 11% in their own home, 25% in a group home, and 2% in a nursing or psychiatric facility (Larson et al, 2107). Where a person lives has a lot to do with how much they access the community.
- During the day, most individuals with IDD are not working and instead receive facility-based (53%) and community-based (44%) nonwork supports (Butterworth et al, 2016). Yet many people with IDD can and want to work. In recent years there has been increased focus on the importance of paid community employment for people with IDD because having a paid job is a critical part of being an active and participating community member.

- Most adults with IDD (42%) require some behavior support, and even more (76%) require support for daily living activities (Anderson et al., 2016). To ensure that people with IDD are active citizens in their communities, it is important that supports focus on engagement, relationships, and community participation.
- Investment in long-term services and supports for people with IDD has increased over time. In fiscal year 2015, an estimated $65 billion was spent for public IDD services; of this total, 76% came from Medicaid dollars (Braddock et al., 2017).

There are approximately 4.31 million people with IDD in the United States, but only about 1.46 million (31%) are known to state IDD agencies, and only 1.21 million (26%) actually receive services through state IDD agencies (Larson et al., 2017). This indicates that most people with IDD don't have or use formal supports from state or government systems. As a result, our knowledge concerning those who are "outside" the service delivery system is limited. However, we do know more about people with IDD within the system who receive formal supports, such as special education, vocational rehabilitation, and social security benefits. Over the past 40 years, more research has been done to understand the experiences and outcomes of people with IDD who use formal supports through public or government programs. When we look at the quality and outcome of services (e.g., paid employment, health) for people with IDD, sometimes it is easy to get discouraged. People with IDD do have different experiences and outcomes than those without disabilities. They are less likely to be employed or own a home, and they have increased rates of certain diseases and often live below the poverty level. These differences do not mean that people with IDD can't experience a high-quality and fulfilling life. We know that many people with IDD across the nation are contributing members of society and actively participate in their communities. This book highlights effective strategies to ensure that people with IDD are included and participate in their communities.

Community Living and Participation

Community can be defined as (1) a group of people living in the same place or having a particular characteristic in common, and as (2) a feeling of fellowship with others, as a result of sharing common attitudes, interests, and goals. Community can be both a feeling and a place. When we talk about community living and participation, we are referring to a set of complex and ever-evolving dimensions related to both the place of community and the feeling of community. These dimensions encompass individual preferences, contexts, and cultural and linguistic lenses. Community living and participation features include:

- where and with whom a person **lives**
- whether and where a person **works**
- the **financial resources** available to a person

- what a person does **during the day**
- the **relationships** a person desires and has with others
- what things of **personal interest** an individual does and with whom
- a person's **health** and **well-being** (physical and emotional)
- whether, where, and with whom a person practices **faith**
- a person's interest and opportunity to engage in **learning** and **personal growth**
- opportunities and ability for a person to make **informed decisions** about and **direct their own life**
- the **human right to assume roles and responsibilities as a citizen** (e.g., neighbor, taxpayer, voter)

Community living and participation are complex and multidimensional. The components that make up community living and participation don't occur in isolation; rather, they are related to and interdependent with each other. The dimensions of

Figure 1.1. Community life is multifaceted.

community living listed above highlight the importance of other key features for success, including:

- **engagement**—the act of being connected and involved in something, which can include civic engagement
- **expectation**—the belief that something can be achieved or will occur
- **a valued social role**—where the person is looked up to and seen as a capable, competent, and valued contributor to the interaction
- **reciprocity**—the exchange of feelings, things, experiences, and ideas for mutual benefit
- **connectedness**—the feeling or state of being joined or linked with a person, group, or idea that includes the feeling of belonging
- **self-direction**—the authority to made decisions and take responsibility for choices, actions, or experiences for oneself
- **choice and control**—the freedom to pick among several options, and to make a decision when faced with one or more possibilities
- **contribution**—one's role in making something happen or advancing something

Figure 1.2. Key features for successful community living and participation.

Although these dimensions and features about community living and participation may seem clear, they are actually hard for many people with IDD to realize and experience. These challenges are related to a number of factors, such as historical challenges and barriers, systems limitations, workforce challenges, reduced expectations, and lack of opportunity. This book includes stories about people with IDD who are living and participating in community life. Each chapter highlights a different dimension and feature of community life. Additionally, each chapter offers information on many community features, as well as an overview of the issues, opportunities, challenges, and experiences of people with IDD. Several chapters focus on critical issues in the field that transcend all features and dimensions of community living, such as person-centered practices, quality life outcomes, and the direct support workforce. The following topics are covered:

1. Community Living and Participation: A Comprehensive Framework
2. One Person at a Time: Using Person-Centered and Positive Support Practices
3. A Place to Call Home
4. Work and Careers: It's More Than Just a Job
5. Friendship, Love, and Fun: Social Inclusion and Relationships
6. Self-Determination and Self-Advocacy: It's My Life
7. Rights, Choices, and Supported Decision Making
8. Health and wellness—Wellness Matters: Supporting Health and Wellness in Adulthood
9. Healthy aging and end-of-life transitions—Planning for Healthy and Engaged Aging
10. Outcomes for quality of life—Practices That Promote Quality Outcomes
11. Securing a direct support workforce—Hiring, Training, and Supporting the Direct Support Workforce

Looking Back: A Brief History of IDD

People with IDD were not historically welcome in the community. Throughout the 19th and 20th centuries, when families could no longer take care of their family member with IDD, their primary option was to place the individual in a large institutional setting, often without the opportunity to ever leave. During this time period, disability was viewed through a medical lens, meaning it was something to be "cured" or "fixed." Institutions were first thought to be a therapeutic way to help people get well again. Instead, over time, they became places where people were warehoused and locked away. People with IDD were kept from their families and the community and often experienced a great deal of abuse, neglect, and maltreatment in institutions. In many situations, people did not even have their basic needs (e.g., food, clothing, safety, health) or human rights met.

Social changes in the 1960s began to shed light on the plight of individuals living in institutions. Exposés, advocacy, and investigations led by the federal government through work done during the Kennedy administration began to lay the groundwork for federal funding to research, support, and advocate for people with IDD. Active parent advocates brought more attention to segregation and the lack of educational opportunities, and provider systems began to develop around offering different types of day, employment, and residential services. The wave of social change occurring in the United States through the civil rights movement also helped move development of a social model of disability to the forefront. This model sees and accepts disability as a natural part of the human experience—one that needs support and not cure. Momentum continued to grow for social change, and important federal laws on education, employment, housing, and healthcare were passed during the 1960s and '70s, paving the way for many of the policies that make community living possible today.

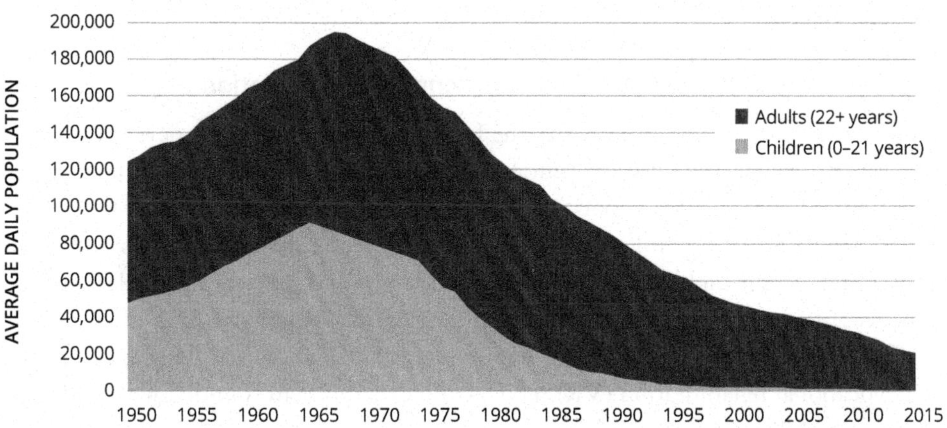

Figure 1.3. Institutionalization trends from 1950 to 2015. Figure reprinted with permission from Larson, S.A., Eschenbacher, H. J., Anderson, L. L., Taylor, B., Pettingell, S., Hewitt, A., Sowers, M., & Fay, M. L. (2017). In-home and residential long-term supports and services for persons with intellectual or developmental disabilities: Status and trends through 2014. Minneapolis, MN: University of Minnesota, Research and Training Center on Community Living, Institute on Community Integration.

It is important to remember this history, as it provides a window into how grim the past was for people with IDD. Through this awareness comes insight and inspiration, which allow us to see the transformation the field continues to make. Over time, attitudes have changed, laws have been passed, and basic human rights have been defended so that people with IDD have opportunities to be a part of their communities, the same as people without disabilities. Today our expectations are higher than ever for people with IDD to live, work, learn, love, and play in the community; this has been made possible, in part, through evolving public policy.

Supporting Community Living Through Policy

A number of important pieces of legislation, litigation, and regulation have created opportunities and provided support for community living and participation for people with IDD. Included among these are commitments made by the federal government to ensure access to community for all people, including individuals with IDD. Shaping policy at the federal and state levels has made it possible for people with IDD to live and participate in the community, instead of living in institutions, receiving segregated education services, and working in sheltered workshops. Although segregated noncommunity services still exist in the United States, legislation, litigation, and policy have played and continue to play a critical role in making sure support systems provide services in the most integrated, inclusive, and equitable settings possible.

Key Legislation Related to Community Living and Participation

Federal and state legislation provides the foundation from which to develop services and support for people with disabilities and their families. Many federal laws guide community living and participation for people with IDD. Typically, these laws came about following strong and planned advocacy by people with disabilities and their allies. This section highlights some of the most significant pieces of legislation that affect access to community living and participation for people with IDD.

The Rehabilitation Act of 1973, referred to as PL 93-112, was designed to revise state vocational rehabilitation (VR) services and expand them to individuals with significant disabilities, including IDD. Earlier VR programs primarily served disabled veterans or people with physical disabilities. The Rehabilitation Act of 1973 includes the following sections:

- **501:** affirmative action and nondiscrimination in employment for federal agencies
- **503:** affirmative action and nondiscrimination in employment for federal contractors and subcontractors
- **504:** nondiscrimination in public services; "no qualified individual with a disability in the United States shall be excluded from, [be] denied the benefits of, or be subjected to discrimination under" any program or activity that receives federal funding (29 U.S. Code § 794 . . . the Rehabilitation Act of 1973, as amended)
- **508:** requirement for accessibility in electronic and information technology developed, maintained, procured, or used by the federal government

The Rehabilitation Act of 1973 is an important early piece of legislation that not only prohibits discrimination against people with disabilities in community spaces, places, and programs, but also actively invests in state VR programs that support the employment and training of people with disabilities, including those with the most significant disabilities. Having a job and access to training is important for all people, regardless of disability, and provides valued social roles. The Rehabilitation Act of 1973 provided foundational guidance and investment in the importance of work and training for people with disabilities.

The Developmental Disabilities Assistance and Bill of Rights Act (DD Act) of 2000, or PL 106-402, has roots in work done by the President's Panel on Mental Retardation initiated by President John Kennedy in 1961. The current DD Act shares the federal government's commitment to and interest in ensuring that people with IDD and their families can access a life in the community. The current law seeks to ensure "that individuals with developmental disabilities and their families participate in the design of and have access to needed community services, individualized supports, and other forms of assistance that promote self-determination, independence, productivity, and integration and inclusion in all facets of community life . . . ." (42 U.S.C. 15001 [b] [2006]). Amendments added in 1984 included a focus on independence, productivity, and integration.

The DD Act authorizes infrastructure critical to programs and services that protect, advocate for, and study the issues faced by people with IDD. Such programs support full community living, access, and participation by (1) studying issues affecting people with IDD, (2) conducting prevalence monitoring and service usage, (3) pursuing litigation to enforce laws, (4) supporting state infrastructure and developing capacity in IDD services and supports, (5) helping shape public policy, and (6) advocating for the needs of people with IDD and their families. Programs within the DD Act include:

- protection and advocacy organizations (P&As)
- state councils on development disabilities (DD Councils)
- University Centers for Excellence in Developmental Disabilities (UCEDDs)
- projects of national significance (PNS)

The Americans With Disabilities Act (ADA) of 1990 is civil rights legislation that prohibits discrimination against people with disabilities in all areas of public life, including jobs, schools, transportation, and spaces open to the public. This law comprises five titles, or sections, that prevent discrimination in different areas:

- **Title I—Employment.** Employers must provide reasonable accommodations for applicants and employees, which could include such accommodations as interpreter services, workstation modification, and job or schedule restricting. This title also prohibits workplace discrimination based on disability.
- **Title II—Public Services.** People with disabilities cannot be denied access to public services, including public transportation.

- **Title III—Public Accommodations.** Public facilities such as restaurants, stores, etc. must be accessible to people with disabilities. New construction and modifications to a businesses or other public spaces must be accessible.
- **Title IV—Telecommunications.** Companies that provide telephone services must provide access to relay services for individuals who use telecommunication devices such as a teletypewriter (TTY).
- **Title V—Miscellaneous.** People with disabilities cannot be coerced, threatened, or retaliated against for asserting their rights under the ADA.

The ADA is the first comprehensive piece of civil rights legislation that protects the needs and rights of people with disabilities so they can pursue a life in the community just as any other person can. The ADA ensures that people have access to the things they need to be active members of a community, including having a job, using public transportation, and accessing local businesses.

The Workforce Innovation and Opportunity Act (WIOA) of 2014, or **PL 113-128,** is an extension of the Rehabilitation Act of 1973. This law was put in place to further modernize public vocational rehabilitation, workforce centers, and community partnerships. It requires additional accountability and tracking of employment outcomes in order to provide job seekers with more informed choices about their work options, build stronger connections with businesses and employers, and improve collaboration and planning between vocational, educational, and community services (U.S. Department of Labor, 2016). Importantly, this legislation prioritizes pathways to competitive, integrated employment for people with disabilities through (1) increased directed funds and guidelines for pre-employment transition services; (2) additional access to supported employment (SE) services; and (3) additional efforts to reduce and limit the use of subminimum wages and facility-based work settings (Murthy et al., 2016.

The Individuals With Disabilities Education Act (IDEA) is intended to ensure that all children with disabilities can access a free and appropriate public education. This law, which has its roots in the Education of All Handicapped Children Act (PL 94-142) of 1975, has been reauthorized several times over the years. It makes access to education and necessary supports a right for all children regardless of ability. IDEA authorizes funds to states to provide special education services (though these funds only pay for a small portion of the total cost of special education). Included in IDEA is provision for transition planning, beginning before age 16, for students with an individualized education plan (IEP) to support the student's move from educational programming and services to adulthood. Transition planning and the IEP should be individualized, based on a student's strengths and should support the development of skills for community life, including work and postsecondary education. In addition, Part B of IDEA allows children and youth from ages three to 21 to receive special education services, and Part C covers programs, including early intervention, for families of young children with disabilities. IDEA includes six pillar concepts:

- individualized education plan (IEP)
- free and appropriate public education (FAPE)
- least restrictive environment (LRE)
- appropriate evaluation
- parent and teacher participation
- procedural safeguards

Collectively, these pillars protect and promote the rights of students with disabilities to an accessible, integrated, and equitable public education. Education plays a critical role in successful adulthood, as it provides a foundation for having a job, pursuing postsecondary education, developing lifelong skills and knowledge, and accessing the benefits of community (e.g., housing, transportation, relationships, engagement, etc.).

The Every Student Succeeds Act (ESSA) of 2015 replaced a previous version of the law called No Child Left Behind (NCLB) with a focus on fully preparing all students, including those with disabilities, for college and careers. ESSA includes the importance of equity for disadvantaged or high-needs students, identification of academic standards that must be taught, data collection through annual statewide assessments, improving access to high-quality preschools, and building local-level innovations in communities and school districts.

ESSA standards are intended to ensure that youth with disabilities have equitable experiences in public education. Such experiences, both for youth with disabilities and for their families, raise the expectation of full participation in school and academic assessments, which, in turn, lead to higher expectations in adulthood. In other words, higher expectations of a person in school support aspects of community living and participation later on, such as having a job, a place to live, fulfilling relationships, and opportunities for economic advancement.

Key Litigation Related to Community Living and Participation

When laws or policies are not being followed or implemented, legal action might be necessary to enforce compliance. Many steps may be taken before litigation occurs, but sometimes it is necessary to ensure that the rights of people with disabilities are not violated.

Olmstead v. L.C. (1999). Although the ADA was signed into law in 1990, people with IDD still face discrimination and institutionalization. As a result of such discrimination, two women with disabilities from Georgia, who sought access to live in the community, filed a lawsuit under the ADA so they could be released from an institutional setting. The case went all the way to the Supreme Court, which ruled in 1999 that unjustified segregation constitutes discrimination. The court also stated:

> [P]ublic entities must provide community-based services to persons with disabilities when (1) such services are appropriate; (2) the affected persons do not oppose community-based treatment; and (3) community-based services can be reasonably accommodated, taking into account the resources available to the public entity and the needs of others who are receiving disability services from the entity. (*Olmstead v. L.C.*, 527 U.S. 581 [1999])

This is an incredibly important case, as it has been used to challenge unwarranted segregation of people with IDD. It also provides a clear message from the highest court in the United States:

> [I]nstitutional placement of persons who can handle and benefit from community settings perpetuates unwarranted assumptions that persons so isolated are incapable of or unworthy of participating in community life . . . confinement in an institution severely diminishes the everyday life activities of individuals, including family relations, social contacts, work options, economic independence, educational advancement, and cultural enrichment." (*Olmstead v. L.C.*, 527 U.S. 581 [1999])

The following are other examples of litigation related to community living:

- *Lane v. Brown* (formerly *Lane v. Kitzhaber*) (2010): Settlement agreement between the U.S. Department of Justice and the State of Oregon regarding access to community-based employment for people with IDD.
- *U.S. v. Rhode Island and City of Providence* (2013): Settlement agreement between the U.S. Department of Justice and the State of Rhode Island and City of Providence to ensure that people with IDD have access to supported employment services, integrated nonwork services, transition services starting at age 14, and state funds that incentivize services in integrated settings.
- *U.S. v. State of Mississippi/Mississippi Service System for People With Developmental Disabilities and Mental Illness* (2016): Lawsuit filed by the U.S. Department of Justice alleging that the State of Mississippi was in violation of ADA Title II and of *Olmstead* by unnecessarily segregating people with mental illness and developmental disabilities in state hospitals, as well as failure to provide community-based services that prevent unnecessary hospitalization or placement. The State of Mississippi was issued a letter from the U.S. Department of Justice in 2011 outlining a number of violations regarding the ADA's integration mandate.

Although litigation is never ideal, it has been an important tool used to protect and fight for the rights of people with disabilities to be free from unwarranted oppression and segregation. Litigation will continue to play an important role in ensuring that the civil rights of people with IDD are not violated.

Regulation Related to Community Living and Participation

Regulation is a rule or directive outlined by regulating agencies, and can include codification of rules and expectations defined within a law. For example, federal laws are codified in the Code of Federal Regulations (CFR), which documents the permanent rules and regulations of federal agencies. Regulation can play an important role in outlining rules, details, and expectations of a federal or state agency or program. There are a number of regulations that outline guidelines for how community-based services and supports should be provided. Because many states and agencies that provide direct services are required to follow these regulations, they function as another tool to ensure access to community-based services and support for people with IDD.

CMS Final Rule on Home and Community-Based Services. In 2014, the Centers for Medicare and Medicaid Services (CMS) issued a "Final Rule" (CMS 2249-F and CMS 2296-F) related to home and community-based settings (HCBS). Because CMS is the largest funder of long-term services and supports for people with IDD, this Final Rule affects many people with IDD and the majority of community-living services and supports. The 2014 Final Rule strengthened expectations and requirements for community settings and services (CMS, 2014). It established requirements for home and community-based settings in Medicaid HCBS programs operated under sections 1915(c), 1915(i), and 1915(k) of the Act (i.e., waiver programs). The new rule provides more outcome-based definitions for what constitutes an HCBS program and seeks to maximize participation in the most integrated community settings so that all recipients can benefit from living in the community. This means that, by 2022, CMS seeks to reimburse states, providers, and vendors in compliance with the rule and phase out services that are not. In addition, HCBS waiver programs must develop a person-centered plan that reflects an individual's preferences and goals, ensures that the support-planning process is led by the individual receiving supports, and allows the individual receiving supports to choose who participates in the process. States are in the process of developing transition plans to help providers come into compliance with the new Final Rule, and have until March 2022 to do so.

Below, we describe other examples of regulation related to community living and participation:

- **Administration on Community Living (ACL) guidance on person-centered planning (2014):** The Affordable Care Act (ACA), section 2402 (a), requires states to ensure that HCBS services maximize independence and self-direction to support community. The guidance outlines standards on person-centered planning and self-direction that must be included in all HCBS programs as appropriate.
- **Final Rule for Independent Living Programs (ILPs; 2016):** Under WIOA, centers of independent living must now provide new core services to facilitate the transition of individuals with significant disabilities from institutional settings to

community-based settings, provide consumer-controlled supports, and support services that prevent institutionalization of those with significant disabilities.

Regulations play an important role in providing guidance and expectations to states, programs, and provider agencies to ensure that their services support and facilitate community living for people with disabilities. Without regulation, these entities might not fully implement a law or might provide unequal access to service or supports. The regulations mentioned are examples of system expectations to support people with IDD accessing community-based services, including housing, employment, healthcare, and transportation.

Community Living and Participation as an Outcome

People typically have better lives when they live in the community; they have more opportunity, are closer to friends and family, and experience better outcomes in general. This is true both for people with IDD and for people without IDD. Research on housing, social inclusion, relationships, healthcare, and employment shows that people with IDD and their family members want to be a part of the community (American Association on Intellectual and Developmental Disabilities, 2015; 2016). They also report better outcomes related to social, emotional, and physical well-being when they are in community settings, have control over their own lives, and can make day-to-day choices for themselves.

The size and location of a setting has a big impact on inclusion and community access. With regard to day, employment, and residential services, the larger a setting, the less satisfied people with disabilities are with it. Although this doesn't mean people with IDD are necessarily unhappy, it means that, when they have less choice about and control over where they live, where they work, what they do, and with whom they do things, they report higher levels of dissatisfaction. The size of a setting also can affect how easily a person can engage and interact within their community. Larger settings often cannot provide the opportunities or support people may need or want to live on their own, have their own job, or move about the community freely. If community living and participation are to be achievable outcomes for both people and systems, it is essential to continually invest in and prioritize services that support fully inclusive lives in the community.

Current Controversies and Challenges

This book will cover a number of controversies and challenges that prevent people with IDD from being fully included in their communities. In order to develop strategies and interventions to address these challenges, it's important to first acknowledge they exist. Although each dimension of community living has its own controversies and challenges, some cross multiple settings, systems, and environments.

Resistance to Full Inclusion

Many self-advocates, advocates, family members, policy makers, and professionals support the community living movement. Yet, still others believe that people have a right or a need to be segregated. This may be based on personal preferences or beliefs that larger and segregated places provide greater safety or protection, or that people with IDD don't belong in the community as other people do. Some may argue that people or their families should be able to choose a segregated life if they want. A growing number of recently created residential programs in the United States purposely segregate people with IDD. There are also varying levels of inclusion in smaller, more integrated programs. Many people with IDD live *in* the community but are not *of* the community—meaning they don't participate directly in community life. This may be because some people (e.g., caregivers, staff, parents, or guardians) are concerned about safety, so they are not comfortable with the extent to which full inclusion gives people with IDD choice and control over all aspects of their lives.

Resistance to community living and participation can also be firmly rooted in fear on the part of people with disabilities themselves: fear of the unknown, fear of the public, fear of embarrassment or shame. Current systems and services are often designed to protect people with IDD, rather than support fully inclusive lives. Therefore, it is important to address and respect the fear they may have without allowing it to prevent them from being able to exercise their rights. People with IDD—just like all other people—should be extended the dignity to take risks, fail, and learn.

Policy Compliance and Enforcement

Earlier in this chapter, various laws and policies were identified to highlight the importance of inclusion and community living. Although policies can lay a foundation, they are still only words on a page if they are not embraced and enforced. True change comes from ensuring that policy is implemented, monitored, and enforced. Unfortunately, there are often limited resources and funding to support the full implementation and enforcement of laws and policies.

Location

One of the most significant indicators of quality, access, and outcomes related to community living is location. The city, county, or state where an individual lives matters a great deal when it comes to the types and quality of services provided, as well as access to those services. States have autonomy in how they use federal funds to support programs for people with IDD, including Medicaid, vocational rehabilitation, and public education. This leads to variability in quality, choice, and outcomes for people with IDD across states and communities, which in turn results in very different experiences, including in terms of access to supports to live and work in the community, for people with IDD and their families.

Workforce Challenges

The direct support workforce is an integral part of the support system for all people with IDD who receive services funded by state IDD agencies. Direct support professionals (DSPs) provide supports that assist people with IDD to be fully included in their communities. These supports make it possible for people with IDD to live, work, access services, and get around in their communities. Without high-quality DSPs, many of the needs, preferences, and aspirations of people with IDD go unfulfilled. A significant workforce crisis exists in the field. Not only are there not enough DSPs, but many are not well equipped to support people in the community due to a lack of competency-based training, support, and mentoring for DSPs. In addition, many DSPs are underpaid, and most do not have access to affordable benefits through their employer. As a result, there are limited avenues to make direct support work a livable career option. Until the workforce can be stabilized, many insurmountable barriers to community access will persist.

Practical Suggestions and Interventions

Community as Place of Intervention

Most people in the United States live and participate in their community. They are members of families; have friends; are engaged in clubs, teams, or groups; have colleagues; and enjoy countless opportunities to grow and learn new things. Although most people with IDD live and thrive in their communities without the service system, many do require long-term services and supports (LTSS). Often when one needs LTSS, they go through specialized providers of services to get them. Such providers sometimes connect people to programs and services that take them away from their family, friends, social connections, and community. People can become reliant on providers to intervene and do for them, instead of being expected to use and participate in typical community programs and services like people without disabilities do. An important question to ask is: By creating a service system, have we inadvertently let the community off the hook in terms of including and supporting people with IDD?

Individuals with IDD have been the focus of an $82 billion services industry since the inception of community services. The focus has been on changing the person to fit within a "system" of formal supports, rather than in community settings or spaces of their choice. Services are purchased by the government and funded through Medicaid (an individual health insurance program) to pay specialized IDD service providers for supports for the person with IDD. Focusing on the individual does not result in communities changing and including people; it results in people changing and people being isolated and not as engaged in their community as they could be.

Many forces resulted in the system we have built in the United States to promote community living and participation for people with IDD. At the individual, service provider, and systems levels, a stigma still exists that focuses on the need to protect vulnerable people with IDD from harm. This promotes services that are risk averse and full of regulations and rules that are expensive and time consuming. There are good reasons for these concerns; they are rooted in the harmful institutional services that were once the only option for people with IDD. Yet, these persisting stigma and attitudes result in the notion that specialized providers are needed in order for people with IDD to be involved and included in the community. This simply is not true. What if specialized providers were paid to support people in truly inclusive settings chosen by the person with IDD, instead of providers focusing on changing the person with IDD?

Shifting our thinking about services and supports from only offering IDD-specific services paid for by the government to a service system that focuses on supporting families is a needed new direction. Such a shift would encourage local community entities, such as businesses, faith communities, recreation programs, and community centers, to be inclusive and set high expectations both for themselves and for people with IDD. This will need to be supported by funding streams that are not tied to individual insurance programs and that allow for creative community development and problem solving. For people with IDD to participate and thrive in the community, the following areas require focus:

- available, reliable, and affordable transportation so people can get to and from places;
- shifted policy that incentivizes providers to help people obtain jobs and other valued roles in their communities, and also allows for self-direction; and
- a robust adoption of the use of technology to promote greater independence, higher expectations, and increased opportunity.

Value-Based Core Elements of Inclusive Community Practice

Person-centeredness is an essential component of any community human service system. Being person centered means considering each person in their individual context, focusing on what is important *to* the person and what is important *for* the person, and then striking a balance in supports and services. This seems like such a simple concept, but systems and providers struggle with it because scaling up practices when each person with IDD has unique needs and desires is tough. Putting the person first, before the needs of the system or providers or staff, can be difficult. It requires systems that are nimble and flexible, and those are often hard to develop.

Looking at each person through a holistic lens is important. Supports and services are not just about health and safety. They are about whatever it takes to support a person to live and participate to the fullest in their community. Considering each person's uniqueness and the intersectionality of various ways in which they identify themselves is important. People with IDD come from different backgrounds and different communities. They may identify as a person with a disability or they may not. Perhaps they identify themselves by their cultural and linguistic identity or by their faith. The intersection of culture, language, faith, and family context influences a person-centered approach. Individuals with IDD should be directing what they want and need, and families should be seen as allies and partners in cultivating person-centered supports. Practices such as informed decision making for people with IDD are important ways to teach people the skills they require to voice what they want and need from services. People with IDD can and do make critical decisions in their lives. We need to improve the service system to ensure that big decisions such as where and with whom a person lives, what they do to earn a living, and with whom they want to build relationships and spend time are made by people with IDD themselves, not by the system (and its representatives) or by legal guardians. Using supported decision making as an alternative to full or partial guardianship is an approach that can increase opportunities for people with IDD to make their own choices and decisions.

Life Course Expectations and Transitions

Community living and participation is not always the same for people. At any given point throughout their life, how they participate in community can and does change. What is important to a person when they are 13 is not the same when they are 45 or 80 years old. What a person's life is like and what community living is for them changes based on the person and over the course of their life. One way to think about this is by understanding, honoring, and using a life course approach to long-term services and supports.

People with IDD and their families are often focused on what is right in front of them in their current life situation. But it is helpful for families and other allies to look ahead and anticipate what life experiences and expectations will be useful to them in moving toward an inclusive community life in the future. We all know that what children experience early in their life can significantly affect life outcomes such as health, well-being, employment, socioeconomic status, etc. The earlier children with IDD can have positive experiences, be challenged and given opportunities to learn, and receive adequate support and services, the more likely they are to have positive outcomes later in life. Using a life course model, individuals and families can focus on the specific life stage their child is experiencing, with an awareness of how that stage and future stages will influence their life trajectory.

Children with IDD and their families usually have to start when the child is very young (between birth and age three) to navigate supports and services, and the systems in which these exist. They must continue to do so during the preschool years; throughout elementary, middle, and secondary school; during young adulthood and the middle adult years; and on into the aging years. Each year offers new transitions and changing ideas, interests, skills, and needs for the person with IDD and their family. It is important that, from a very early age, individuals are taught and families aspire to have expectations and a vision for how they will create a quality life in which the person with IDD will live and participate in their community. This requires providing opportunities, supports, and life experiences that direct a life trajectory toward community living and participation. Throughout this book, as we discuss the dimensions and features of community living, we will also provide examples of how such dimensions evolve and change throughout the life course.

Personal Illustration: Josh Harris

Josh Harris lives with his family in Minnesota. Now 25 and a graduate of Eagan public schools, he enjoys baseball, watching the Rachel Maddow show, attending church, and spending time with his family. Josh has a breathing tube, making it difficult for him to speak, but with excellent receptive language he takes in everything going on around him.

Born prematurely with multiple and complex medical issues, Josh was not expected to survive. He underwent 10 surgeries in his first year and spent much of his time in pediatric intensive care units. "He's had a long, difficult journey medically, said Debbi Harris, Josh's mother. "But he takes it in stride and he's kind of my hero."

When Debbi enrolled Josh in school, she was told that he would not be able to participate in activities because he required nursing care, something the school district would not provide. "[The school district] literally brought in big-time lawyers in fancy suits and briefcases. There were maybe 27 people in this particular IEP meeting to make sure, I guess, that Josh didn't come to school unless we provided nursing." Working with The Arc, Debbi fought this and made sure Josh was part of a regular classroom. The decision was made that the school district had to send letters out to all families whose children required nursing case, letting them know their children were welcome and nursing care would be provided or reimbursed by the district.

Social inclusion was a concern. But Josh did make a friend, Eric, who he still sees today. Josh has become a strong presence in his community, and his family makes sure he is engaged and included.

The road to inclusion has been challenging, and perhaps too often the focus has been on staffing crises or medical complications. "One thing I don't ever really get to say," said Debbi, "is that I'll just go downstairs and Josh will be sleeping, and I'll just look at him, and I'll just think, I am the most fortunate mom in the entire world and he is absolutely perfect. That's what I think."

Conclusion

Community living and participation is a multifaceted construct. Community is not only a place, but also a feeling. It conveys a message of reciprocity, connectedness, and engagement. For people with IDD, community living includes:

- where and with whom a person **lives**
- whether and where a person **works**
- the **financial resources** available to a person
- what a person does **during the day**
- the **relationships** a person desires and has with others
- what things of **personal interest** an individual does, and with whom
- a person's **health** and **well-being** (physical and emotional)
- whether, where, and with whom a person practices **faith**
- a person's interest and opportunity to engage in **learning** and **personal growth**
- opportunities and ability for a person to make **informed decisions** about and **direct their own life**
- the **human right to assume roles and responsibilities as a citizen** (e.g., neighbor, taxpayer, voter) given to each person

People with IDD should be included in all facets of community living and participation. Not only do most people with IDD want to be a part of the community; they also bring rich and diverse perspectives and experiences that benefit others. Many individuals with IDD access formal services for support, but these services do not always facilitate or enhance access to the community. In the pursuit of equality and equity of access to community living and participation for people with IDD, they must be seen as competent individuals capable of making decisions, taking risks, and living their lives just as people without disabilities do. Addressing fear, raising expectations, and respecting the civil rights of people with disabilities can lead to increased pathways to community living and participation.

Discussion Questions

- What are the most important aspects of your life in the community? How do these aspects compare with the lives of people with IDD with whom you interact?
- What are the roles and responsibilities of communities when it comes to including and supporting people with IDD? In what ways can local businesses, restaurants, faith communities, libraries, schools, community centers, etc. promote community living and participation for people with IDD? What can you do to hold these community places accountable for inclusion and ensure they do their part?
- What is the key difference between being *in* the community and being *of* the community?

Resources

- National Goals in Research Policy and Practice. Book. *Critical Issues in Intellectual and Developmental Disability: Contemporary Research, Practice, and Policy,* published by AAIDD, provides a concise review of what we know, from both research and practice, about intellectual and developmental disabilities and what the knowledge means for future developments in public policy, research, and practice. https://aaidd.org/news-policy/policy/national-goals-2015#.
- *Of the Community.* Documentary film. Forty years ago, large institutions warehousing thousands of people were common. Today, most people with intellectual and developmental disabilities (IDD) are living with their families or in homes and apartments in their communities. But are they active members of their community? *Of the Community* explores community living today. https://rtcmedia.vhx.tv/products/of-the-community
- HCBS Advocacy. Website. This website provides the most current and up-to-date information on CMS's Final Rule activity related to HCBS services. Individual state plans are also available on the site. https://hcbsadvocacy.org/learn-about-the-new-rules/
- Charting the LifeCourse Resources. Website. This online toolkit provides resources that can be used by individuals, families, practitioners, and systems to implement a life course framework. http://www.lifecoursetools.com/planning/

References

Americans With Disabilities Act of 1990, 42 U.S.C.A. § 12101 et seq. (1993).

Anderson, L. L., Larson, S. A., Kardell, Y., Taylor, B., Hallas-Muchow, L., Eschenbacher, H. J., . . . Bourne, M. L. (2016). *Supporting individuals with intellectual or developmental disabilities and their families: Status and trends through 2014.* (Rep.). Minneapolis, MN: University of Minnesota, Research and Training Center on Community Living, Institute on Community Integration.

American Association of Intellectual and Developmental Disabilities. (2017). *Frequently asked questions on intellectual disability.* Retrieved frhttps://aaidd.org/intellectual-disability/definition/faqs-on-intellectual-disability.

American Association on Intellectual and Developmental Disabilities & Association of University Centers on Disability. (2016). *Community living and participation for people with intellectual and developmental disabilities.* Retrieved from: http://aaidd.org/news-policy/policy/position-statements/community-living-and-participation.

American Association on Intellectual and Developmental Disabilities (2015). *Critical issues in intellectual and developmental disabilities: Contemporary research, practice, and policy.* Washington, DC: Author

Americans With Disabilities Act of 1990, 42 U.S.C.A. § 12101 et seq. (1993).

Butterworth, J., Smith, F. A., Winsor, J., Ciulla Timmons, J., Migliore, A., & Domin, D, (2016). *StateData: The national report on employment services and outcomes.* (Rep.). Boston, MA: University of Massachusetts Boston, Institute for Community Inclusion.

Boyle, C. A., Boulet, S., Schieve, L. A., Cohen, R. A., Blumberg, S. J., Yeargin-Allsopp, M., . . . & Kogan, M. D. (2011). Trends in the prevalence of developmental disabilities in US children, 1997–2008. *Pediatrics, 127*(6), 1034–1042. doi:http://dx.doi.org/10.1542/peds.2010–2989d

Braddock, D., Hemp, R., Rizzolo, M. C., Tanis, E. S., Wu, J., & Haffer, L (2017). *The state of the states in intellectual and developmental disabilities* (11th ed). Washington, DC: The American Association on Intellectual and Developmental Disabilities.

Butterworth, J., Smith, F. A., Winsor, J., Ciulla Timmons, J., Migliore, A., & Domin, D, (2016). *StateData: The national report on employment services and outcomes.* Boston, MA: University of Massachusetts Boston, Institute for Community Inclusion.

Centers for Medicare and Medicaid Services. (2014). *Medicaid program; State plan home and community-based services, 5-Year period for waivers, provider payment reassignment, and home and community-based setting requirements for community first choice and Home and Community Based Services (HCBS).* [Sections 1915(k)and 1915(c) Waivers (Section 1915(c) of the Act)]. Retrieved from https://www.federalregister.gov/documents/2014/01/16/2014-00487/medicaid-program-state-plan-home-and-community-based-services-5-year-period-for-waivers-provider

Centers for Medicare and Medicaid Services. (2014). Final Rule for Home and Community Based Services, 42 CFR 430, 431 et al.

Developmental Disabilities Assistance and Bill of Rights Act of 2000. Pub. L. No. 106-402. (2000).

Every Student Succeeds Act., Pub. L. 114-95 U.S.C. (2015).

Individuals With Disabilities Education Improvement Act, Pub. L. 108-446 U.S.C. (2004).

Larson, S. A., Eschenbacher, H. J., Anderson, L. L., Taylor, B., Pettingell, S., Hewitt, A. S. , . . . Fay, M. L. (2017). *In-home and residential long-term supports and services for persons with intellectual or developmental disabilities: Status and trends through 2014* (Report). Minneapolis, MN: University of Minnesota, Research and Training Center on Community Living, Institute on Community Integration. Retrieved from https://risp.umn.edu/publications.

Missouri Family to Family. (2015). *Charting the lifecourse: Experiences and questions booklet, a guide for individuals, families, and professionals.* Kansas City, MO: University of Missouri-Kansas City Institute for Human Development, University Center for Excellence in Developmental Disabilities.

Murthy, V.D., Rast J.E., Roux A.M. (2016) National Autism Data Center fact sheet series: Issue 9. Philadelphia, PA: Life Course Outcomes Research Program, A.J. Drexel Autism Institute, Drexel University.

Patient Protection and Affordable Care Act, 42 U.S.C. § 18001 (2010). *Olmstead v. L.C.*, No. 98–536, 527 581 (1999).

Rehabilitation Act of 1973. 29 U.S.C. § 701 et seq. (1973).

Schalock, R. L., Borthwick-Duffy, S. A., Bradley, V. J., Buntinx, W. H. E., Coulter, D. L., Craig, E. M.Gomez, S. C., Lachapelle, Y., Luckasson, R., Reeve, A., Shogren, K. A., Snell, M. Ed., Spreat, S., Tassé, M. J., Thompson, J. R., Verdugo-Alonso, M. A., Wehmeyer, M. L., & Yeager, M. H. (2010). *Intellectual disability: Definition, classification, and systems of supports.* Washington, DC: American Association on Intellectual and Developmental Disabilities.

U. S. Department of Labor. (2016). *The Workforce Innovation and Opportunity Act final rules: An overview.* Washington, DC: Retrieved from https://www.doleta.gov/WIOA/Docs/Final-Rules-An-Overview-Fact-Sheet.pdf

Workforce Innovation and Opportunity Act of 2014, Pub. L. No.113-128 (2016).

CHAPTER TWO

One Person at a Time: Using Person-Centered and Positive Support Practices

Jody Van Ness, Kelly M. Nye-Lengerman, Rachel Freeman, Erin Flicker, and Claire Benway

Advance Organizers

- All people deserve to be treated with respect and you can show this by listening to people about what is important to them.
- Positive support and person-centered practices are approaches that focus on the person first and not the system because they have person-centered values.
- Person centered practices focus on listening to what people want for their lives in order to best support them in planning and give control to the person.
- It is important to start with understanding what is important *to* and *for* the person.

Person-centered practices and other positive support strategies mark a significant shift in how services and supports are provided to people with IDD and their families. As described in Chapter 1, services were historically system-driven and focused on what was best for an organization or state agency. Systems were, and still are, concerned about compliance, control, and safety. As a result, people were given little or no choice about their life and were seen as passive recipients of services. The system was fraught with abuses and the systematic dehumanization of people with IDD. Little to no attention was paid to the preferences of people with IDD or their families. But, as the 1970s saw the rise of the disability rights movement, recognition of the importance of self-determination for people with IDD grew and families increased their expectations of services. As a result, transformative shifts occurred within policy, services, and government. Today, more than ever before, services are designed with the person with IDD in mind and are increasingly individualized. Although there is still a long way to go to achieve full inclusion of people with IDD in society, person-centered practices and positive supports provide the necessary approaches to achieve this goal.

For many people, including those with IDD, an optimal quality of life is elusive when others are making the decisions that affect them or are not respecting their wishes. It can be even more difficult to achieve when the people around them are not listening to what they are trying to say. People with IDD are often ignored and excluded from their communities because of their differences and/or their need for additional accommodations (O'Brien & Mount, 2015). Given individual support needs or vulnerabilities of people with IDD, the organizations, family, support staff, and allies that support them may unintentionally isolate them further from opportunities for inclusion in their communities. Person-centered practices and other positive support models can bring forward strength-based ideas and address concerns based on what is important both *to* and *for* an individual.

The goal of positive supports and person-centered practices is to change the way we support all people by reframing our interactions so as to ensure that we empower them to achieve their highest potential and make their own decisions about their life whenever possible. Navigating life with IDD can be challenging. Person-centered planning brings together a team, including family members, support professionals, and other important people in an individual's life, to celebrate the person's strengths, listen closely to identify important clues for improving their quality of life, and help build and facilitate a life the individual will consider worth living.

Person-centered practices and positive supports are not new ideas. In fact, they have been around for a very long time. However, many of the new laws, policies, and court decisions supporting community living for people with IDD have brought renewed attention to how the system, and support professionals within that system, can now approach services differently to ensure that people with IDD are heard, respected, and given the dignity to make decisions about their own lives.

Sometimes it can be confusing to keep all the different terms straight. Figure 2.1 outlines three levels of change involved in person-centered practices—individual, organizational, and system—as well as different approaches—thinking, planning, and implementation. Most importantly, person-centered practices and positive supports focus on the person, are strengths based, and support valued social roles and reciprocity.

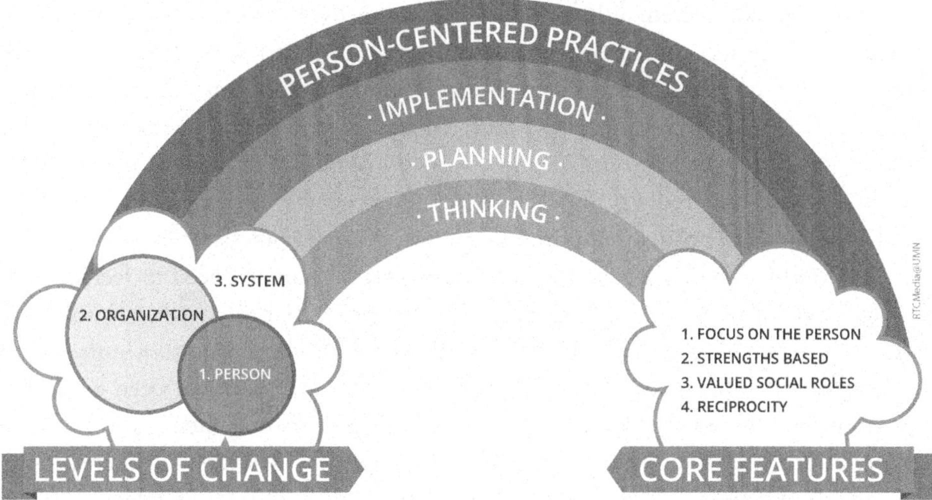

Figure 2.1. Overview of person-centered practices and positive supports.

A Value-Based Approach

By design, services and supports have been deficit based, focusing on a person's challenges and weaknesses and trying to change them. Person-centered practices and positive supports encourage seeing the person's strengths, preferences, and positive attributes as the starting place. Being person-centered is a journey, not a destination. As discussed in The Learning Community for Person Centered Practices (2017), it takes both the practice and the application of skills and tools that reflect and reinforce values that:

- work for all humans
- help us support individuals rather than fix them
- work at every level
- build a culture of learning, partnership, and accountability
- affirm our belief that everyone can learn
- help people achieve better lives, not just on paper, but in reality (O'Brien, 2002; O'Brien & Mount, 2015)

It's also important to keep in mind that person-centeredness is not just for the individual professional or family member. Being person-centered does take individual effort, but organizations that support people with IDD and their families also need to look at how they provide services. There are explicit and subtle ways in which organizations can approach the implementation of person-centered practices: How are intake meetings conducted? What kind of language is used on forms? Do staff receive adequate training and competency checks on person-centered skills? Person-centered individuals and organizations work together to build more person-centered systems. Although policies may require person-centered activities, the organizations and individuals actually carry them out. All must work in harmony to support people with IDD in a person-centered way. Later in this chapter, we will discuss various organizational approaches to positive supports and person-centered practices.

Person-centered practices takes into account that all humans need to feel valued. It is important that individuals with IDD have valued social roles—that is, roles on which society places value. Some examples are friend, teacher, volunteer, nurse, parent, neighbor, coach, employee, etc. Many people with IDD have not been given the opportunity or support to develop valued social roles. Person-centered and positive support efforts are trying to change that and ensure that services will increasingly foster the development of valued social roles in the community for people with IDD instead of isolation and segregation. Valued social roles and reciprocity with others are developed by (O'Brien, 2002; O'Brien & Mount, 2015; The Learning Community for Person Centered Practices, 2017):

- engaging in personal relationships
- sharing places and activities
- contributing
- making choices
- being treated with respect

Person-centered thinking is defined as a set of value-based skills and personalized approaches that focus on a person's strengths (Helen Sanderson Associates, 2018; Support Development Associates, 2018). Person-centered thinking can be used not only with people with IDD, but with anyone. Person-centered values translate to all different aspects of a person's life (e.g., housing, employment, friendship). Each area may call for unique ways of using person-centered thinking, but the same foundational principles always apply: focusing on the person, working from a base of strength, and supporting valued social roles and reciprocity.

To be person-centered in one's thinking, it is also important to understand the inherent biases we all have. All team members should take time to reflect on their thoughts and feelings about the individual being supported. Being person centered does not mean that team members have to change or compromise their beliefs, but it may mean they work to recognize their own biases and do not default to their own opinion about what is important to and for the individual.

When supporting a person with IDD, it is important to understand that being person-centered does not mean that the individual gets whatever they want whenever they want it. When providing support to any individual, one must consider what health and safety needs that person has. The critical consideration must be balancing

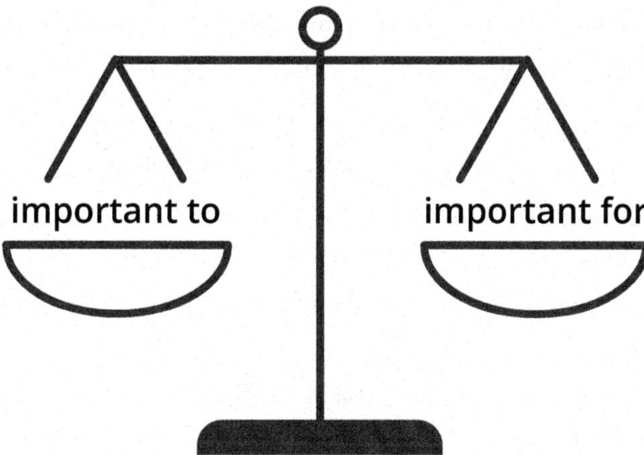

Figure 2.2. Important to and important for must be kept in balance. The scale shown above includes person-centered concepts, principles, and materials used with permission from The Learning Community for Person Centered Practices. Retrieved from http://tlcpcp.com. http://tlcpcp.com/.

what is important *to* the individual with what is important *for* them. It is within that balance that quality of life emerges.

One way, but not the only way, to better understand how to keep what is important *to* and important *for* in balance is through person-centered planning. Person-centered planning is, in effect, putting person-centered practices into action. Person-centered planning is an active, collaborative process that consists of a support team or circle, chosen by the person being supported, discussing, developing, and implementing a plan of support so that the person can lead the life of their choosing. Person-centered planning most often takes the shape of a series of meetings, facilitated by someone outside the support team. A variety of person-centered planning tools are available to assist with this process; some of them will be referenced later in this chapter.

Central to the person-centered planning process is focusing on the person's strengths and preferences to support a higher quality of life and keeping what is important *for* the individual in balance with what is important *to* them. For many people, a good person-centered planning process leads to greater inclusion in and connectedness to the community, and an increase in valued social roles and relationships. However, person-centered planning isn't just about fun and finding out what people like. Of equal importance is helping them to understand and support risks, independence, and choices, while the person leads the life of their choosing. The result of this process is a plan, or guide, for supporting the person to live a life of their choosing. Such plans are living documents and must be reviewed, updated, and discussed regularly. In fact, different milestones and stages in people's lives may require sound person-centered planning.

A growing number of organizations, and the service providers they employ, are embracing person-centered values as part of their organizational culture. Sometimes these values mark a significant shift from the way an organization has been run in the past, but sometimes they require only a subtle change in the way an organization does business and makes decisions (Smull, Bourne, & Sanderson, (2009). At the core, person-centered values focus on the individual, seek to build community capacity, deepen connections between people, and support informed choice. In an organization, this can play out in different ways. The following statements are examples of organizational person-centered values:

- Our mission focuses on building relationships with community partners.
- Staff are trained to be community facilitators and to help build natural supports.
- We strive to move from an expert-driven organization to a collaborative team approach alongside the individual and community.
- Our intake process ensures that individuals and families have choices about how our supports can best meet their needs.
- We provide a menu of services to meet individual needs, rather than a "one-stop shop" approach.
- Board members include people with IDD and/or their family members.
- Our organization's services are provided in the community where people live and work.

Whether you are a professional at an organization, a family member, a staff person, or an ally, finding the balance between what is important to and what is important for the individual you support should be the guiding principle. This goal alone bonds team members with a common purpose and provides the coherence needed to help individuals with IDD create ordinary lives and make changes together as a community.

Current Controversies and Challenges

Individuals, Families, and Support Professionals

For some, many of the values and ideas of person-centered practices are easy to support and to be excited about. For others, these practices represent a significant change and a direct challenge to the way a person with IDD has lived. And for many more, they are somewhere in between. It may be easy to say in practice that people with IDD should have more choices and freedoms, but it can be difficult for some to apply in real-life settings. Being person centered-means giving control to the person with IDD, and not actively having power over them in everything they do.

Offering choices, and providing quality information to make those choices, is central to person-centered practices. Where do you want to live? What do you want to do? Who do you want to spend time with? What makes you happy? These are all great questions. How many of them can you answer? Now think about some people with IDD whose choices and opportunities have been limited or dictated by the system (providers, family members, support workers). If the way in which you could live had been given to you without your consent, and no one ever asked or really listened to what you wanted, would you be able to answer those questions? Some people with IDD have not been provided with key life experiences or choices that inform these kinds of questions. It is common for us to choose what we know, to choose what we think others want us to choose, and to choose what feels realistic. For many people, these critical questions are met with "I don't know" or a blank stare. Additionally, various levels of intellectual capacity and ability may also color an individual's understanding or experience. For example, if you didn't know what working in the community was, would you know what to say if someone asked you, "Do you want to work in a competitive job in the community?"

In this era of increased choices and inclusion for people with IDD, there is also fear—fear of the unknown, fear of risks, fear of injury, fear of failure, fear of litigation. Parents and guardians are not in the business of facilitating failure, and support professionals have been trained to mitigate and reduce risk at all costs. As a result, the pursuit of self-directed, self-controlled lives for people with IDD is different, and even unheard of, in some cases. Fear and resistance can drive decision making for parents, guardians, and support professionals; and person-centered practices can come into direct conflict with business as usual and the *status quo*. It is not uncommon for parents or guardians to speak on behalf of a person with IDD, or for a support professional to feel they know what a person they support really wants. What person-centered practices ask of families and support professionals is to consider different alternatives that give power and control to the person, or share it with them, and to make sure that the person with IDD is living the life they choose with the supports necessary to do so. As with any self-directed life, there are risks—to take risks is to be human. Denying people with IDD the opportunity to take some risks can, in effect, strip them of a crucial aspect of their humanity.

Power dynamics in a relationship vary with the people involved. For some people with IDD, other people are given power over them because of their disability, intellectual capacity, history, etc. At the heart of person-centered practices is the idea that power sharing and decision making can and should be a joint effort. In fact, whenever possible, the person with IDD should be in control of their own life, body, and environment. Most people, with or without disabilities, seek and require the input of others to help them make decisions. One of the challenges in the pursuit of person-centeredness is rebalancing power and control. Parents, guardians, or other support professionals may have become accustomed to having power and don't fully recognize the control they have over a person with IDD. Before rebalancing these dynamics, awareness is critical.

Person-centered practices, such as person-centered planning, can help delve into many questions: Who is the person, really? What do they want for themselves? How can we support their experiences in such a way that they can make informed decisions about life and their preferences? How can we as a team support their risk taking and even allow them to fail, safely? There are no easy answers to any of these questions because person-centered planning is an individualized journey, but a number of practical interventions and solutions to some of these challenges will be discussed later in this chapter.

Organizations and Systems

Organizations that support individuals with disabilities face various controversies and challenges in implementing person-centered and positive support practices. One important challenge is the growing pressure to use evidence-based practices in education and human services. Evidence-based practices in human services involve the integration of science-based knowledge paired with applied expertise and guided by stakeholder goals, interests, values, and preferences within home, work, and community settings (American Psychological Association, 2016). Implementing evidence-based practices in an effective manner can be quite challenging. Sending people to a training to learn about a practice does not ensure that each individual will immediately be able to use the new skills in everyday settings. An overreliance on the use of trainings and workshops to introduce new practices is called the "train and hope model" because no direct strategies are used to help staff members determine how to embed a new practice into busy and sometimes complicated routines and work schedules. All too often, little to no evaluation or measurement is used to monitor the impact or changes after a training. This is especially true for organizations attempting to implement more than one type of practice while facing resource and staffing shortages.

Another of the current controversial discussions relates to the role of data-based decision making in a person-centered organization. Data-based decision making draws upon different types of evidence or data collected to make decisions. Rather than relying on experience, opinion, or inertia, data becomes the foundation of how an organization responds to an issue. The pressure to use evidence-based practices naturally reinforces the need to evaluate whether a practice is resulting in positive change in people's lives. Historically, leaders have disagreed about the use of outcome-based measurement to assess person-centered practices (Holburn, 2002; O'Brien, 2002). One of the founders of person-centered planning summed this up by saying he doubted whether this practice "could be tested like a drug to establish its causal power" (O'Brien, 2002). The danger, some people feel, is that an overreliance on checklists, data-collection forms, and other bureaucratic documentation focuses an organization's efforts in a direction that may make it harder to mobilize people to make real and significant social change. Other leaders in person-centered practices describe how some organizations place an emphasis on documentation as part of annual compliance processes rather than viewing person-centered plans as active blueprints for change (Smull, Bourne, & Sanderson, 2009). The goal of person-centered planning becomes automated, with less thought and intention given to the creative act of social change.

This controversy about collecting outcome data and using documentation systems may, in part, explain why person-centered planning is not yet considered an evidence-based practice (Claes, Van Hove, Vandevelde, van Loon, & Schalock, 2010; Ratti et al., 2016). More research is needed to understand how effective person-centered planning and person-centered practices are for supporting people with IDD. However, values inherent in person-centered planning as a practice can emphasize a more qualitative, organic, and informal approach to knowledge gathering.

Life Course Expectations and Transitions

The types of person-centered practices and positive supports a person needs change over time. The way in which person-centered strategies are used to empower young children and families is different from the strategies for older adults with IDD. Anticipating and adapting to people's changing needs across the lifespan requires cross-agency collaboration. Family members, foster care parents, early childhood and preschool staff, professionals involved in elementary through high school education, special education personnel, mental health clinicians, residential and employment providers, juvenile justice professionals, and community members may all be involved in someone's life at different times. Each person on a support team brings educational experiences, ideas, preferences, and cultural views that influence what types of positive supports they will introduce as options for a person to consider. Team-based and family-focused strategies that empower and support a person across developmental life stages will change as new challenges, learning opportunities, and experiences arise.

A proactive approach in person-centered planning is to anticipate key transitions in life and make changes to person-centered and positive support methods in order to better meet the needs of people receiving support. Young children transition to kindergarten and elementary school settings. Students move from elementary to secondary educational settings. Older children prepare for employment in the community. Young adults encounter significant changes as they become more independent from their families over time. As we age, our needs and priorities shift.

Some transitions are unexpected and require additions or modifications to person-centered and positive support practices. A family member may pass away suddenly. New jobs become available requiring a family to relocate to a different neighborhood or across the country. Major illnesses or other health problems arise. Person-centered practices and positive supports should be assessed on a regular basis in order to anticipate and adjust to quality-of-life changes that occur in life.

Practical Suggestions and Interventions

Levels of Change

As previously noted, person-centered strategies apply to everyone. Being person-centered requires that we build partnerships with the individuals we support and with their team. As individuals, we can grow our own person-centered skills by being mindful of the values they are built around and the way we communicate with and listen to others. As part of an organization, we can make sure our services are provided in a supportive, respectful way that honors choice. Lastly, as part of a system, we can develop policies that support and prioritize choice and inclusion, and that build in mechanisms for accountability. Everyone who uses person-centered practices can create meaningful change. (See Figure 2.3.)

An important consideration when thinking about person-centered approaches is that change occurs at different levels. We can do things at an individual or personal level that will have a big impact. For example, using respectful language, listening actively, sharing control and power, and recognizing our own biases make a positive difference in the lives of people we support. These individual-level practices are called Level 1 changes.

Organizations or service providers can also make changes that support person-centered practices. Examples include rewriting agency documents in plain language, using alternative assessment methods during an intake, offering and requiring staff training and competencies in person-centered practices, and developing employee performance measures around outcomes defined by the persons supported. These types of changes are referred to as Level 2 changes. Organizational change is a journey, but small investments can have a significant impact over time. Later in this section, you will learn about more specific organizational approaches.

Individuals and organizations are parts of systems. Systems have rules and policies that are made at higher levels of government or by funders. Level 3 changes occur when policies and structures that affect a large number of people and organizations are changed. Examples of level 3 changes are a federal agency adopting new person-centered planning guidelines, a state agency offering training on positive behavior supports, and a licensing entity requiring evidence of person-centered services. Level 3 changes are often the hardest and take the most time. However, each level of change has an impact and is a worthy investment to improve choice, quality, and access to the full benefits of community for people with IDD.

LEVEL 1	Any changes that result in a positive difference in the lives of the people who use services or in your own work life
LEVEL 2	Any changes an organization makes to its practices, structure or rules that result in positive differences in the lives of people. *(Organization level/Managers/Supervisors/CEO/Administrative Support)*
LEVEL 3	Any change in practice, structure and rules made at the system level. These changes have an effect on many organizations and therefore many peoples' lives. *(Larger State Level or National Organizational or Leadership Level Issues)*

Figure 2.3. Levels of change in person-centered practices. The levels of change shown above includes person-centered concepts, principles and materials used with permission from The Learning Community for Person-Centered Practices (2017), The Learning Community for Person Centered Practices. Retrieved from: http://tlcpcp.com/

Action Through Language

The words we use matter. One of the most powerful and practical ways individuals, organizations, and systems can be person-centered is through use of language. Words can convey respect, dignity, choice, and inclusion. They can also purposely or inadvertently convey oppression, segregation, and control. The words we use often affect our actions and, over time, these actions become habits. To break the cycle of system approaches that focus only on what is important *for* an individual, it is necessary to change our actions and habits. This process can be facilitated through our words.

The system (policies, rules, etc.) has its own language or "systems speak." Words like *vulnerable*, *needy*, *disabled*, *challenged*, *behaviors*, *program*, and *barriers* frame individuals according to their deficits. Although it may be necessary to use these terms or words for certain types of paperwork or reporting, it is necessary to think critically about how, when, where, and why we use these terms. Unfortunately, eligibility for programs and services often requires highlighting deficits and vulnerabilities; however, that doesn't mean that is who a person really is. Reframing our thinking through the use of our (and our organization's) words can change how we see, approach, and support people with IDD.

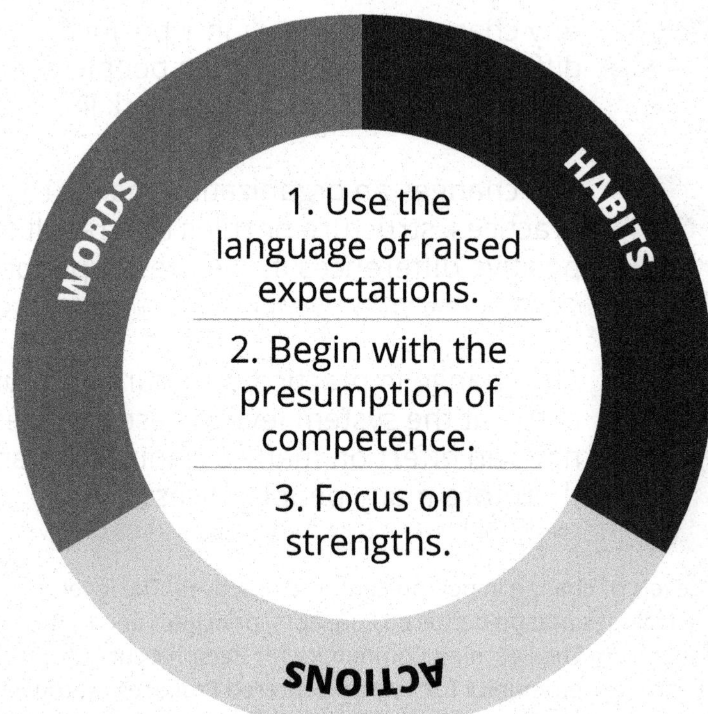

***Figure* 2.4.** Words, thoughts, and actions for person-centeredness.

We can reframe thinking through words that start with the person's strengths and positive qualities: *creative*, *diverse*, *support*, *opportunities*, *future*, *choices*, *strong*, and *informed.* This is strength-based by nature, respectful, and promotes heightened expectations of *contribution*. Every interaction is an opportunity to raise expectations and share strengths. It is also helpful to use open-ended questions, affirmations, and reflections, and then summarize when possible to be sure we understand what is important to and for the individual.

Planning Tools and Approaches

For many of us, planning for the future starts early in life, and so should it for individuals with IDD. Determining what is important to and for an individual begins in early childhood. Adults build children's skills using their preferences as powerful motivators, and we provide opportunities for them to explore their interests and talents. As children move toward young adulthood, person-centered tools can help them frame their journey, often in visual and concrete ways.

A number of organizations and services have developed person-centered planning tools that can be used to get to know a person, explore strengths and preferences, and understand support needs. These tools can be powerful, yet somewhat nontraditional, ways to get at what a person needs or wants out of life. Examples of tools from organizations such as Support Development Associates (*Person-Centered Thinking, Planning, and Practices* [2018]) and Helen Sanderson Associates (*Person-Centered Thinking* [2018]) include the following:

- positive person profiles/one-page profiles
- good day/bad day
- learning logs
- relationship maps
- what's working/not working
- four-plus-one questions
- communication charts
- the donut

The added structure of these tools support the processing of information and the abstract thinking skills needed to find a solution or reach a decision. These tools work across settings and experiences: housing, employment, choices, problem solving, healthcare decisions, and ways to be and feel included in the community. See the resources section at the end of this chapter for links to different tools for person-centered planning.

During transition periods, such as graduation to adulthood, processing and planning for major life events becomes critical. Many individuals with IDD struggle with understanding the big picture or the *gestalt* of the world beyond age 18 or 21. Using concrete and visual tools for future planning can support individuals in sharing what is really important to them and for them. The way this generally works is that the individual supported, along with their family, allies, and support providers, serving as an action team, complete questionnaires or interviews regarding what they know about the individual's skills, interests, and ideas for the future. The team then meets, processes the information, and creates an action plan or map for the future, making certain the individual served is represented based on a strengths-based perspective, with their hopes and dreams at the center of the conversation. A number of models are available to meet the needs of someone interested in a person-centered plan. Familiarity with the various methods can help facilitators identify strategies that will work best for people across the stages of life. Experienced facilitators tend to combine elements from different person-centered methods to tailor planning to the unique needs of each person. Table 2.1 outlines eight unique tools for gathering information and creating a person-centered plan.

Figure 2.5 shows a model of how primary, secondary, and tertiary prevention strategies form a continuum of increasingly intense person-centered and positive support approaches.

Table 2.1. *Methods and Examples of Person-Centered Approaches*

Method	Description of Method and Major Characteristics
Person-Centered Thinking and Planning (2-day training event)	Based on The Learning Community for Person Centered Practices person-centered thinking (PCT) tools for exploration and discovery. Results in a one- to two-page description of what is important to and for a person. Useful when a more complex planning process is not necessary.
Picture of a Life	Based on PCT tools with both graphic and written descriptions to summarize a person's most desirable places to live, work, and relax, with an action plan for moving forward. This method is helpful for transition planning.
Essential Lifestyle Planning	A person-centered plan is created by identifying the "essential" values of a person and including how a person can be supported to honor those values. Originally developed for people who are described as having significant challenging behavior, now a process considered useful for everyone.
Personal Futures Planning	A brainstorming approach that assists a person and a group of people who know the person well in designing a life of meaning. It includes information about the ways in which a person can make contributions in the community. The facilitator encourages creative thinking and uses pictures or drawings to represent planning.
Planning Alternative Tomorrows with Hope (PATH)	Planning starts with a dream that is described with pictures or drawings. The steps necessary for implementing the dream are written down, with targets established for achieving goals.
Discovering Personal Genius (The Discovery Process)	A planning process dedicated to creating sustainable and satisfying person-directed employment. Brainstorming is not confined to traditional job development options that might already be available.
Group Action Planning	A model created by leaders in person-centered planning who have family members with IDD and a history of problem behavior. Emphasis is placed on recruiting "reliable allies" who provide ongoing support and assist in monitoring and adjusting goals over time as part of a team process.
Making Action Plans (MAP)	Tools first used to help children integrate into inclusive school settings. This method is now used widely by both adults and children. Steps include describing a person's history and dreams, nightmares, gifts, strengths, and talents. Strategies for achieving dreams and avoiding nightmares are discussed, with an action plan documenting steps.

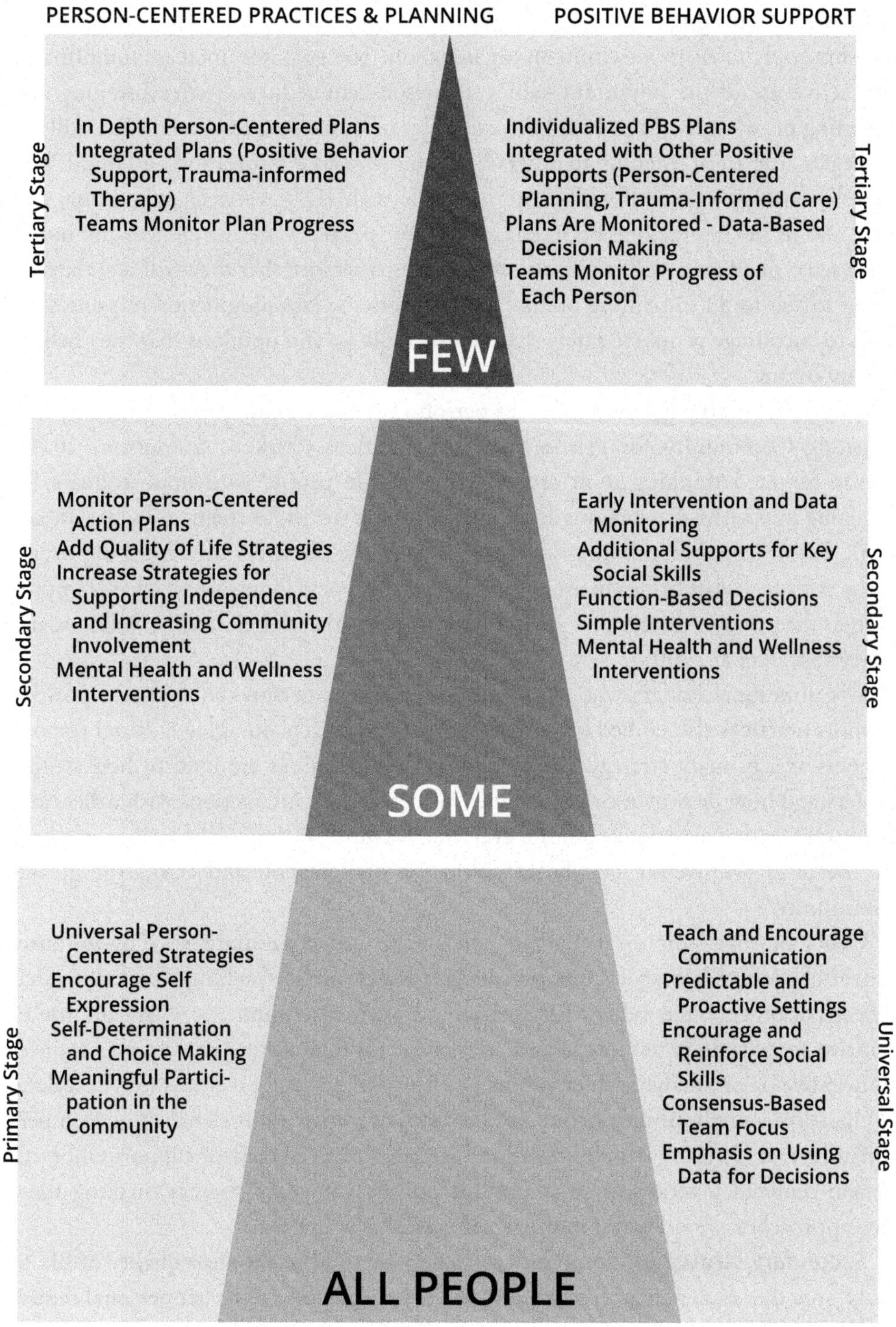

	PERSON-CENTERED PRACTICES & PLANNING		POSITIVE BEHAVIOR SUPPORT	
Tertiary Stage	In Depth Person-Centered Plans Integrated Plans (Positive Behavior Support, Trauma-informed Therapy) Teams Monitor Plan Progress	FEW	Individualized PBS Plans Integrated with Other Positive Supports (Person-Centered Planning, Trauma-Informed Care) Plans Are Monitored - Data-Based Decision Making Teams Monitor Progress of Each Person	Tertiary Stage
Secondary Stage	Monitor Person-Centered Action Plans Add Quality of Life Strategies Increase Strategies for Supporting Independence and Increasing Community Involvement Mental Health and Wellness Interventions	SOME	Early Intervention and Data Monitoring Additional Supports for Key Social Skills Function-Based Decisions Simple Interventions Mental Health and Wellness Interventions	Secondary Stage
Primary Stage	Universal Person-Centered Strategies Encourage Self Expression Self-Determination and Choice Making Meaningful Participation in the Community	ALL PEOPLE	Teach and Encourage Communication Predictable and Proactive Settings Encourage and Reinforce Social Skills Consensus-Based Team Focus Emphasis on Using Data for Decisions	Universal Stage

Figure 2.5. Stages of person-centered practices and planning. Freeman, R. (2016). Strategies for implementing positive support strategies in agencies and organizations. Impact, 29(2), 12–15. Used with permission.

Primary strategies. Primary strategies encourage the use of person-centered methods that apply to *everyone* within an organization. The goal is to increase mindfulness and active use of the important values of person-centeredness. Active listening and reflecting on what has been heard are examples of universal person-centered skills or strategies. The art of listening to others helps improve communication and builds better relationships with staff who support people with IDD, between supervisors and staff, and in any interactions between two or more people. Offering choices and building a sense of alliance with a person reduces the possibility that they will feel they are being forced to do something or controlled by others. Nonjudgmental responses are used to encourage people to safely share ideas, feelings, and opinions that they believe are important.

One primary strategy, referred to as person-centered thinking, was created by The Learning Community for Person Centered Practices (Stirk & Sanderson, 2012). Person-centered thinking tools are used to provide people with opportunities for engaging in positive interactions and exploring what works for them and what doesn't work. Person-centered thinking strategies assist in the discovery of what is important *to* the person—what brings them joy and makes life worth living—and what is important *for* the person—things that are necessary for the sake of their health, wellness, and safety (Smull et al., 2009).

Organizational leaders who successfully implement person-centered and positive support practices also embed learning opportunities for encouraging cultural responsiveness as a primary strategy. These learning opportunities are used to help people understand how their own cultural values influence their interactions with others and encourage an active dialogue among everyone within a setting. Celebrations of diversity occur at a universal level both within the organization and across the greater community.

Other positive supports encourage the use of universal strategies. For instance, universal positive behavior support strategies focus on (1) teaching social skills that reflect person-centered values; (2) creating a positive environment where the use of positive social skills is reinforced and celebrated; (3) establishing consistent responses to negative or problematic interactions to ensure that social problems don't escalate; (4) increasing predictability, choice, and control over important elements of each person's life; and (5) using data for decision making. Positive behavior support embraces person-centered practices as an important universal primary strategy, making these two approaches a good fit for multi-tiered systems of support.

Secondary strategies. Secondary strategies are used to monitor quality of life to make sure that each person is making progress in achieving his or her personal desires and goals. Ongoing monitoring of quality-of-life outcomes provides a way to intervene as early as possible when a person's efforts to achieve optimal quality of life have not been successful using primary strategies alone. Additional group or individual strategies are added to help improve quality of life. Examples of secondary strategies include social and community-based learning opportunities, problem solving when a person's work or home life is not ideal, and helping people explore new hobbies, meet new people, and attend community events.

In positive behavior support, secondary strategies might include monitoring incident report patterns and other indicators that social interaction problems are occurring, and then inviting people to participate in group or individual interventions such as anger management, learning to identify emotions, or health and wellness interventions. The goal in positive behavior support is to identify the function of the behavior, the reason a problem is occurring, and ways to help people replace problematic interactions with positive social responses before these problems become chronic or more severe.

Tertiary strategies. Tertiary strategies are individualized and more intensive than primary or secondary strategies. The goal is to build capacity within an organization to ensure that anyone receiving services who wants a person-centered plan will be able to access a facilitator of his or her choice. Ideally, plan facilitators are familiar with more than one type of person-centered strategy, such as Essential Lifestyle Planning, PATH, or MAPS (O'Brien, Pearpoint, & Kahn, 2010), and can work with a person receiving services to tailor the planning process to address that individual's unique needs and characteristics. Tertiary strategies involve active and ongoing planning processes and a team approach for reviewing every person's plan regularly to make sure they do not become compliance documents that are filed away and not actually used. In addition, the team meets regularly to problem solve, create action plans, review progress, and celebrate successes over time.

The person-centered planning review process may identify the need for other positive supports. In such a case, tertiary teams include additional positive support strategies in the person-centered planning process instead of creating a completely separate set of meetings. This may require adding new members to the person-centered planning team who can guide the individual in adding action items to the plan. For example, positive behavior support can be helpful when team members and staff need to change their own behavior to encourage positive social interactions. The person and his or her team use positive behavior support to review specific routines that are problematic in the person's life. A process called functional behavioral assessment (FBA) is used to identify the reasons problems are occurring during that routine. Together, the person and team use the FBA information to add additional interventions and action items to the planning process.

Organizational Approaches

Organizations that support individuals with IDD and other disabilities must consider all of their services and systems when implementing a new procedure, such as person-centered practices and positive supports, in order to do so effectively. Everyone within an organization should be considered part of the process (Lohrmann, Forman, Martin, & Palmieri, 2008).

Creating organization-wide teams. One way to avoid relying too much on the "train and hope model" we mentioned earlier in this chapter is to form an organization-wide team of members who can work together to implement new practices. Research suggests that a team approach is more effective because it combines the experience of multiple viewpoints and shares responsibility for leadership and decision making (Fixsen, Naoom, Blasé, Friedman, & Wallace, 2005; Sindelar, Shearer, Yendel-Hoppey, & Liebert, 2006). These individuals are all considered important stakeholders who provide guidance and feedback on the planning process (Lohrmann et al., 2008). The team systematically assesses the strengths of the organization and develops an action plan for moving forward. Research in education and human services suggests that active administrative leadership and support is one of the key elements that predict successful implementation efforts (Fixsen. Naoom, Blase, Friedman, & Wallace, 2005; Kincaid, Childs, Blase, & Wallace, 2007).

Assessing the readiness and interest of the people who will be involved in the process is an important first step in implementing a new practice. Teams may start by sharing details about a particular practice during staff meetings or special events that bring stakeholders together. Implementation of a new practice requires more than one person dedicated to the change process. Champions are needed at each level of an organization—leadership, management and supervision, people with IDD receiving supports, and direct support staff all contributing to the success of implementation. If the majority of people indicate interest, the team can get started with the self-assessment process.

Implementing a new practice requires a thoughtful review of policies and procedures, onboarding and ongoing training systems, hiring processes, coaching and mentoring systems for support staff learning new skills, and information that will help teams assess and evaluate the implementation process. Champions of person-centered practices and/or other positive supports need to be recruited to take on leadership of different elements of the action plan. Many organizations will have pockets of innovation and areas of strength related to a new practice that teams can build on and expand over time.

Teams use self-assessment to clearly identify a person-centered vision and connect it to organizational mission and vision statements. Sometimes changes are made to the original organizational mission to better align values. It is important to identify these values by selecting desired outcomes for people with IDD supported within an organization, staff members, the organization itself, and the larger community in which the organization exists. Action planning is tied directly to each outcome for these four target areas. The alignment of outcome statements and action planning connects key values with everyday efforts to implement person-centered practices and positive supports.

The team creates a plan outlining how the outcomes will be achieved across 3 years, setting goals for each year. Once the team has finalized the self-assessment and action plan, ongoing meetings are scheduled in advance across the year, taking into account existing meetings and communication strategies. Whenever possible, teams use the meetings and organizational systems already in place to implement new practices. The idea is to "work smarter, not harder" by incorporating action-plan items into everyday work routines and systems.

Coaching and staff support. Research indicates that coaching and support systems for staff members are considered an important element for implementing any new practice (Joyce & Showers, 2002; Reinke, Stormont, Herman, & Newcomer, 2014). Teams implementing person-centered practices set up strategies to support staff and evaluate the overall effectiveness of coaching and mentoring systems. Coaches are used to make sure that universal primary strategies such as person-centered thinking (Smull et al., 2009) are introduced and used by staff members. The coaching role is used to support opportunities to practice new strategies and reflect on how they can be integrated into different work situations and settings. These coaching systems become more formalized when methods are added to document staff members' completion of trainings, create competency-based assessment and feedback, and review coach progress regularly.

Data-based decision making. The goal of organization-wide planning is to bring data-based decision making into team meetings for review by a wider group of stakeholders. Many organizations regularly collect different types of organization-wide data that are reviewed by smaller subsets of people at the leadership level, by management, and/or within human resources. The organization-wide team needs this information to guide implementation and to evaluate a new practice's impact on the organization. Staff tenure and retention, cultural responsiveness evaluation, satisfaction surveys for all stakeholders (people supported, families, staff), incident reports, workers' compensation, and sick leave can all be used to assess the effectiveness of the overall organizational processes since the introduction of a new practice. Secondary and tertiary strategies rely heavily on the ability to create easy and efficient summaries of incident report, quality of life, and other data for progress-monitoring purposes.

The final goal of data-based decision making is to create a way for the team to assess whether a new practice has been implemented effectively. The degree to which a practice has been implemented in the way it is intended is referred to as *fidelity of implementation*. A team may observe that the quality of life for people with IDD is improving, incident reports are decreasing, or other positive outcomes are evident. Evidence showing fidelity of implementation increases the ability of an organization-wide team to assess whether the outcomes or changes may be related to implementation of a new practice.

Personal Illustration: James Good

At age 21, James Good thought it was time he spread his wings. His mother knew he'd need support and contacted Trillium Services, an agency in Duluth, Minnesota, that provides residential and supported employment services to children and adults with developmental disabilities. James made the transition to living in a group home and, 1 year later, began thinking seriously about his future. "I had my first PATH in 2008," recalled James.

A PATH (Planning Alternative Tomorrows with Hope) is a tool used in person-centered planning. The person supported shares his or her dreams for the future and graphic facilitation is used to develop and illustrate achievable and realistic goals. "When you look at a PATH," said Kari Aaneson, Executive Director of residential services at Trillium, "it really starts with the North Star, and that's hopes and dreams for the person. And really, there are no barriers."

One of the themes in James's PATH was travel. "The biggest thing that he wanted to work on was going to a football game," recalled Mike Molitor, a direct support professional at Trillium who has worked with James since 2007. "So, through PATH we helped him with the steps—who he wanted to invite, where he would stay." But through deeper listening, Mike and others in the support circle discovered that traveling to a football game was secondary to James's memory of watching football on Sundays with his dad. "And so, going to a football game kind of helped James connect with his father," said Mike. Trained as a PATH facilitator in 2004, Mike has seen over and over again how person-centered planning can positively affect people's lives. "The first thing I have to do is listen, and listen deeply. How to be a really good listener starts with developing a relationship with each person, and getting to know them."

Trillium has had a culture of person-centeredness from its beginning. "When the owners started the agency," said Kari, "one of them was in a cohort project through the University of Minnesota where they went around to different states, and they taught person-centered planning." In addition to PATH, the agency has trained its staff in MAPS (Making Action Plans) and ELP (Essential Lifestyle Planning). They are now using Liberty Plan, an alternative person-centered planning tool that places more emphasis on previous accomplishments and gifts. "We try and really keep up with the latest in the field," said Kari, "and challenge our thinking on what person-centered thinking can be, and how far it can go." Trillium has coaches on staff who work onsite with direct support professionals, reinforcing the use of person-centered thinking tools.

Trillium's person-centered culture has certainly enhanced the quality of the agency, which boasts a staff retention rate of 92%. "Really, it's just trying to help people lead the best lives they possibly can for themselves," said Kari, "and the lives they choose for themselves." The agency's focus on the individual resonates deeply with staff, many of whom make their careers at Trillium.

Being person-centered at Trillium means nurturing respectful relationships with the people they support. "I think it means listening more than speaking," said Kari, "and listening not only to that person, and what their dreams and hopes are in life, but listening to those who have known them the best in their life, so listening to parents, listening to family members, especially for individuals who do not use words to speak for themselves."

Trillium has close to 300 employees, serving 180 individuals. Mike, who worked with James from the beginning, moved to a different department within the agency so he could continue supporting James after he had moved into his own apartment. "There's a template that you can follow," said Mike, "but the road to person-centeredness is going to look different for every person. You really have to open your heart, and you have to open your mind, to find that correct path for each person."

Being person-centered as an agency also means knowing when to step out of the way. "Sometimes as providers, we can hold people back, and that is a very disturbing thought," said Kari. "Coming from someone who's worked in the field for 21 years, to think that I've ever held someone back is not the best thought I've ever had. And sometimes, [being person-centered] means just being able to think about things in a different way, be as creative as you possibly can be, step outside the box, work with the rest of the team members."

After living in a group home for a few years, James gained self-confidence and independent living skills and was ready to live on his own. "I knew how to cook dinner, I knew how to clean," said James. "I pretty much knew how to do everything so I was like the big guy who taught other people stuff, you know." In his second PATH, in 2011, plans were made to help James explore his options and find the right place to live. The search took a few years but James is now living in a place of his own.

Soon after moving into his own apartment James initiated his third PATH. "Now I'm going for my driver's license and owning a car and hopefully having a family someday," said James. These goals may have seemed unrealistic when James first moved out of his mother's house. Now, they are entirely within his reach. Soon after passing his driver's test in 2017, and after investigating countless vehicles with his PATH coach, James purchased a used Ford Focus with a sunroof. "The very next morning, something important happened in James's life," said Mike. "He drove to work for the first time."

James feels gratitude for the people in his circle of support that believed in him, and he's ready to pay it forward. "I'm hoping that someday I can actually help one of the guys I lived with do the same thing, think about moving out and getting on with your life, cause that's the way that I did it."

Conclusion

Person-centered and positive support practices can be used by individuals, organizations, and systems to support people with IDD to reach optimal quality of life while living and participating fully in their communities. Positive behavior supports and person-centered planning are just two examples of these approaches. These types of approaches are not new, but they are very necessary, because many services and supports for people with IDD and their families have been driven by the system's needs and preferences, rather than by the person supported. Being person centered as an individual, an organization, or a system means that we value and respect the individual first by focusing on their strengths while, at the same time, supporting valued social roles and reciprocity. At the core, person-centeredness is about supporting people with IDD to live the lives they choose for themselves, even if those lives and choices look different than what family members or other professionals might choose.

Person-centeredness is an ongoing journey at any level, not just a destination. There are different methods and approaches for learning about and implementing person-centered practices and positive approaches. The effectiveness of an individual, organization, or system in empowering each person with IDD to achieve an optimal quality of life depends on investment, commitment, action, and metrics. Although the efforts and outcomes look different depending on the level of change, the values of person-centered practices remain constant. All people using person-centered practices can create meaningful change.

Discussion Questions

- How would you evaluate whether quality of life is improving for someone?
- What values do you believe are most important in a person-centered organization?
- How can a team integrate person-centered practices and positive supports within an organization?
- Will training be available to individuals supported and their families and allies to ensure they understand the spirit of the changes and their role(s) within the process?
- Imagine you are introducing a new positive support practice to people in your organization. What strategies would you use to assess whether people are ready to implement a new practice? How would you know that staff members and people supported by the organization want to participate?
- Diversity can result from team members' different educational backgrounds and past training and work experiences. How can having a diverse team within an organization help advance the implementation of person-centered practices and positive supports?

Resources

- The Learning Community for Person-Centered Practices (TLC) and Support Development Associates (SDA) are national leaders in the field of person-centered practices. Their websites provide information, training, and opportunities to connect with others on person-centered practices. http://tlcpcp.com/ and http://sdaus.com/
- Feature Issue on Person-Centered Positive Supports. This issue of *IMPACT* explores various approaches and perspectives on person-centered practices and positive supports. https://ici.umn.edu/products/impact/292/
- Minnesota Positive Support Practices. Although designed for Minnesota, this website contains various resources and tools for increasing positive supports, which support people to make positive changes in their lives. This site is inclusive for all types of disabilities. mnpsp.org
- Helen Sanderson Associates. This website provides an overview of person-centered planning as well as free person-centered planning tools and resources. http://helensandersonassociates.co.uk/person-centred-practice/
- Association for Positive Behavior Support (APBS). APBS is a national association focused on best practices and implementation of positive behavior supports. Positive behavior support is a set of processes that combine information from social, behavioral, and biomedical science and applies this information at the individual and/or systems level to reduce behavioral challenges and improve quality of life. http://www.apbs.org/

References

American Psychological Association. (2016). *Policy statement on evidence-based practice in psychology*. Retrieved from http://www.apa.org/practice/guidelines/evidence-based-statement.aspx)

Claes, C., Van Hove, G., Vandevelde, S., van Loon, J., & Schalock, R. L. (2010). Person-centered planning: analysis of research and effectiveness. *IDD, 48*, 432–453. http://dx.doi.org/10.1352/1934-9556-48.6.432

Fixsen, D. L., Naoom, S. F., Blase, K. A., Friedman, R. M., & Wallace, F. (2005). *Implementation research: A synthesis of the literature*. Tampa, FL: University of South Florida.

Freeman, R. (2016). Strategies for implementing positive support strategies in agencies and organizations. *Impact, 29*(2), 12–15.

Helen Sanderson Associates. (2018). *Person centered thinking*. Retrieved from http://helensandersonassociates.co.uk/about/how-can-we-help-you/our-courses/person-centred-thinking/

Holburn, S. (2002). How science can evaluate and enhance person-centered planning. *Research & Practice for Persons with severe Disabilities, 27*(4), 250–260. http://dx.doi.org/10.2511/rpsd.27.4.250

Joyce, B., & Showers, B. (2002). *Student achievement through staff development* (3rd ed.). Alexandria, VA: Association for Supervision and Curriculum Development.

Kincaid, D., Childs, K., Blase, K. A., & Wallace, F. (2007). Identifying barriers and facilitators in implementing schoolwide positive behavior support. *Journal of Positive Behavior Interventions, 9*(3), 174–184. http://dx.doi.org/10.1177/10983007070090030501

The Learning Community for Person Centered Practices. (2017). *The Learning Community for Person Centered Practices*. Retrieved from http://tlcpcp.com/

Lohrmann, S., Forman, S., Martin, S., & Palmieri, M. (2008). Understanding school personnel's resistance to adopting schoolwide positive behavior support at a universal level of intervention. *Journal of Positive Behavior Interventions, 10*(4), 256–269.

Lucyshyn, J., Dunlap, G., & Freeman, R. (2014). A historical perspective on the evolution of positive behavior support. F. Brown, J. Anderson, & R. De Pry, (Eds.*), Individual positive behavior supports: A standards-based guide to practices in school and community-based settings* (pp. 3–25). Baltimore, MD: Brookes.

O'Brien, J. (2002). Person-centered planning as a contributing factor in organizational and systems change. *Research & Practice for Persons with severe Disabilities, 27*(4), 261–264.

O'Brien, J., & Mount, B. (2015). *Pathfinders: People with developmental disabilities and their allies building communities that work better for everybody*. Ontario, Canada: Inclusion Press.

O'Brien, J., Pearpoint, J., & Kahn, L. (2010). *The PATH & MAPS handbook: Person-centered ways to build community*. Toronto, Canada: Inclusion Press.

Ratti, V., Hassiotis, A., Crabtree, J., Deb, S., Gallagher, P., & Unwin, G. (2016). The effectiveness of person-centred planning for people with intellectual disabilities: A systematic review. *Research in Developmental Disabilities, 57*, 63–84. http://dx.doi.org/10.1016/j.ridd.2016.06.015

Reinke, W. M., Stormont, M., Herman, K. C., & Newcomer, L. (2014). Using coaching to support teacher implementation of classroom-based interventions. *Journal of Behavioral Education, 23*(1), 150–167. http://dx.doi.org/10.1007/s10864-013-9186-0

Sindelar, P. T., Shearer, D. K., Yendol-Hoppey, D., & Liebert, T. W. (2006). The sustainability of inclusive school reform. *Exceptional Children, 72*(3), 317–331. http://dx.doi.org/10.1177/001440290607200304

Smull, M. W., Bourne, M. L., & Sanderson, H. (2009). *Becoming a person-centered system.*, VA: National Association of State Directors of Developmental Disability Services, Alexandria. Retrieved from: http://www.nasddds.org/resource-library/person-centered-practices/becoming-a-person-centered-system-a-brief-overview-smull-bourne-and-sanderson/

Stirk, S., & Sanderson, H. (2012). *Creating person-centered organisations: Strategies and tools for managing change in health, social care, and the voluntary sector*. London, UK: Jessica Kingsley Publishers.

Support Development Associates. (2018). *Person-centered thinking, planning, and practices.* Retrieved from http://sdaus.com/work#pctpp

CHAPTER THREE

Housing: A Place to Call Home

Sheryl A. Larson, Heidi Eschenbacher, and Sandra L. Pettingell

Advance Organizers

- Most people with IDD in the United States live at home with their families.
- Medicaid is the primary funding mechanism for residential supports.
- While many states have closed all institutions, today nearly 40,000 people with IDD still live in institutional settings (e.g., nursing homes, psychiatric facilities, large intermediate care facilities).
- Having a place to call home is important throughout the lifespan.

Historical Views

Most people with IDD in the United States live with family members throughout their lives. However, for people not living with a family member, living arrangements and options have changed dramatically in the last 50 years. In 1967, 194,650 people with IDD (half of whom were children) lived in state IDD institutions located in all 50 states and the District of Columbia (see Figure 3.1). By 2015, only 20,642 (4% of whom were children) remained in large state IDD institutions, with another 21,392 living in nonstate IDD facilities serving 16 or more people (Larson et.al., 2017).

Forces for change. In the 1940s and 1950s, families joined forces to protest that institutions serving children and adults with IDD were understaffed, overcrowded,

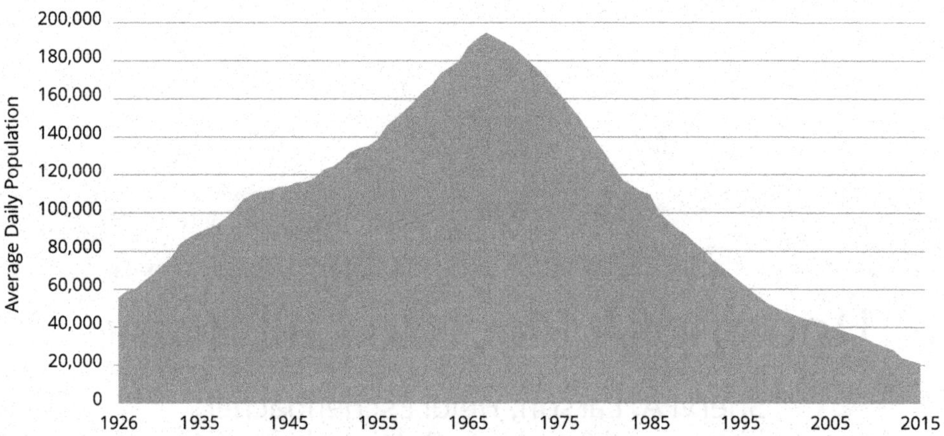

Figure 3.1. Average Daily Population of State-Operated IDD Institutions 1926 through 2015. Source: Figure reprinted with permission from Larson, S.A., Eschenbacher, H. J., Anderson, L. L., Taylor, B., Pettingell, S., Hewitt, A., Sowers, M., & Fay, M. L. (2017). *In-home and residential long-term supports and services for persons with intellectual or developmental disabilities: Status and trends through 2014.* Minneapolis: University of Minnesota, Research and Training Center on Community Living, Institute on Community Integration.

and inadequate in terms of the care they provided. Their concerns received national attention when Senator Robert Kennedy visited the Willowbrook State School in New York in 1965, when Blatt & Kaplan's photo essay Christmas in Purgatory was published in 1966, and when Geraldo Rivera's documentary, *Willowbrook: The Last Great Disgrace,* was televised in 1972 (Blatt & Kaplan, 1966; Minnesota Governor's Council on Developmental Disabilities [MNGCDD], 2016). Living conditions for people in institutions were deplorable. Educational services were limited or not available, facilities were overcrowded, communicable diseases such as Hepatitis B spread uncontrolled, many people spent their days with little or nothing to do, and for some, even basic food, clothing, and sanitation needs went unmet. For many children and adults with IDD, institutions provided nothing more than "three hots [meals] and a cot [a place to sleep]."

In 1963, President John F. Kennedy, whose sister Rosemary had IDD, established the President's Panel on Mental Retardation and urged Congress to develop services and supports for people with IDD in communities instead of in custodial institutions (J.F. Kennedy Presidential Library and Museum, 2016). Visionary thinkers such as Bengt Nirje and Wolf Wolfensberger argued that all people, regardless of the type or severity of their disabilities, should live in physically accessible and socially inclusive settings in typical neighborhoods (Kugel & Wolfensberger, 1969; MNGCDD, 2016). They argued that people with IDD should

- have daily, weekly, and annual schedules like those of other people their age;
- work, play, live, and go to school with people experiencing the full range of human abilities;
- spend time in the company of both males and females;
- maintain employment in jobs earning enough money to meet their needs; and
- be treated with dignity and respect, with the right to make choices about all aspects of life.

Seminal litigation and legislation. Pressure for reform mounted as class action lawsuits filed in state court sought improvements in institutional conditions and argued that people with IDD should move from institutions to homes in community settings (e.g., *PARC v. Commonwealth of Pennsylvania,* 1972; *ARC v. Rockefeller,* 1972; *Wyatt v. Stickney,* 1971; and *Welsch v. Likins,* 1972). Legislation was passed prohibiting discrimination based on disability in federally funded programs (the Rehabilitation Act of 1973), and providing access to free appropriate public education in neighborhood schools for all children regardless of disability (PL 94-142; the Education for All Handicapped Children Act of 1975, now the Individuals with Disabilities Education Act).

Medicaid financing. The Medicaid Intermediate Care Facilities for Individuals with Intellectual Disabilities (ICF/IID, previously ICF/MR) program was authorized in 1967. The program offered federal financial assistance to states covering half or more of the costs of institutional care for people with IDD in facilities that met strict standards designed to reduce overcrowding, improve living conditions, and provide individualized treatment. The effect of these judicial and legislative actions was profound. States moved people, especially children, out of institutions into other settings and improved the environment and services in institutions so they would qualify for federal ICF/IID funding.

The proportion of people living in state-operated IDD facilities who were in ICF/IID-certified settings was 59% by 1977, and 85% by 1982 (Lakin et al., 1985). The proportion of individuals age 21 years or younger dropped from 49% in 1965 to 22% in 1982 (Lakin et al., 1993). Also by 1982, nearly half (49%) of all LTSS recipients with IDD who did not live with a family member lived in a nonstate setting, and 38% shared a home with six or fewer people.

In 1981, Congress authorized the Medicaid 1915(c) Home and Community Based Services (HCBS) Waiver to fund LTSS in community rather than in institutional settings. HCBS recipients live in their own home, with a family member, with a host or foster family, or in a community group home. Unlike the ICF/IID program, which bundles housing and services into a one-size-fits-all package, Medicaid HCBS Waiver–funded supports are offered a la carte. People select only the services they need in the amounts they need. Unlike ICF/IID services, Medicaid HCBS funds may not be used to pay for room and board.

States specify the service menu and eligibility criteria for their Medicaid Waiver programs. The HCBS service menu varies by state but may include supports for family caregivers, respite, personal care, in-home skill development, case management, residential services (in a group home, for example), supports for employment and community participation, behavioral supports, medical supports such as in-home nursing or therapies such as occupational or speech therapy, transportation, and environmental modifications. In many Medicaid Waiver programs, participants can choose to direct their own supports, leading the planning process and managing budgeted resources, or they can opt to have their supports managed by a provider agency or another entity. Between 1982 and 2000, 138 large state-operated IDD facilities closed. By 2000, only 116,411 people lived in ICF/IIDs, while 291,255 people received Medicaid Wavier–funded LTSS. Of the Medicaid Waiver recipients, 36% lived with a family member.

Over time, attitudes, legislation, and funding have transformed what home can mean for many people with IDD. Looking back, a place to call home was not regarded as essential, but now, more than ever, people with IDD have options about what home looks like for them. However, even today many people with IDD do remain isolated in residential settings, and it is important to prioritize inclusion, choice, and access so people with IDD are able to have a place to call home.

Current status. Of the 1.2 million people receiving LTSS through state IDD agencies in 2015, 56% lived with a family member, 11% lived in a home of their own, 5% lived with a foster family, and 26% lived in a group IDD setting. The remaining 2% lived in a nursing home or psychiatric facility (see Figure 3.2). Only 10% lived in facilities housing seven or more people with IDD.

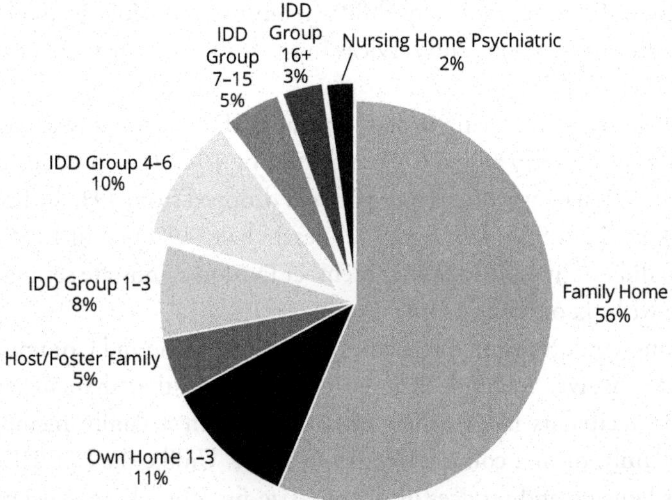

Figure 3.2. Residence Type and Size for People Receiving Long-Term Supports or Services from State IDD Agencies on June 30, 2015 (Estimated Totals). Source: Larson et al. (2017).

Misperceptions and Assumptions

People have different ideas about what home should look like. Common misperceptions about housing for people with IDD concern location, funding, and access. People with IDD are our neighbors and, increasingly, live in community-based settings, including in their own homes. Publicly funded LTSS for people with IDD in the United States are complex and sometimes misunderstood. One common misconception is that all people with IDD in the US are entitled to government-funded LTSS as adults. While all children with IDD are entitled to a free and appropriate public education, Medicaid and state LTSS recipients must meet income, disability, and level-of-support-needs criteria. The institutional Medicaid ICF/IID program is technically an "entitlement program," meaning that anyone who is eligible must be offered the option of receiving services in an ICF/IID. However, only 77,444 people chose that option in 2015. Most other Medicaid and state-funded programs, including the Medicaid Waiver Home and Community Based Services program, serve only a portion of the eligible population. In fact, while 774,964 people with IDD received Medicaid Waiver–funded supports in 2015, an estimated 199,641 people with IDD living with family members were waiting for services.

A second misconception is that most people with IDD move from their family's home into a group home as adults. In reality, most adults with IDD (at least 53%, according to one study) live in the home of a family member. Even among adults who receive Medicaid-funded services, 34% live in the home of a family member (Larson, Doljanac, & Lakin, 2005; Larson et al., 2017). In addition, this misconception is furthered by the idea that people with IDD can't live alone and in their own homes. This is not true. Many people with IDD live independently, whether alone, with a partner, or with family.

Another misconception is that services for people with IDD are the same throughout the United States. The reality is that services differ dramatically by state. A person who receives services in one state may not be eligible for services if they move to another state. If a person moves to a new state are found eligible, there is no guarantee that they will continue to receive the same services that they are received in their previous state.

A final misconception is that some people with IDD are so different from the rest of the population that the only and best place for them to live is in a segregated state-operated institution serving 16 and several hundred people. While all states had state-operated IDD institutions at some point in the 20th century, today 15 states no longer have any large state IDD institution. In those states, people with a full range of support needs are served in the home of a family member or in another community setting. Even in states that continue to operate institutions, fewer people are admitted each year than are discharged. People with IDD can and do live in homes in communities. Dozens of deinstitutionalization studies have shown that people who move from an institution to a community home develop and use more skills, are more likely to make choices about both the little and the big things in life, and are active participants in their communities (Larson, Lakin, & Hill, 2013; Ticha et al., 2013).

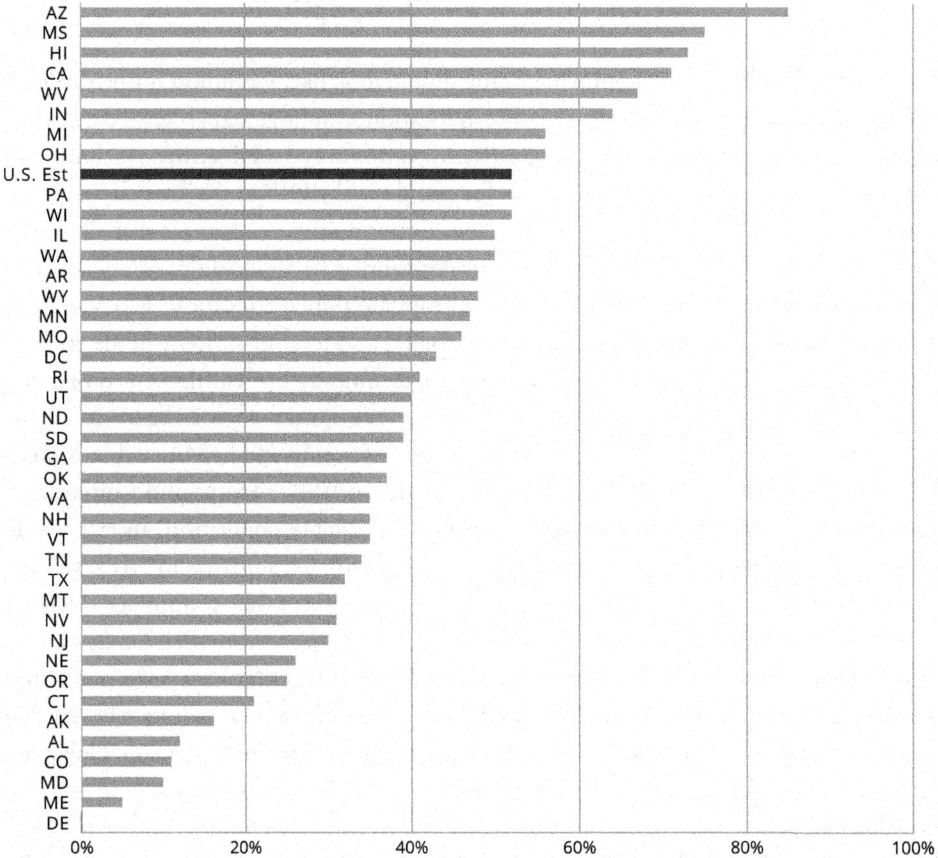

Figure 3.3. Percent of Medicaid Waiver Recipients with IDD Living with a Family Member by State as of June 30, 2015. Source: Larson et al. (2017).

Current Controversies and Challenges

Changing Expectations for Medicaid HCBS: The 2014 Settings Rule

In 2014, Medicaid set new rules that require person-centered planning practices, define the characteristics of home and community-based services (HCBS) for which Medicaid resources can be used, and prohibit the use of Medicaid HCBS funding for services in residential or non-residential institutions. The rules describe protections for people living in provider-owned housing. You can read more about person-centered practices in chapter 2.

Some families are concerned that the institutional settings in which their family member lives or receives services will no longer qualify for Medicaid funding. However, the rule does not ban the use of *any* Medicaid funding for institutions; it says that Medicaid HCBS funding cannot be used to pay for services provided in institutional settings. Medicaid continues to fund institutional services in intermediate care facilities for individuals with intellectual disabilities and nursing homes.

Shifting Funding Models: Medicaid-Managed LTSS Care

Medicaid began as a fee-for-service program. Recipients could choose any provider that would accept Medicaid payments. Providers were reimbursed for each service. Increasingly, states are choosing to use Managed Care Organizations (MCOs) to operate Medicaid-funded medical and long-term supports and services. Managed care plans require participants to receive services from a specific network of providers. Services from providers not in the network are restricted or may not be reimbursed at all. MCOs are reimbursed on a per-member per-month rate for all recipients regardless of the number or type of services provided.

Managed LTSS may improve service coordination, eliminate unnecessary duplication in services, and shift some of the financial risk of providing expensive services from state agencies to an MCO. However, when Medicaid LTSS are converted from fee-for-service to managed care, LTSS recipients face new challenges. In a fee-for-service model, people can select a different provider for each service. For example, an adult living in a home of their own could use self-directed supports to hire family members to provide in-home supports, a hospital network for physician services, a specialized mental health provider, a local governmental agency for care coordination services, and other agencies for respite care, transportation, and employment supports. In managed care, the person may be required to select all of those providers from a single network.

People with IDD receive LTSS in many different settings. MCOs enrolling participants who are shifting from a fee-for-service model may be asked to contract with dozens or even hundreds of residential service providers. If they do not, former fee-for-service enrollees may have to move to a home operated by a different service provider, receive employment supports from a different vendor, find a different roster of personal care attendants, and/or select a new team of medical or therapeutic specialists so that all of their care comes from approved providers.

Deinstitutionalization and Home and Community-Based Services

Even though 90% people with IDD receive services in home or community-based settings, more than 40,000 people with IDD continued to live in institutions, nursing homes, or psychiatric facilities in 2015 (Larson et al., 2017). There are 145 state-operated IDD facilities serving 16 or more people on a single campus. While 15 states have closed all state-operated IDD facilities serving 16 or more people, nine states have closed none. The number of people living in institutions will continue to decline, but fully converting to community-based supports may take decades. The speed of change will depend on several factors, including the success or failure of congressional proposals to significantly reduce overall federal Medicaid spending. States facing decreasing federal Medicaid dollars may choose to close expensive services (such as state-operated IDD facilities), cut the amount spent per person for services, and/or reduce the total number of people they serve to adjust to any cuts made.

Waiting Lists and Alternatives

With nearly 200,000 people waiting for Medicaid Waiver–funded LTSS, the demand for services far exceeds the supply. To meet the needs of those known to be waiting, the number of Medicaid LTSS recipients with IDD would have to increase by 23% (Larson et al., 2017). The unmet demand for LTSS increases each year as 65,048 students with IDD exit school due to graduation, completion of a certificate, or loss of eligibility for special education services (U.S. Department of Education, 2016).

People who are waiting for Medicaid Waiver–funded LTSS have a variety of options. Many live with family members throughout their adult lives. Some families remodel their homes to make a separate living area for an adult who lives with them. Others use assistive technology to monitor and support family members who remain at home while a family member is at work, or they find a neighbor who can check in with the person periodically. Some people with IDD share a home with a friend or family member, and cover the friend or family member's rent in exchange for their providing specific supports.

Some families frustrated with long waiting lists for public IDD LTSS have developed apartment complexes or subdivisions, gated communities, farmsteads, assisted living facilities, or other congregate settings in which groups of people with IDD live and receive services while physically separated from their communities. Such options often aim for an adult with IDD to live more independently than they could if they stayed with family members. Advocates in the disability community have expressed concern that these residential options are a return to separating people with IDD in institutional settings (American Association on Intellectual and Developmental Disabilities & Association of University Centers on Disability, 2016). The challenge of such settings is that routines and patterns of life need to work for everyone sharing the environment. The more people who share the environment, the less opportunity each individual will have to direct their own life. Segregated settings also create barriers to working, playing, living, and going to school with people across the full range of human abilities.

Life Course Expectations and Transitions

Having a place to call home is important throughout the lifespan. For young children, a stable forever home free of abuse and neglect is a top priority. Early experiences can facilitate the development of a person's skills and preferences. Families, educators, and support professionals can support full participation, increased expectations, and meaningful choices early in life that will set the stage for living independently as an adult. Strategies to facilitate independence can include activities across the lifespan.

Families can enhance the lives of school-age children with disabilities by supporting participation in the full array of activities enjoyed by all children of that age. Individuals with disabilities may require more assistance to participate or may participate in a slightly different way, but should be fully included in the family and the community in which they live.

Financial planning should begin during the early school years to maximize a person's opportunity to participate in postsecondary education, training, and employment and choose a place to live that they will consider home as an adult. Tax-advantaged Achieving a Better Life Experience (ABLE) savings accounts can be used to save money for the future without jeopardizing eligibility for publicly funded healthcare, income, employment, education, or other supports in adulthood. Other financial tools such as special-needs trusts or pooled trusts can also be used for this purpose.

In adolescence, young people with disabilities need support to participate in activities and events that help them make friends and to participate in the community beyond the family. They also need opportunities and perhaps support to participate in family and household activities, and to become as independent as possible in getting from one place to another by driving, using public transportation, or accessing other transportation options. Adolescents should be active partners in planning for postsecondary education and employment, and for contributing to the broader community.

Adolescents who have work or internship opportunities before they leave high school are more likely to be employed as adults. Having earned income can make it possible to participate in postsecondary education options and to live in a setting other than the home of a family member in adulthood. Strong community connections made during adolescence and young adulthood can create a network that provides informal supports throughout a person's adult life.

In adulthood, individuals with IDD may need formal or informal supports in areas such as finances, making important decisions, medical care, daily living skills, managing a household, and navigating romantic relationships, work, and living arrangements. Families can help adults with IDD to identify natural supports or services that can facilitate living in the community. Supports may include healthcare, housing, income support, or other services that empower living in the community. Adults with IDD may be eligible for low-income housing subsidies such as Section 8 Housing Choice Vouchers or Section 811 supportive housing for people with disabilities through Housing and Urban Development agencies.

Practical Suggestions and Interventions

Families can help their loved one with IDD to cultivate dreams and to plan and prepare for adult roles by establishing a solid foundation of skills, experiences, and relationships to make the person's dreams achievable. Families can work together to establish and pursue goals in the areas of finance, living arrangements, relationships, employment, and education. They can develop a person-centered housing plan that describes a menu of services, supports, and technologies the individual will need for independent living.

Parent support groups, advocacy organizations, Centers for Independent Living, and provider organizations offer valuable supports for families. Some of them are listed at the end of this chapter. Participating in trainings and other activities sponsored by those organizations can be a good way to connect with other families who have had similar experiences or needs. Centers for Independent Living, Developmental Disability Councils (which advise the governor in each state), and University Centers of Excellence in Developmental Disabilities offer valuable resources.

If needed supports are not available, persons with IDD and their families are urged to share their stories with local, state, or national elected governmental officials who are in a position to change the service system. As individuals and their families become familiar with Medicaid and other publicly funded services, they may learn about new services for which they are eligible. Individuals and families can offer praise for supports that are working well and suggestions for improvement for those that are not. It is important to remember that the choices, decisions, and dreams of the person with IDD should drive plans and services. People with IDD and their family members should speak up when they have an idea about how to make it easier to participate fully in important activities and events.

Individuals who provide supports, whether they are family members, friends, or paid support staff, share a mission to keep the person with IDD at the center of all decisions, learn what their goals and dreams are, and find ways to support them to achieve those goals. It is important to respect the person's right to privacy and their active participation in making choices about both the little things and the big things in life. Direct support professionals (DSPs) or those who provide support need to remember whose home it is! By learning more about self-determination, supported decision making, and person-centered planning and practices the person can become more comfortable expressing their preferences and desires. DSPs and others should support the person in developing and sustaining friendships and other relationships. The more information and individual and family have about options, the more they can make informed decisions about where they live and what they need from LTSS.

Personal Illustration: Kelsey Peterson

A few years after high school, Kelsey decided she was ready to move out of her parents' home. She lived with my wife and me for several years as an adult," said Kelsey's father, Steve Peterson, "but we moved to a condominium, a 55-and-older building. And she really wasn't happy there, because we're all retired people and there were no young people around." Kelsey and her family started looking into other options, seeking a home in the suburbs of St. Paul, Minnesota, that provided the companionship of friends. Kelsey moved into a group home, where she lived for five years. "That was fine at first," said Steve, "but she wanted more independence. And she didn't need staff around 24/7."

With the support of a Dakota County social worker, Kelsey and her parents explored other options and decided to work with Residential Transitions Incorporated (RTI), a provider committed to assisting persons with disabilities to achieve their highest level of personal independence. Kelsey now lives in an apartment and RTI is supporting her in making the transition from group home living to independent living. RTI has several staff across the street from Kelsey's apartment complex and they come for about an hour a day to assist with independent living skills, including help with paying bills and interpreting medical information. Kelsey lives with a friend with whom she shares the living expenses. "We just have fun. We hang out, play cards, cook. We enjoy our cooking a lot."

"I like it here because I get help only when I need it," said Kelsey. Because of her epilepsy, she requires someone to be present when she showers. In the event of a seizure, staff are trained to ensure she is safe. Episodes generally last less than one minute. "But they won't call 911 unless you really need it. That's what I like about it. In my group home, they called 911 a lot and I didn't need it."

Today, Kelsey's supports are more person centered. She receives support when she asks for it, and staff understand that she is in control. Her parents also want her to assume greater control over her affairs. "My wife and I, we know that someday we won't be here, and that's why we're trying to give her a little more responsibility every six months or so. We do help her manage her financial and medical responsibilities. But, slowly but surely, we're turning those over to her."

Like many people with disabilities, Kelsey had difficulty finding employment. This past summer, with the support of RTI, she obtained a job with the City of West St. Paul Parks and Recreation Department. Having a job that she finds meaningful and enjoys adds to Kelsey's growing independence. "I teach little kids how to do sports and I love it," said Kelsey. She and her parents hope this seasonal job will lead to something more permanent, such as working for the YMCA.

Steve is optimistic. "I see a very bright future for Kelsey. She has a very nice young man she's been dating for quite a while; there's a possibility there for a long-term relationship. And I can see her living someday in a townhome, having some pets. And possibly living up north, because she does like the up-north environment, and the quietness."

"Home means finding a dream," said Kelsey. "This home is my short-term dream. My other dream is to someday live on the Whitefish Chain," a chain of lakes in northern Minnesota. "You know, I don't really think life could be better. Just keep on following your dream. That's my thing."

Conclusion

Now, more than ever, people with IDD live independently, own their homes, and are our neighbors. Where a person lives and the choices they have about their home are essential ingredients of community living and participation. Home is a place where a person chooses what to do, with whom, and when. It is where a person decides what to eat and when, how the space is decorated and arranged. Home is a place where it is safe to dream, to try, to fail, and to dream again. Supports and services are simply tools to assist the person to live life the way they want to. The reality is that services don't make a home; it's the people, choices, and activities within this space that give it the most meaning.

Discussion Questions

- If a person's goal is to obtain affordable, accessible housing, what can direct support staff do to help the person achieve that goal?
- Some families of people living in institutions today are afraid of what might happen if their family member moved to a community setting. Others are working hard to create new segregated congregate settings for their family member with IDD. What strategies can be used to help those families get enough information about the alternatives to make an informed choice between an institution and a home in a community setting?
- How can family members assist adults with IDD to make choices about where to live and with whom?
- How does the location of a home facilitate or hinder employment in community jobs, earning community wages, with coworkers who have a range of abilities?
- How can people with IDD be supported so there is a good match between the setting and the individual's preferred lifestyle, including levels of privacy and control in decision making and activities?

Resources

- CSH: The Source for Housing Solutions: An organization providing training and education, policy solutions, consulting and assistance, and lending supporting housing solutions. http://www.csh.org/
- The Arc: A national advocacy and provider organization for people with IDD and their families. Its website lists local chapters throughout the U.S. and offers resources on housing issues and long-term supports and services. http://www.thearc.org/
- Residential Information Systems Project: A research project of national significance funded by the Administration on Intellectual and Developmental Disabilities located at the University of Minnesota. It provides annually updated state profiles, technical reports, and online interactive data on living arrangements of people with IDD receiving LTSS. http://risp.umn.edu
- Self-Advocacy Online: A website hosted by the Research and Training Center on Community Living at the University of Minnesota telling the stories of people with disabilities. http://www.selfadvocacyonline.org
- Technical Assistance Collaborative: A technical assistance provider focusing on affordable housing, healthcare, human services, and public policy and advocacy. Its website offers reports on housing, such as *Priced Out in 2014*, a database of housing vouchers for people with disabilities, and other resources on housing options. http://www.tacinc.org/

References

Administration on Intellectual and Developmental Disabilities (2016). *Fact sheet: President's Committee for People with Intellectual Disabilities.* Washington, DC: Author. Retrieved from https://www.acl.gov/sites/default/files/programs/2016-11/PCPIDfactsheet.pdf

American Association on Intellectual and Developmental Disabilities & Association of University Centers on Disability. (2016). Community living and participation for people with intellectual and developmental disabilities. Retrieved from: http://aaidd.org/news-policy/policy/position-statements/community-living-and-participation#.WlGS9FQ-d-U

Blatt, B., and Kaplan, F.M. (1966). *Christmas in purgatory: A photographic essay on mental retardation.* Republished in 1974, Syracuse, NY: Human Policy Press.

Centers for Medicare and Medicaid Services (2014). *Final Regulation:* 1915(i) State Plan HCBS, 5-Year Period for Waivers, Provider Payment Reassignment, Setting Requirements for Community First Choice, and 1915(c) HCBS Waivers—CMS-2249-F/CMS-2296-F 42 CFR § 441. Available at http://www.medicaid.gov/HCBS.

Flynn, R.J., & Nitsch, K.E. (1980). *Normalization, social integration and community services.* Baltimorem MD: University Park Press.

Hill, K. (2012). Permanency and placement planning for older youth with disabilities in out-of-home placement. *Children and Youth Services Review, 34,* 1418–1424.

John F. Kennedy Presidential Library and Museum (2016). *JFK and people with intellectual disabilities.* Retrieved from http://www.jfklibrary.org/JFK/JFK-in-History/JFK-and-People-with-Intellectual-Disabilities.aspx.

Kugel, R, & Wolfensberger, W. (Eds., 1969). *Changing patterns in residential services for the mentally retarded.* Washington, D.C. President's Committee on Mental Retardation.

Lakin, K.C., Hill, B.K., & Bruininks, R.H., (1985). *An analysis of Medicaid's Intermediate Care Facility for the Mentally Retarded (ICF-MR) program.* Minneapolis, MN: University of Minnesota, Department of Educational Psychology.

Lakin, K.C., Blake, E.M., Prouty, R.W., Mangan, T., & Bruininks, R.H., (1993). *Residential services for persons with developmental disabilities: Status and trends through 1991.* Minneapolis, MN: University of Minnesota Center on Residential Services and Community Living, Institute on Community Integration/UAP.

Larson, S.A., & Lakin, K.C. (1991). Parent attitudes about residential placement before and after deinstitutionalization: A research synthesis. *Journal of the Association for Persons with Severe Handicaps, 16,* 25–38.

Larson, S.A., Doljanac, R., & Lakin, K.C. (2005). United States living arrangements of people with intellectual and/or developmental disabilities in 1995. *Journal of Intellectual and Developmental Disability, 30,* 236–239.

Larson, S.A., Eschenbacher, H.J., Anderson, L.L., Taylor, B., Pettingell, S., Hewitt, A., Sowers, M., & Bourne, M.L. (2017). *In-home and residential long-term supports and services for persons with intellectual or developmental disabilities: Status and trends through 2015.* Minneapolis, MN: University of Minnesota, Research and Training Center on Community Living, Institute on Community Integration.

Larson, S.A., Lakin, K.C., & Hill, S.L. (2013). Behavioral outcomes of moving from institutional to community living for people with : U.S. studies from 1977 to 2010. *Research and practice for persons with severe disabilities, 37*(4), 1–12.

Larson, S. A., Lakin, K. C., Anderson, L. L., Kwak, N. (2001) Demographic characteristics of persons with MR/DD living in their own homes or with family members: NHIS-D analysis. *MR/DD Data Brief, 3*(2). Minneapolis, MN: University of Minnesota, Institute on Community Integration.

Lightfoot, E., Hill, K., & LaLiberte, T. (2011). Prevalence of children with disabilities in the child welfare system and outcome of home placement: An examination of administrative records. *Children and Youth Services Review, 33*, 2069–2075.

Minnesota Governor's Council on Developmental Disabilities (2016). *V. The reawakening 1950–1080 b. 1950–1970 Improving the institutions*. Video: Senator Robert Kennedy visiting institutions ('snake pits") in New York. St. Paul, MN: Retrieved from http://mn.gov/mnddc/parallels/five/5b/4.html.

Newman, L., Wagner, M., Knokey, A.-M., Marder, C., Nagle, K., Shaver, D., Wei, X., with Cameto, R., Contreras, E., Ferguson, K., Greene, S., and Schwarting, M. (2011). *The post-high-school outcomes of young adults with disabilities up to 8 years after high school. A Report From the National Longitudinal Transition Study-2* (NLTS2)(NCSER 2011–3005). Menlo Park, CA: SRI International. Retrieved from www.nlts2.org/reports/

Rizzolo, M.K., Larson, S.A., & Hewitt, A.S. (2016). *Long-term supports and services for people with IDD: Research, practice and policy implications. Critical issues in intellectual and developmental disabilities: Contemporary research, practice, and policy*. (pp. 89–107). Washington, DC: American Association on Intellectual and Developmental Disabilities.

Scheerenberger, R. (1983). *A history of mental retardation*. Baltimore, MD: Brookes Publishing Co.

Ticha, R., Hewitt, A., Nord, D. & Larson, S.A. (2013). System and individual outcomes and their predictors in services and support for people with IDD. *Intellectual and Developmental Disabilities, 51*, 316–332.

U.S. Department of Education (2016a). *EDFacts Data Warehouse* (EDW): "IDEA Part B Exiting," SY 2014–15. Retrieved from https://www2.ed.gov/programs/osepidea/618-data/static-tables.

U.S. Department of Education (2016b). *EDFacts Data Warehouse* (EDW): "IDEA Part B Child Count and Educational Environments Collection," 2015–16. Retrieved from https://www2.ed.gov/programs/osepidea/618-data/static-tables.

Westcott, H.L. & Jones, D.P.H (1999). Annotation: The abuse of disabled children. *Journal of Child Psychology and Psychiatry, 40*, 497–506.

CHAPTER FOUR

Work and Careers: It's More Than Just a Job

Amy Gunty, Joe Timmons, and Kelly M. Nye-Lengerman

Advance Organizers

- Having a job at which one earns money is considered a typical role for an adult.
- People with intellectual and developmental disabilities benefit in many ways from employment.
- Valued social roles provide opportunities for positive interactions that keep people connected. People who are unemployed or underemployed have limited opportunities for social, economic, and personal growth.
- Barriers to employment need to be addressed by employers, advocates, disability organizations, and systems.

This chapter explores the history of employment and non-employment day services for people with IDD, including a review of policies and laws that support employment for people with IDD, and common barriers that prevent full employment participation. Information is provided regarding best practices, interventions, and strategies that promote meaningful employment of individuals with IDD in their communities.

For most adults, being an employee is a highly sought after and valued social role. People who are unemployed or underemployed lack this opportunity and can, therefore, miss out on some of the good things in life that come along with having a job, including:

- developing relationships and friendships;
- being extended dignity, respect, and acceptance;
- feeling a sense of belonging and purpose;
- developing and exercising skills;
- sharing perspectives about what is going on in the community and society;
- having opportunities to participate in activities and relationships; and
- earning income to meet material needs.

Throughout history, families, service providers, community members, and systems have not expected people with IDD to have meaningful jobs in the community. Instead, people with IDD have been viewed as needing specialized care and supervision, which has often led to overprotection and limitation of their freedom and inclusion in society. In this manner, people with IDD have often been systematically denied the ordinary opportunities most adults find in the workplace. Yet, most people with IDD have the interest, desire, and willingness to work in the community (AAIDD and The Arc, 2012).

People with IDD work and spend their days in various types of settings, covered later in this chapter. Today more people with IDD than in past decades earn at least minimum wage working in the community, but a significant number still lack that opportunity. In fact, many unemployed people with IDD spend their days in sheltered or facility-based settings, which may include prevocational or training programs that do not actually lead to competitive employment (Butterworth et al., 2016). Because having a job is a critical part of community life and participation, a revitalized push has emerged recently to focus on policies and practices that support and invest in community-based employment options for people with IDD.

Given the social and economic benefits of employment to both people and communities, the case can be made that pathways to fulfilling careers and integrated, meaningful employment should be accessible to all people, and that services and supports should facilitate, rather than prevent, employment. Employment for people with IDD should be an expectation rather than an exception. Indeed, policies are shifting to reflect a move toward such expectations becoming universal. It is critical that these shifts continue.

History of Employment and People With IDD

Segregation of people with IDD in institutions was the norm until the last third of the 20th century. In addition to providing housing for many, these institutions were the primary providers of day supports for people with IDD (Nielsen, 2013; The Minnesota Governor's Council on Developmental Disabilities, n.d.). This segregation was based on the belief that people with disabilities of all kinds were helpless and that keeping them out of society was best for everyone. Others believed that disabilities were a form of punishment for families who deserved their fate (because they were sinful, evil, or possessed). These ignorant misperceptions led to a reality in which people with IDD were seen as not having skills or social standing and were often treated as less than human. In many communities, people with IDD experienced systematic abuse and limited opportunities for learning, independence, or any type of ordinary life (Nielsen, 2013).

Institutions were large, self-contained facilities in which the residents often performed work that kept the facility running and for which there was little or no pay: keeping the grounds, cooking and cleaning in the kitchen, doing laundry, providing farm labor. Later in the 20th century, if a person with IDD was employed outside an institution, it was almost always in a segregated setting, doing monotonous, menial labor for little or no pay.

During World Wars I and II, more people became disabled due to war injuries, which created a greater demand for institutional care and vocational services. Segregated programs known as sheltered workshops increased in number. These were places where injured or disabled veterans could work, and were considered a charitable way of giving people things to do during the day. Over time, sheltered workshops also became available to other residents of institutions who had not previously served in the military. According to the U.S. Department of Labor (1979), the number of sheltered workshops in the United States increased from 85 in 1948 to about 3,000 in 1976.

Children and youth with disabilities generally did not have opportunities to learn in public-school settings before the 1970s—a circumstance that contributed to the abundance of segregated day programs (Nielsen, 2013). Most people believed that school was of no benefit to a child with a significant disability, and that their presence would only hinder other students' learning. Therefore, many children and adolescents with disabilities were kept out of public schools. But they still needed somewhere to go during the day. This led to an increase in the number of day programs designed to provide education and prevocational training to people with IDD. While many such programs were initially connected to institutions, some were in segregated community settings. Parents who wanted more for their children with disabilities started many of these day programs because they knew their children could learn, grow, and work.

Sheltered workshops and day programs were designed to provide opportunities for learning and purposeful activity, but over time, they began to look like warehouses where participants typically had no voice in deciding where and how they spent their days. If work did occur, most workers with disabilities were paid a sub-minimum wage. Much of the time, these programs were considered training, but the training went on for years without resulting in integration into society or integrated employment in the community (Friedman & Rizzolo, 2017).

Legislation to Support Employment and Education

A shift began in the 1970s, with the passage of two important laws protecting the rights of people with disabilities. The Rehabilitation Act of 1973 mandated that people with all types of disabilities have access to supports and resources to gain employment or access training. The Rehabilitation Act did not eliminate sheltered workshops, but it prohibited discrimination in any activity or program with connections to the federal government. (In this way, it was a precursor to the Americans with Disabilities Act of 1990.) Its aim was to ensure that people with disabilities would have opportunities to participate in community life, including the ability to participate in employment, purchase goods and services, and take part in government programs and services (The Rehabilitation Act of 1973).

Then, two years later, the Education for All Handicapped Children Act (EAHCA) of 1975 became law. The EAHCA provided protection for children and youth with disabilities by requiring all schools receiving federal funding to give children with disabilities access to education as similar as possible to the education their peers without disabilities received. It also mandated the creation of systems for parents to report concerns about the education their children with disabilities were receiving. It goes without saying that education is a crucial pathway to employment because it provides foundational knowledge and skills that support future vocational abilities. Overwhelming evidence also shows that access to education plays an important role in long-term employment outcomes. Because the EAHCA provided equal access to education for children with disabilities, they now had the opportunity to obtain foundational knowledge and skills in the same way their nondisabled peers did.

After the ratification of these laws, many people continued to advocate for more rights and civil liberties for people with IDD. In the 1980s and 1990s, this shift was seen clearly, as the Department of Education offered major federal grants to states to assist in creating supported employment (SE) programs. In 1988, as these programs were implemented, the Association of People Supporting Employment First (APSE) was founded. This organization advocates for competitive, integrated employment for all people with disabilities and disseminates information about underlying principles of and best practices for helping people with disabilities find, maintain, and thrive at integrated employment. Over time, SE (initially developed in these state grant programs) has expanded to include other approaches to employment for people with IDD, including customized employment.

Recently, federal policy and legislation has continued to protect the civil rights of people with disabilities, with the adoption of the Workforce Innovation and Opportunity Act (WIOA) in 2013 and the Centers for Medicare and Medicaid Services' (CMS) Final Rule for home and community-based services (HCBS) in 2014. WIOA aims to strengthen society's workforce by helping youth and adults who encounter substantial barriers to employment, including those related to disability, to find high-quality, meaningful work in their communities. WIOA also includes amendments to the Rehabilitation Act of 1973 that prioritize services for youth, limit access to sub-minimum wage employment for youth, and encourage business partnerships and community collaboration. The CMS Final Rule on HCBS states that programs paid for by Medicaid under Home and Community Based Services (including waivers) must take place in integrated community settings (i.e., in a space alongside people without disabilities). You can read more about WIOA and the CMS Final Rule on HCBS in chapter 1.

The changing landscape and increased employment expectations for people with disabilities developed into the Employment First movement, which identifies employment as the preferred outcome for people with disabilities and encourages those supporting people with disabilities (e.g., special education teachers, case managers, employment specialists, families) to consider employment as a first option before considering alternatives (APSE, 2017). Over time, many states have adopted an Employment First philosophy through executive orders, state legislation, state departmental policies, and other activities (Gunty, Dean, Nord, Hoff, & Nye-Lengerman, 2017). These efforts recognize that people with IDD have skills and talents that can contribute to the richness and well-being of communities. Advocates and self-advocates continue to work for integrated, community-based employment as the first and preferred option for all people. Families and advocates want, expect, and demand greater access to community living and participation, including employment, for their family members and friends with disabilities, and continue to fight in court for equal rights (e.g., *Olmstead v. L.C.*, 1999).

Current Employment Settings

A variety of employment providers and day activity settings exists for people with IDD. They may receive services from Community Rehabilitation Providers, Day Training & Habilitation programs, or supported employment (SE) providers. Most day and employment services are paid for through Medicaid Home and Community Based Services (sometimes called waiver programs), but funding may also come from county or state agencies (e.g., vocational rehabilitation), school districts, or non-profits.

The settings in which people spend their time are generally classified into four types: paid community employment, paid facility-based employment, community-based non-work, and facility-based non-work. The proportion of people with IDD who spend their days in each type of setting varies by state (Butterworth et al., 2016).

People with IDD may be employed in paid community jobs or paid facility-based jobs, and many participate in multiple employment settings over the course of a year that are paid for by state IDD agencies. Those with a job in the community (i.e., they work alongside peers without disabilities) that pays at least minimum wage participate in paid community employment and account for about 19% of people with IDD nationally (Butterworth et al., 2016). Facility-based employment occurs when a person works in a segregated or semi-segregated setting. People with IDD usually earn sub-minimum wage for this work. Facility-based employment may also be referred to as a sheltered workshop. About 23% of people with IDD participate in this type of employment nationally (Butterworth et al., 2016). It is important to note that many people with IDD are self-employed, own their own businesses, or employ others. Over the past several years, self-employment opportunities have grown and provide a viable alternative to other activities or settings. In addition, there are millions of individuals with IDD who are not using formal employment supports and who are not part of the formal service system (Larson, Salmi, Smith, Anderson, & Hewitt, 2013). Unfortunately, it is difficult to know much about where people who are not a part of the formal IDD service system work, how much they earn, and what their working conditions are like because it is hard to identify these people in national household survey data (Nord et al., 2016).

People with IDD can also participate in community-based or facility-based non-work settings in which they do not earn wages (Butterworth et al, 2016). Activities in non-work programs vary by service provider. Community-based non-work takes place, as the name indicates, in the community, where people with IDD take part in activities alongside people without disabilities. In these programs 40% of people with IDD have accessed this setting (Butterworth et al., 2016). When people with IDD attend a day program at a facility in which they come into contact only with other participants with disabilities and staff, they are identified as participating in facility-based non-work. This is similar to sheltered workshops, but the participants are not paid. About 53% of people with IDD have participated in facility-based non-work nationally in 2015 (Butterworth et al., 2016). It is important to note that people with IDD can participate in multiple settings. For example, it is possible for an individual with IDD to be employed in a job in their community part-time and also to participate in community-based non-work for another portion of their week.

Over time, despite investment in SE and other public programs, the rate of employment has remained relatively flat. In addition, there has actually been an increase in the number of people with IDD supported in non-work programs (Butterworth et al., 2016). Despite new policies and initiatives across the United States, employment remains elusive for many.

What is an employment outcome?

Many policy and practice changes involve discussion about improving "employment outcomes" for people with IDD. There are different ideas about what constitutes an employment outcome. Currently, in disability employment research outcomes are most often identified as wages/earnings, hours worked, availability of employee benefits, and setting type. When the language of a policy, practice, or intervention states that it is designed to increase or improve employment outcomes, it most often means that it should result in increased earnings, work hours, access to benefits, and proportion of jobs in integrated, community settings. However, other types of outcomes should not be discounted, even if they are not always measured. They include having choices, engaging in interesting work, finding personal satisfaction, gaining independence, utilizing available supports, and developing social relationships and connectedness. Chapter 10 provides additional information on measuring quality of life outcomes.

Misperceptions and Assumptions

In order to improve employment outcomes for individuals with IDD, it is important to confront some assumptions many people have. Long-held beliefs can be difficult to overcome. The following five common assumptions should be addressed:

"Employers won't [or don't want to] hire people with IDD." *Correction:* Employers are looking to improve their businesses; they seek out talented people to help them achieve this. People with IDD have skills that can be valuable to all types of employers. Employers simply need to be aware of how to provide supports that lead to success. Over time, each successful employment placement of a person with IDD serves as an example for other businesses and demonstrates that hiring employees with all kinds of backgrounds and skills can be good for business.

"People with IDD don't need to make a living wage; they have other benefits." *Correction:* Access to equal and fair earnings is a civil right long denied to people with IDD, who have often been paid below the minimum wage. While certain governmental benefits are available to people with IDD, they do not negate this civil right. In many cases, in facility-based work or sheltered workshops, people with IDD perform repetitive tasks for which they are paid according to how many times they finish the task rather than how much time they spend working. While individual rates of productivity vary in all types of work, the majority of jobs are no longer paid based on employee productivity. People with IDD are one of the only groups who can be discriminated against in this way. Whenever someone, including a person with IDD, is placed in a job that is matched to the person's interests and preferences, the result is deeper engagement, higher productivity, and greater satisfaction.

"People with IDD need a lot of support in the community and can't be alone." *Correction:* All of us receive some kind of support in our employment from our supervisors, coworkers, friends, and family members. Anyone who does something that makes it more likely that we will succeed at work provides us with employment support. Some people with IDD have higher support needs, yet many others are quite able to be independent in many settings. If a person is not given the opportunity to demonstrate their capabilities, exercise independence, and experience different opportunities in life, it is very difficult to determine how much support they need or do not need. The right supports allow people with IDD to demonstrate their strengths and skills and to be as independent as possible.

"Some people with IDD are too disabled to work." *Correction:* People often rise to the expectations set for them. If society expects people with IDD to be unable to work, that will become a self-fulfilling belief. Raising expectations for people with IDD is the first step to fighting the effects of stereotypes and discrimination. Individuals ought to be able to expect that they can find work that is meaningful to them and that allows them to fully participate as a contributing member of society. Families can expect that their loved ones will have a meaningful job and career. Community members can expect that people with IDD will contribute to their communities socially, economically, and politically. Employers can expect that people with IDD will contribute valuable skills that add to their businesses. Integrating people with IDD more fully into their communities through employment starts with raised expectations and focuses on supporting one person at a time, one job at a time.

"People with IDD need to have services from a formal provider to make employment successful." *Correction:* The majority of people with IDD do not receive formal services. A provider can be useful in supporting a person with finding and maintaining a job, but it is not always required. Friends, family, employers, and personal networks can also provide these types of supports. Most important in all of this is that the majority of people with IDD do desire to work.

Supporting people with IDD in developing valued social roles for themselves can contribute to a decrease in the stigma associated with IDD and lead to improved opportunities to make connections toward meaningful employment. When people with IDD have valued social roles, others get to know them as unique individuals and see how they enrich the community. Interactions in which people with IDD are respected for their contributions will nudge people in the community to re-evaluate their assumptions about and expectations of people with IDD.

The messages in the assumptions discussed above are communicated subtly to individuals throughout their lifetimes. These messages and low expectations can be internalized, at times leading people with IDD to develop limited beliefs about themselves, such as that they cannot work or that they do not deserve opportunities to work. Without opportunities to take risks and develop increasing independence, people with IDD do not always have realistic views of their capabilities, nor do they feel empowered as active, self-determining individuals who can make informed choices about their lives.

Current Controversies and Challenges

Changing the assumptions listed above is just one part of the struggle to create more opportunities for people with IDD to work in competitive, integrated employment. Other controversies and challenges also contribute. Stakeholders have various perceptions about the challenges related to employment. This section addresses some of the forces and circumstances that are debated in the field of IDD, while the subsequent sections identify solutions to some of these problems.

The Individual

People with IDD often leave school with little vocational experience or training to establish a foundation for the transition to work or postsecondary education. Many young people without disabilities use part-time jobs or volunteer experiences during high school to demonstrate to prospective employers that they have necessary employment skills such as interacting well with others (e.g., customers), solving problems, and working as a team. However, many schools have limited resources to support work-based learning through part-time jobs or volunteer work for youth with IDD. Therefore, after finishing high school, youth with IDD are not able to demonstrate their capabilities to prospective employers in the same way youth without disabilities can.

Furthermore, current service systems for youth and adults with IDD are structured to teach and support people in groups, rather than as individuals. These group supports and services are a holdover from years of institutionalization when people thought it was easier and less expensive to keep people with IDD in segregated group settings. Without customized and individualized training and work experiences, it is difficult to help people with IDD find and retain jobs and be more fully included in their communities.

Family

Family members are inundated with the same messages and assumptions about their loved one with IDD as is the person with the disability. They are often socialized to think of their family member with IDD as needing to be taken care of and protected. Families can develop low expectations of their family member due to societal structures, messages, and beliefs. Many families have not encountered adults with IDD who are thriving in integrated employment settings, so they lack the ability to visualize a future in which their family member is supported in such a way that he or she is as independent as possible, thriving in a competitive, integrated job.

Additionally, family members are often concerned about their loved ones working because of the perceived risks that come with employment. Families generally worry about two types of risks: The first is financial—that if a person works, they may lose important government benefits, including cash benefits (e.g., Supplemental Security Income or Social Security Disability Insurance) and healthcare benefits (e.g., Medicaid). The complexity of how benefits and work interact can be confusing, and when families have fought to receive benefits, this potential loss due to earnings from competitive, integrated employment may feel too risky.

The second risk felt by many families relates to health and safety. Family members may see community-based employment as scary or dangerous, fearing that their loved one may be unsupported, taken advantage of, bullied, or harmed in some other way. These fears are common examples of the difficulty of balancing what is important *to* a person and what is important *for* that person.

Community Members

Not surprisingly, employers are important community members when we consider employment for people with IDD. Most employers focus on their bottom line, working to increase profits and decrease costs. Hiring people with IDD might require employers to engage in strategic, creative thinking. Many employers have difficulty understanding how hiring a person with IDD could be good for business. Business leaders often expect there to be higher costs for insurance or extra expenses for specialized equipment when they hire someone with IDD. They may not understand the logistics of reasonable accommodations in SE for individuals with IDD.

Generally, business owners and managers have identified jobs and related tasks with specific job descriptions. These developed positions may not be a good fit for a person with IDD. When businesses are open to learning about accommodations and supports, and when they are willing to work with a job developer to find tasks that call for the strengths, skills, and interests of people with IDD, they will likely find their business enhanced in many ways upon hiring people with IDD.

Attitudes about people with IDD in the community and the workplace are slowly changing. Unfortunately, some people still have difficulty seeing individuals with IDD as having unique strengths. Much of this stems from a lack of experience and limited personal relationships with people with IDD. Without opportunities to spend time with people with IDD, people do not see how they can contribute to the well-being of the community. As people with IDD have opportunities to be in the community, other community members will develop personal experiences and relationships with them, which will in turn allow those community members to be more responsive and accepting of the valued social roles people with IDD can fulfill.

Providers

Providers who are paid to support people with IDD encounter all of the challenges mentioned above in the form of resistance and a lack of confidence from individuals, families, and businesses; and they do so in a system that is constantly changing due to legislation, policies, budgets, and, sometimes, litigation. Funding streams supporting providers are often not large or flexible enough to provide the individualized services in the community needed to produce the best outcomes. In some cases, providers receive more funding when they support people with IDD in non-work or non-community settings, dis-incentivizing community-based employment services. High levels of stress and many barriers to overcome result in a high rate of professional turnover. This often means that few people stay in the field or at an agency long enough to develop real expertise in supporting people with IDD to find and keep competitive, integrated employment.

Life Course Expectations and Transitions

For anyone, transitioning from school to work can be a formidable task, and for youth and young adults with IDD, this transition can be particularly stressful. This is a time when the individual steps away from the protection and structure of school (and, for most, an individualized education program [IEP] or 504 plan), to an environment full of unknowns. This transition includes moving from mandated services provided by a school district to more limited services provided by adult service structures. This period is often referred to as the transition cliff, where a youth and family fall into a number of unfamiliar service agencies, often in silos with no apparent connection among them. In some cases, there are no long-term supports available to the person after high school. There are, however, things that youth and young adults with disabilities and those who support them can do to ease the stress and difficulty inherent in this transition.

Transition planning that identifies and prioritizes employment as a goal should begin as early as possible. This can be achieved through a customized, person-centered IEP process that focuses on the job seeker's skills and preferences, which will support a good employment fit. The IEP goals can target the development of vocational skills, exploration of preferences and interests, and participation in paid and unpaid work experiences.

Both formal and informal tools can support this process as the student with IDD makes use of ingredients such as career exploration, skill and preference development, individual exploration, job shadowing, and informational interviews. These ingredients serve different purposes. For example, observing or shadowing people working in a variety of roles and settings gives a student a realistic view of what particular jobs are like. Engaging in volunteer activities or paid work experiences that fit a student's interests can help them find and develop skills for employment while identifying supports that enhance their success in those roles.

Families and their networks are essential during this time. Schools have limited connections to real work and volunteer opportunities in communities. From age 14 on, families should use their own social networks to support their loved one with IDD in finding and maximizing volunteer and employment opportunities. Relying solely on schools to do this networking often leads to dead ends. Families have a lot of options for setting a successful course for their family member with IDD, and they can push school systems to understand the significance of these opportunities. It is also important to start early and have conversations to plan for other important components of successful adulthood, such as transportation, benefits, and supports that will be needed after the person is hired into a job or enters postsecondary school.

Practical Suggestions and Interventions

The Individual

Empowering people with IDD who want to be employed in a community setting requires supporting their exercise of self-determination, through which they develop a sense of their ability to play an active role in their own lives, making informed choices about what their lives will look like. It is essential that individuals be given opportunities to acquire knowledge about what it means to be employed, and the skills necessary to become and stay employed. This knowledge and these skills are developed when the individual is able to ask questions, seek out a mentor, observe other people in similar circumstances, and get real work experience.

While service providers offer some of these opportunities, families and allies can enhance the experience by providing additional opportunities. The more people working with the individual to connect them to experiences where they can gain exposure, knowledge, and skills in action, the better. Furthermore, most people find jobs based on connections and networking, and this is also true for people with IDD. Developing the individual's network and expanding their connections is important because it allows them to personally connect with people who might either hire them or have connections to someone else who might hire them.

Throughout the entire process of finding and maintaining employment, everyone involved must remember that it is the person with IDD who will be employed, and that this employment will be one aspect of that person's life. Therefore, supporting the person with IDD to be self-determining will have the strongest and most lasting effects, not only with regard to employment outcomes, but also for overall life satisfaction, well-being, and the ability to thrive.

Family

Setting expectations. In order to support employment as a key component of community living for people with IDD, it is essential that families hold the expectation that their loved one with IDD will work in an integrated setting. The best way to develop this expectation is for families to see other people with IDD who are employed in their own communities. This will give families a frame of reference from which to think about what it might look like for their loved one to be employed, and what skills and experiences their loved one needs in order to prepare for that eventual outcome.

Supporting risks. Over the course of a person's life, family members can allow for their loved one to take appropriate risks and can support them in doing so. Understandably, families are concerned about the safety of the person with IDD, but—though it might seem counterintuitive—supporting risk-taking over the course of an individual's life actually enhances their ability to keep themselves safe. As individuals engage in appropriate risks over time, they learn from the consequences of the risks taken, which will enable them to cultivate the skills for balancing risk (possible cost) with reward (possible benefit). Furthermore, supporting individuals in taking risks provides them the opportunity to experience the dignity of risk, through which they are able to build self-confidence and experience the sense of empowerment that comes from making decisions (including risky ones). The dignity of risk and its accompanying strengthened sense of empowerment and control position the person with IDD to enter integrated employment with the skills needed to navigate the risks and rewards inherent in a community workplace.

Families are in the position to be the strongest advocates for people with IDD who are seeking employment. Families can ask questions and challenge the status quo, seek out information about employment, and push to find support for the person to be employed in a community setting. One way for families to do this is to seek out other families of people with IDD who are employed in community settings. These connections allow families to learn about the process other families went through, including possible barriers and available supports. It also allows families to band together to be a collective voice pushing for full inclusion of people with IDD in their community through employment.

Communities as a whole might not always assume that a person with IDD is employable. Families can fill in this gap by demanding that people with IDD be seen as capable, knowledgeable, and skilled. When families meet barriers to employment that come from assumptions and stereotypes, they can challenge the assumptions by asking what prevents their family member from being employed. The ensuing conversation is enhanced when the family is able to articulate (or assist the individual to articulate) the person's interests and skills and how those might fit in the context of different business or employment settings.

In the absence of formal support to help a person with IDD find work in the community, families can leverage their own networks and skills to facilitate the process themselves. Because families know the job seeker the best, they are in a unique position to see places where the person could make a difference in a community. As has been mentioned, most of the time people—including those with IDD—find jobs through person-to-person networking. As families connect with people they know, they can have conversations around what their loved one with IDD is good at and interested in, and can use these conversations to probe for places in the community where their loved one could fulfill certain needs.

In all these ways, families are an integral part of the process of finding meaningful, competitive, integrated employment for people with IDD. The work of families can in turn be facilitated by a community that is also supportive of integrated work for people with IDD.

Community Members

Communities can support employment for people with IDD in multiple ways. Members of the community, particularly business leaders and human resources professionals, can seek out education about what it means to employ a person with IDD, and can then consider what tasks within their businesses might be well suited for people with IDD. When a variety of businesses are open to hiring people with IDD, this creates an opportunity for better job matches that are more satisfying for the job seeker and the employer alike.

Business leaders can also seek out people who know job seekers with IDD in order to facilitate better connections. Business leaders might join professional organizations that work for and support integrated employment for people with IDD. The membership base of such professional organizations is often composed of service providers, without representation from the business community. However, business leaders can take the initiative to share a business perspective in discussions on supporting employment for people with IDD.

Furthermore, once a person with IDD has been hired, it is important to have high expectations of that individual. People with IDD should be held to professional standards. When businesses and customers hold such expectations, it communicates an assumption of competence, which allows the employee with IDD to rise to the expectation and demonstrate their full abilities. People should never be allowed to act in an unprofessional manner simply because they have a disability. People with IDD may need extra support to meet the expectations of professional conduct, or they may require an explicit explanation of expectations that are generally considered "common sense," but they can fulfill expectations of professionalism and should be given the opportunity to do so.

Multifaceted community support creates an environment where people with IDD are not only accepted but valued as important members of the community. This perspective champions the notion that each person in the community has a unique point of view, set of skills, and breadth of interests, and that, when all people are integrated into the community, the community itself becomes richer.

Providers

There are certain practices that providers can and should engage in to support improved employment outcomes for people with IDD. These practices might require some amount of organizational change. The change process must focus on clear and consistent organizational goals communicated regularly to stakeholders; engagement of different entities (job seekers, families, businesses) throughout the process; and development of a strategy to concentrate on one job seeker, one job match at a time (Timmons & Lyons, 2016).

The comprehensive model of employment supports (Figure4.1) provides an overview of activities and support strategies that providers utilize to increase the likelihood of successful employment outcomes for job seekers with IDD (Migliore, Nye-Lengermen, Lyons, Bose, & Butterworth, 2018. This model builds upon the job seeker's needs, preferences, and strengths, which are at the foundation of the placement process. At the center of the model is matching job seekers with IDD with jobs. The model illustrates that supporting job seekers is a cyclical, ongoing process that includes building trust, getting to know the job seeker, finding jobs or tasks, and planning supports. When providers assist job seekers with IDD in finding a job by continuously engaging in the activities highlighted in this model, they are better able to facilitate a job match.

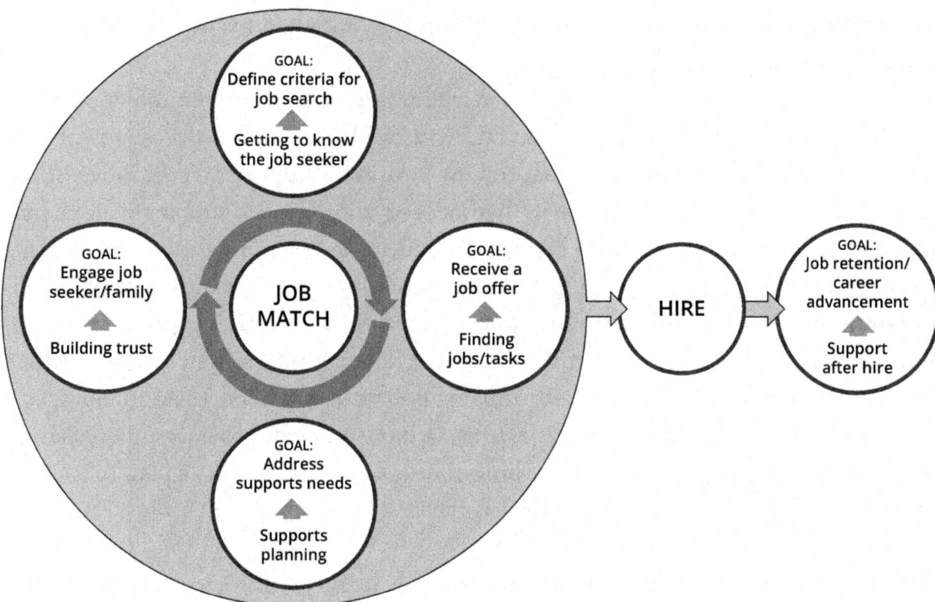

Figure 4.1. A Comprehensive Model of Employment Supports. Reprinted with permission from Research and Training Center on Advancing Employment, ThinkWork, at the University of Massachusetts Boston's Institute for Community Inclusion.

It is important that providers build trust with job seekers and their families. As mentioned, families (and other allies) are ultimately concerned about their loved one's safety and well-being, so they need to trust that the provider will uphold their loved one's well-being throughout the entire process of finding competitive, integrated employment. To build trust, providers need to spend time getting to know job seekers and their families/allies. This may be a significant shift for provider organizations, as it requires providers to spend informal time with the job seeker to truly understand the individual's strengths, interests, and support needs. This investment of time, however, will lead to a greater ability to negotiate with employers to identify a position that is a good fit for the person with IDD. It will also allow the provider to better represent and discuss the job seeker from a strengths-based perspective, while enabling job seekers to develop the skill of discussing their own strengths and talents.

Providers also need to network and form relationships with businesses and their leaders. Often, the jobs in which people with IDD are employed are not posted, pre-existing positions. Rather, the provider gets to know a business and discovers opportunities to customize jobs to meet the needs of both the employer and the job seeker. Creative thinking is key to customizing employment and finding jobs for people with IDD. Jobs can be split up (job sharing), tasks can be modified, and accommodations can be made to carve out a customized position that is a good fit for the person with IDD and also serves the business.

Alongside all of these roles, a provider facilitating community employment also plans for the supports a person with IDD will need to be successful in his or her position. This involves looking for natural, or informal, supports within the existing structure of the business or position. When needed, more formal supports can be put in place to allow the employee to be as independent and successful as possible. Formal supports include job coaching, assistive technology, services provided by direct support professionals, and transportation services. Some formal supports last for a short time at the beginning of employment (e.g., during the training period), while others last longer. Funding for most formal supports comes from government agencies; occasionally, businesses provide it. Once a job is offered, providers may need to assist the person with IDD to evaluate long-term supports and make a plan for modifying them when needed so the person has the best chance possible for job retention and advancement.

At the center of all of these activities is the job seeker with their strengths, skills, interests, and preferences. The provider must constantly enlist person-centered thinking and planning to ensure that what is important *to* the job seeker is balanced with what is important *for* them, within the context of the business's needs, goals, and objectives. This critical balance takes into account what makes a person happy, engaged, and energized in the context of keeping them healthy and safe. Each person who is part of a job seeker's life should have an understanding of person-centered thinking and how it contributes to a successful job search and subsequent employment.

When a provider employs a person-centered mindset, the ultimate job match is more likely to be a good fit for both the job seeker and the business. This in turn allows the individual to become a participating member of the community by fulfilling a valued social role as an employee and coworker.

Career Planning and Assessment

Before actively beginning a job search, it is usually valuable to engage in career planning and assessment activities that assist a job seeker to set employment goals based on their experience, interests, and skills. Assessment should not focus on identifying deficits or weaknesses, but rather on uncovering what a person is good at. The priority should be to discover strengths, preferences, and areas for growth. Career planning uses information collected during assessment to match a person's interests, skills, strengths, and aptitudes to available or newly developed positions. Person-centered career planning is a creative process that focuses on one person at a time rather than on what exists in the system or is easiest for the system. Several developed models provide a structure to assist in this type of exploratory assessment, including a discovery process, or Discovering Personal Genius (Griffin & Hammis, 2011).

Based on the results of the assessment process, the job seeker might even discover new interests and abilities, while making realistic choices about their job search. Because quality assessment is strengths based, people with IDD should not be evaluated for things they haven't done or learned. Rather, best practices stem from a foundation of expecting people to be considered for employment based on what they can do and what they know. Assessments should also examine the supports that have allowed people to be their best selves in formal and informal work experiences, in order to identify what supports will be needed on the job. These can include natural supports, such as supervisor feedback, coworker training and assistance, procedures and routines in the workplace, and transportation assistance from family or neighbors, as well as formal or paid supports, such as job coaching, direct support professionals, and adaptive technology.

Supported Employment and Supported Employment Services

SE is defined as "competitive, integrated employment, including customized employment . . . that is individualized and customized consistent with the strengths, abilities, interests, and informed choice of the individuals involved, for individuals with the most significant disabilities" (WIOA, 2014). Evidence exists for the effectiveness of SE for job seekers with disabilities (Wehman, Chan, Ditchman, & Kang, 2014). Customized employment results when a job seeker, with assistance, negotiates with an employer to adapt the duties of a position to meet both employer and employee needs. Self-employment is a form of customized employment designed for the job seeker to be both employer and employee—as an entrepreneur. The following principles are common among SE approaches (Drake, Bond, & Becker, 2012; Wehman, 2012):

- **Goal of competitive employment:** The intention is to help the job seeker find competitive, integrated employment in the community.
- **Centrality of individual choice:** The job seeker and his or her strengths and skills are at the center of the job search, and job seekers are given space to make informed choices about their jobs and careers.
- **Importance of benefits counseling:** Career planning includes an exploration of available benefits and how employment might impact those benefits.
- **Rapid job search:** Job seekers need not spend years in the initial stages of the job search, but are actually able to find a good match within a reasonable amount of time.
- **Availability of job carving:** People supporting the job seeker aim to find a job that is a good fit for them, which may involve working with a business to create a customized job description for the job seeker.
- **Time-unlimited support:** Support is planned so as to last as long as necessary, and includes both natural and formal supports.

Accommodations

Accommodations are adaptations that make things simpler for an individual or group. These can be technologically simple, like installing a door lever instead of a knob, or they can be more technologically complicated, like a computer that talks or a Braille printer. A reasonable accommodation is:

> any modification or adjustment to a job or the work environment that will enable a qualified applicant or employee with a disability . . . to perform essential job functions. Reasonable accommodation also includes adjustments to ensure that a qualified individual with a disability has rights and privileges in employment equal to those of employees without disabilities. (EEOC, 2002)

Combined with supported and customized employment, accommodations can be part of the negotiation process. Funding for more expensive accommodations may come from the employer or from government agencies such as vocational rehabilitation offices. Career planning and assessment, SE, and accommodations are foundational approaches from which additional interventions can be developed.

Systems

Systems play a multifaceted role in supporting competitive, integrated employment for people with IDD. They do this through the development of policy, which sets the foundation for provider training, expected practices, necessary documentation for services, and funding structures. For example, when a state agency adopts an Employment First policy, competitive, integrated employment is identified as the first and preferred outcome for people with IDD. This sets the expectation that providers will know how to help people with IDD find competitive, integrated employment; that they will use this knowledge with each individual they support; and that they will document how they did so.

Systems can also facilitate communication between provider-supported employment and businesses by increasing the expectations for providers to be in the community, getting to know job seekers and businesses on a deeper level. This will enable them to facilitate job matches with the potential for high levels of satisfaction for both the job seeker and the employer. When employment professionals spend more time in the community, they are also better able to identify natural supports, or tasks where less support is necessary, which makes it less intimidating for businesses to employ people who need extra support.

Policy also sets the stage for systems to support the employment of people with IDD by providing funding for programs and services focused on community-based employment. Through policy, priorities and directives can be outlined to incentivize programs and services that support competitive, integrated employment over facility-based settings. Funding structures, then, need to align with the desired outcome of competitive, integrated employment, offering incentives to service providers, individuals, and businesses that support competitive, integrated employment for people with IDD. The majority of people with IDD report that they want to be employed in the community (Butterworth et al., 2015; Nye-Lengerman, Pettingell, Nord, & Hewitt, submitted). It stands to reason, then, that if funding is available to support the realization of these desires, people with IDD will utilize it.

Action at all of these levels will contribute to a community in which people with IDD are able to have valued social roles through integrated employment in which they contribute meaningfully to the well-being of the community. This employment then becomes a pillar and facilitator of even more profound integration into community living for people with IDD.

Personal Illustration: Tamir Tsogbaatar

Tamir Tsogbaatar is passionate about technology. "I realized very quickly that he is a technology trend expert," recalled Barb McGovern, a Customized Employment Specialist with ProAct, Inc., an organization providing job training and SE.

Born in a small village in Mongolia, Tamir was educated in a school established for him by his mother. "I was born with Cerebral Palsy and hemiplegia, and there was no adaptive technology there to help me," said Tamir. "There was no equipment, there were no wheelchairs, there were no doctors to help me." Fortunately, there were caring teachers who supported Tamir and other children with disabilities. He moved to Minnesota at age 11 and completed high school and a transition program.

When Barb met Tamir, his job was doing recycling, earning 37 cents per hour. Because of mobility and communications challenges, expectations for Tamir had not been ambitious. "There wasn't an understanding of what he could do, what his true work skills were," said Barb.

Tamir's dream was to work at Best Buy because of their focus on technology. Barb worked with Tamir in completing online applications and developing interviewing skills. "He was able to talk about all of his strengths and his motivation, and his desire to join the Best Buy team," said Barb. When they visited a number of local Best Buy stores, she was surprised to see that most managers recognized Tamir as a customer.

Barb arranged a meeting for Tamir at a Best Buy store in Apple Valley, Minnesota. General Manager Ron Szelag was impressed with Tamir's enthusiasm for technology. "He loves to game," said Ron. "He loves the technology, so that set him apart." Following a formal interview, Tamir was offered the position of Merchandise Specialist.

"I hired him and he's been cross-trained in multiple areas," said Ron. "He can sell TVs, downstock, merchandise, price set. He's been with me a year now and he's just a fantastic employee." Tamir enjoys the work, the collaborative atmosphere, and the exposure to new products. "What I like most," said Tamir, "is when new technologies come up and I can share what they can do for people."

Tamir's speech is at times difficult to understand. After beginning his new job, he investigated several dictation devices and now uses Active Voice, an app that learns his speech patterns and helps him communicate more effectively with customers. Being in a position where he speaks with customers daily has improved his enunciation skills. "His speech has greatly improved," said Barb. "Most folks don't have any trouble understanding him at all." Ron agrees, noting that other staff soon had no difficulty understanding Tamir's speech. "In terms of formal accommodations," said Ron, "I haven't really had to make any."

In his previous work in recycling, Tamir's wages were tied to physical proficiency and productivity. At Best Buy, he is paid $11 per hour, the same rate as other Merchandise Specialists. "Tamir got a 3,000% increase in his wage!" exclaimed Barb. Beyond the salary increase, Tamir has also been supported in pursuing a career in an industry of his choosing.

Having a job at Best Buy has allowed Tamir to realize his dreams. "Tamir identified this as his dream job from the beginning," said Barb. "He is able to connect with customers and share his passion for technology." And the job has increased Tamir's belief in his abilities. "Working here, it makes me more independent," he said. Ron appreciates having an enthusiastic employee who shares his passion for technology. "It's good for your customer, good for your bottom dollar, good for your bottom line, period."

Conclusion

Having a job is a valued social role. Employment is a pathway to independence, economic self-sufficiency, respect, purpose, dignity, and full community participation. Almost all people can benefit from having a job, regardless of disability. The employment of people with IDD reduces many of the stigmas and misconceptions that others have about people with IDD. Employment is a powerful way to combat stereotypes. As more people with IDD have community jobs, other community members experience meaningful interactions with them and see their strengths and skills. This cultivates within the community a sense of the value of all people, which then leads to the development of more opportunities for people with IDD to be a meaningful part of their communities.

While most people with IDD are not working in the community, there is a recent, strong surge of interest at the individual, family, provider, and policy level in focusing on competitive, integrated employment. It is critical for both systems and providers to invest in and prioritize employment supports, as many people with IDD utilize them. At all levels of service and in the community, the message of high expectations is critical for improving employment outcomes for people with IDD. The inclusion of people with IDD in the workforce has benefits across the social, economic, and cultural fabric of society.

Discussion Questions

- What are some examples of activities or expectations for individuals with IDD at different ages that would promote positive messages about and prepare them for employment?
- What community resources are available to support people with and without disabilities in finding employment? How can people with IDD benefit from these supports?
- When families depend on their family member with IDD having something to do during the day so they can work, what happens if day programs or other services are not an option?
- What incentives and disincentives contribute to a person with IDD deciding to seek or not seek paid employment in the community?

Resources

- APSE (Association of People Supporting Employment First): APSE, founded in 1988, is the only national organization with an exclusive focus on integrated employment and career advancement opportunities for individuals with disabilities. APSE has 3,000+ members and is a growing, national non-profit membership organization. Their members include individuals with disabilities, families, disability professionals, and businesses. www.apse.org/
- LEAD Center: The LEAD Center focuses on promoting innovation in policy, employment, and economic advancement to advance individual and systems-level change for all people with disabilities. It provides policy research and recommendations, training, and technical assistance, as well as demonstration projects designed to break down silos in existing systems. http://www.leadcenter.org/
- Office of Disability Employment Policy (ODEP): ODEP is a non-regulatory federal agency that promotes policies and coordinates with employers and all levels of government to increase workplace success for people with disabilities. ODEP's mission is to develop and influence policies and practices that increase the number and quality of employment opportunities. www.dol.gov/odep
- Think Work: ThinkWork is a hub for an array of resources on the opportunities and challenges related to employment for people with IDD at the Institute for Community Inclusion at the University of Massachusetts Boston. www.thinkwork.org
- Social Security Administration Red Book: The Red Book serves as a general reference source about the employment-related provisions of Social Security Disability Insurance and the Supplemental Security Income Programs for educators, advocates, rehabilitation professionals, and counselors who serve people with disabilities. https://www.ssa.gov/redbook/

References

AAIDD and The Arc. (2012). Employment: Joint position statement of AAIDD and the Arc. Retrieved from https://aaidd.org/news-policy/policy/position-statements/employment#

Americans with Disabilities Act of 1990, Pub. L. No. 101-336, 104 Stat. 328 (1990).

Association of People Supporting Employment First (APSE). (2017). Defining Employment First. Retrieved from http://apse.org/employment-first/https://www.cdc.gov/ncbddd/disabilityandhealth/disability-barriers.html.

Butterworth, J., Smith, F. A., Winsor, J., Ciulla Timmons, J., Migliore, A., & Domin, D, (2016). *StateData: The national report on employment services and outcomes.* Boston, MA: University of Massachusetts Boston, Institute for Community Inclusion.

Butterworth, J., Hiersteiner, D., Engler, J., Bershadsky, J., & Bradley, V. (2015). National core indicators: Data on the current state of employment of adults with IDD and suggestions for policy development. *Journal of Vocational Rehabilitation, 42*(3), 209–220. doi:10.3233/JVR-150741

Centers for Medicare and Medicaid Services (2014). *Final Regulation:* 1915(i) State Plan HCBS, 5-Year Period for Waivers, Provider Payment Reassignment, Setting Requirements for Community First Choice, and 1915(c) HCBS Waivers—CMS-2249-F/CMS-2296-F 42 CFR § 441. Available at http://www.medicaid.gov/HCBS

Drake, R. E., Bond, G. R., & Becker, D. R. (2012). *Individual placement and support: An evidence-based approach to supported employment.* Oxford University Press.

The Education for All Handicapped Children Act of 1975, Pub. L. No. 94–142 (1975).

Friedman, C. & Rizzolo, M. C. (2017). "Get us real jobs:" Supported employment services for people with intellectual and developmental disabilities in Medicaid Home and Community Based Services Waivers. *Journal of Vocational Rehabilitation, 46*(1), 107–116. doi: 10.3233/JVR-160847

Griffin, C., & Hammis, D. (2011). Discovering personal genius: Self-employment for transition-age youth. *National Gateway to Self-Determination, September*(2), 13–16.

Gunty, A. L., Dean, K., Nord, D., Hoff, D., & Nye-Lengerman, K., (2017). *Employment First: An update on national progress.* Policy Research Brief, 26(2), Minneapolis, MN: Research & Training Center on Community Living at the University of Minnesota.

Larson, S. A., Salmi, P., Smith, D., Anderson, L., & Hewitt, A. (2013). *Residential services for persons with intellectual or developmental disabilities: Status and trends through 2011.* Minneapolis, MN: Institute on Community Integration, University of Minnesota.

Migliore, A., Nye-Lengerman, K., Lyons, O., Bose, J., & Butterworth, J. (2018). A comprehensive model of employment supports for job seekers with IDDIDD. *Journal of Rehabilitation.*

Minnesota Governor's Council on Developmental Disabilities. (n.d.). *Parallels in time: A history of developmental disabilities.* Retrieved from https://mn.gov/mnddc/parallels/index.html

National Association of Workforce Boards and the Public Consulting Group (2014). *The Workforce Innovation and Opportunity Act—Driving innovation, collaboration, and performance.* Retrieved from http://www.nawb.org/documents/Publications/WIOA_Overview.pdf

Nielsen, K. E. (2013). *A disability history of the United States.* Boston, MA: Beacon Press.

Nord, D., Butterworth, J., Carlson, D., Grossi, T., Cohen Hall, A., & Nye-Lengerman, K. (2016). *Employment for people with IDD: What do we know and where are we going? in National goals for research for people with IDDIDD.* Washington, DC: American Association on IDDIDD.

Nye-Lengerman KM, Pettingell SL, Hewitt AS, & Nord DK. (submitted Apr 2018). Utilization of employment services by people with intellectual and developmental disabilities: An analysis of National Core Indicator data. *Research and Practice Persons with Severe Disabilities.*

Olmstead v. L.C., No. 98–536, 527 581, (1999).

Rehabilitation Act of 1973, Pub. L. No. 93-112, 87 Stat. 355 (1973).

Timmons, J., & Lyons, O. (2016) Essential elements in organizational transformation: Findings from a Delphi Panel of experts. *Bringing Employment First to scale, Issue 8.* Boston, MA: University of Massachusetts Boston, Institute for Community Inclusion.

U.S. Department of Labor. (1979). Summary of major findings of the US Department of Labor sheltered workshop study. *Amicus, 4*(5,6):276-.

U.S. Equal Employment Opportunity Commission (EEOC) (2002). *Enforcement guidance: Reasonable accommodation and undue hardship under the Americans with Disabilities Act.* Retrieved from https://www.eeoc.gov/policy/docs/accommodation.html

Wehman, P., Chan, F., Ditchman, N., & Kang, H. (2014) Effect of supported employment on vocational rehabilitation outcomes of transition-age youth with IDDIDD: A case control study. *IDDIDD, 52*(4), 296–310. doi:10.1352/1934-9556-52.4.296

Wehman, P. (2012). Supported Employment: What is it? *Journal of Vocational Rehabilitation 37*, 3. 139–142. doi:10.3233/JVR-2012-0607

Workforce Innovation and Opportunity Act of 2013, Pub. L. No. 113-128 (2013).

CHAPTER FIVE

Friendship, Love, and Fun: Social Inclusion and Relationships

Angela N. Amado, Jody Van Ness, Jennifer Hall Lande, and Rebecca Dosch Brown

---

Advance Organizers

- Having friends and social connections is important at any age.
- People with IDD may experience challenges in making social connections with others.
- Inclusion is more than just sharing space.
- Support services and systems can sometimes be a barrier for making and keeping friends.

Societal attitudes about people with disabilities have changed over time. More people with disabilities are active members of their communities than in the past. Attitudes have shifted from seeing people with disabilities as "less than" or dangerous to appreciating them as full citizens with many contributions to make. Community members who have befriended people with IDD have noted the gifts they receive from their friends, such as joy, humor, love, kindness, and reminders of what's important in life. People with IDD contribute their skills and talents in workplaces, faith communities, schools, and community organizations. Attitudes are also shifting toward valuing diversity as an important element in strong communities. Increasing diversity involves including people with IDD in every aspect of community life.

Acceptance of the physical presence of people with disabilities in businesses, neighborhoods, and congregations is now commonplace. However, significant change is still needed in order for people with IDD to enjoy full community inclusion, including close relationships with other community members and a full sense of community belonging and membership. It is possible for people with IDD to have rich social networks and valued community social roles. When communities become truly inclusive, treasuring relationships with and the contributions of citizens with IDD, everyday community life will be enhanced for everyone.

The Importance of Relationships

Our first relationships are with our family. As we grow, we develop friendships with peers and form relationships in other environments, such as with schoolmates when we're young and with coworkers as we reach adulthood. We also develop relationships and friendships in the wider community with neighbors, friends in clubs we belong to, fellow congregation members, and professional colleagues. During adolescence, most people also develop more intimate partnerships, such as with boyfriends or girlfriends. More recently, many people also have "Facebook friends" or other online acquaintances, with whom they communicate but may not have met face-to-face.

Relationships can be classified according to their frequency of interaction and their depth. In many person-centered planning approaches used with people with disabilities, supporters draw "relationship maps"—typically, concentric circles with the deepest relationships in the innermost circle and acquaintances in the outer circle. You can read more about person-centered approaches in Chapter 2.

Relationships affect physical, mental, and emotional health. People with fewer relationships may experience higher-than-average levels of depression, or other physical or emotional issues. A University of Chicago study found that friendships benefit health by helping people develop resilience and master the ability to bounce back after adversity (Perry, 2014). A study of U.S. nurses found that those who had no close friends were four times as likely to die from cancer as women with many friends (Kroenke, Kubzansky, Schernhammer, Holmes, & Kawachi, 2006). High-quality relationships and close friendships are also a vital component of psychological health. Our thoughts, behaviors, and emotions are driven by a motivation to form meaningful relationships with others. Consequently, individuals who experience ongoing, persistent challenges in developing and maintaining high-quality relationships are susceptible to feelings of chronic social isolation and loneliness.

Besides the health and other benefits that accrue from friendship, recreation specialists have documented that the degree of fun we have is related to the people with whom we engage in activities. Whether we are biking, eating out, or going to the movies, it's more fun to share these experiences with people we like.

Valued Social Roles

When examining relationships and social networks, it is important to understand the different types of social roles an individual with IDD experiences. "Social roles" are ones we have in relationship to others—friend, spouse, coworker, boss, congregation member, colleague, and many others. These roles often have social value attached to them. When people are seen only or mainly as their disability, they feel they are in a devalued social role—as the object of pity or ridicule, or as one of "them." Historical patterns of isolation both reflect and contribute to the devaluation of people with disabilities in the eyes of the wider public. Wolf Wolfensberger (2000) was a key developer of the idea that one of the most powerful ways to make a difference in quality of life for people with IDD was to assist them to have more valued social roles. In recent years, for example, many actors with Down syndrome, cerebral palsy, and autism have played major roles in films and on television. The Americans With Disabilities Act (ADA) has paved the way for people with disabilities to have ordinary jobs in workplaces, where it can be seen that they contribute unique skills and talents. Many people with IDD have taken on other valued social roles, such as church greeter, member of a Kiwanis or Rotary club, or candidate for public office. Promoting such socially valued roles is an important part of cultivating relationships among people with IDD and the wider community.

Developing Intimacy

Close personal relationships are a key ingredient in quality of life for all people, including those with intellectual disability (Wolfensberger, 2000). At the same time, research suggests that people with IDD often experience significant challenges in developing close relationships and maintaining meaningful friendships (Friedman & Rizzolo, 2017). Children with IDD typically participate in significantly fewer social activities with friends and report fewer reciprocal friendships than their peers without disabilities (Solish, Perry, & Minnes, 2010). Adults with IDD consistently identify fewer friendships than do people without disabilities, and their identified relationships are often with other people with IDD (Emerson & McVilly, 2004; Gilmore & Cuskelly, 2014). Older adults and senior citizens with IDD report that their closest relationships are with paid support staff, family members, and other individuals with IDD (Bigby & Knox, 2009).

Studies have found evidence of frequent isolation and loneliness among people in the services system, as well as the paucity of a variety of relationships in their social networks. A study by Verdonschot, de Witte, Reichraft, Buntinx, and Curfs (2009) found an average of three people in the social network of individuals with IDD, with one of the three a staff member. These findings contrast with studies of the general population, which found that people without disabilities have approximately 125 people in their social networks (Hill & Dunbar, 2003).

Current research reveals that loneliness and feelings of isolation are a common experience for adults with IDD. Previous studies consistently suggested that up to half of people with IDD experienced frequent feelings of loneliness (e.g., Stancliffe et al., 2007), compared to reported rates of loneliness of 15–30% in the general population (Gilmore & Cuskelly, 2014). In other words, despite the fact that many people with IDD are integrated into their community and participate in community social activities, they still report having few close friends and meaningful social connections in the community (Bogenschutz & Amado, 2016).

Historical Views

Historical patterns of attitudes toward people with disabilities include significant patterns of devaluation. Institutionalization and "special" programs that have isolated people with IDD have contributed to the need to overcome many negative attitudes in the larger community.

Although the physical inclusion of people with IDD has greatly expanded, they are often still seen as needing special assistance, as occupying devalued social roles, and as not being equal to other citizens. Additionally, although formal supports have been designed to help people with disabilities, many human services programs have effectively separated the population into two "worlds"—the disability world and the community world. As David Pitonyak (2014) wrote, "Loneliness is the only real disability." Tay and Diener (2011) found that, even when people lacked basic food or shelter, they could be happy if they had friends; people who do not have much money (as holds true for many people with IDD) can still feel happy if they have a strong network of loved ones and friends, along with a sense of purpose. Although services have addressed skill development and physical care, there remains a huge need to support people in developing "enduring, freely chosen relationships" (O'Brien & O'Brien, 1987). Professionals don't have to wait for other things to be "in order" before they support deliberately working on relationships that can provide benefits such as fun and happiness to a person. Research has shown that there are simple, pragmatic ways to build more inclusive spaces where participants can gain a strong sense of belonging.

Misperceptions and Assumptions

There are many barriers to relationships between individuals with and without disabilities, and to individuals with IDD being valued as full citizens. Two types of barriers are misperceptions and assumptions. The following statements are often heard about people with IDD:

"They want to be with their own kind." The historical separation of individuals with IDD from neurotypical community members, which began with institutionalization, is perpetuated in current times with the grouping and congregation of individuals with IDD in many service designs. This notion of people belonging with "their own kind" has often led community entities such as congregations, community education programs, and some service organizations to start "special" programs for people with disabilities. Such designs fail to allow people with disabilities to contribute to the wider community, and fail to let community members get to know individuals with IDD beyond acquaintanceship or superficial levels of acceptance.

"It should happen naturally." Promoting relationships between individuals with and without disabilities often takes overcoming major attitudinal divides. Although it is ideal for people to get to know one another naturally, it often takes more conscious effort and intentionality to bridge the divides between the disability world and the community world.

"They need 'special' people." Service design in the last century has often led to community members thinking that people with disabilities are "taken care of" within the services system. A common notion is that people with disabilities need "special" people to support them. Members of the general public often do not recognize the importance of their own role in making communities inclusive. Human services have sometimes stripped neurotypical people of the knowledge of their own capacity to know, befriend, and support their fellow citizens with IDD.

"Presence is the same as participation. Community activity is the same as relationship." The physical presence and acceptance of people with disabilities where nondisabled people also live, work, play, and worship is critical for full community living. However, more effort needs to be expended in order to build relationships and contribution. When service regulations require "community participation," it often takes the shape of human services agencies taking people to places like restaurants, movies, shopping, and church services, but this is only physical inclusion. "Community activities" are not the same as authentic reciprocal relationships, real friendships, belonging, and membership. In a major British study of four communities that had made a significant commitment to implementing person-centered planning approaches, the individuals experienced an increase in choice and in community activities, but not in the inclusiveness of their personal social networks (Green, Moore, & O'Brien, 2006). It will require going beyond normal practices and take more concerted effort to realize such increases.

"People with IDD cannot have intimate relationships." The belief that people with IDD are not sexual often interferes with promotion of more intimate and loving relationships. Many individuals with IDD are held back from developing intimate relationships by others' attitudes, including the idea that they are not sexual beings, they are not ready, and sex is too dangerous for them. There is real and legitimate fear on the part of many families that their child might be taken advantage of or abused.

Although vulnerability is of great concern, fear must be balanced with the recognition that people with IDD have the right to express themselves sexually and have loving and intimate partners.

Current Controversies and Challenges

Important forces are currently supporting the movement toward more meaningful community integration and social inclusion for people with IDD, as well as addressing existing barriers and issues to make greater inclusion possible. Legislation such as the ADA (1990) and litigation such as the Olmstead v. L.C. decision (1999) have brought people with IDD into local neighborhoods, places of employment, businesses, recreation programs, and congregations. The Workforce Innovation and Opportunity Act (2014), state Employment First policies, and regulations for people who receive Medicaid waiver services have increased the community presence of individuals who previously were in segregated living and work settings. You can read more about these pieces of legislation in Chapter 1. Community inclusion starts with physical presence, and system drivers such as these have enabled that presence. However, one of the major challenges is that social inclusion goes far beyond the physical presence in the community. Social inclusion also means that people with IDD physically, emotionally, culturally, and financially participate in and contribute to the community in the same ways as those without disabilities.

Attitudinal Challenges

Attitudes represent a major challenge in bringing people with IDD and other community members together. As previously noted, misperceptions and assumptions can exacerbate controversy or fear. The fear of parents or guardians for their loved one's safety must be balanced with the dignity of risk—affording real opportunities while providing sufficient safeguards. Both families and professional support providers must strike a balance between promoting social inclusion and preventing harm or abuse of people with IDD—all while considering an agency's concerns about liability.

Agency and System Support Issues

Agencies committed to greater social inclusion for the individuals they support have many challenges to address, including larger policy issues that can present barriers. A significant barrier to more personal relationships is when people in a congregated program (such as a group home or day program) have to go in groups to community places. When community members see groups of people with IDD, the notion is strengthened that such people belong "with their own kind," or that they need help from "special" people. People with IDD who are always grouped with others with IDD do not have the opportunity to be known as individuals. Human services systems must find ways to provide more individualized support to address this challenge.

Opportunities to be known as a unique person are maximized when a single individual joins a community group. But this is difficult in group situations, such as small group homes or congregated day programs where there might not be sufficient staff or flexible enough schedules to allow an individual to be supported one-on-one in connecting with their own places. For example, staff in a group home may be reduced from two staff to one at 9 p.m. If an event really gets going at 10 p.m., how will a person who wants to stay late be able to do so? These are the types of difficult questions that agencies face when trying to support people with IDD in an individualized way.

Another policy issue concerns confidentiality. Some staff believe they cannot introduce people to community members because of confidentiality rules. At the same time, regulations governing the funding of social service programs require community participation and promotion of natural supports, which means that community members do need to be introduced to people receiving services. Staff need to understand that, as long as they have guardians' permission, they can indeed introduce people widely; agencies need to obtain such permission and discuss social integration plans with people with IDD and their guardians. Agencies may need to evaluate and even change their practices and policies to address how to introduce and what to say about the people they support, especially those who cannot speak for themselves. In addition, agency policies and practices need to be assessed for the degree to which they appropriately support dating, sexual relationships, and marriage. Agency rules frequently interfere with such relationships.

Physical challenges, such as transportation, might also be an issue. For example, if someone who lives with their family wants to go to a karaoke club on a Tuesday night, who besides their family can take them? If three or four people live in a group home with one staff person, and the other residents do not want to go to the club, how will the person who wants to go get there? Transportation is also an important issue to address in support of more intimate relationships. For example, people who want to date one another often live in different places; how can they be supported so that they can spend time together?

In smaller communities, recreational opportunities often run past the time when public transportation stops operating. A young person with disabilities often can't get to a community organization meeting or opportunity unless their family or staff takes them. Creative approaches with transportation often involve finding and making requests of others who are going to the same place, asking a congregation or service organization to provide rides, or, on a larger scale, advocating for the expansion of public transportation.

At the governmental level, several policy issues hinder social relationships. The movement toward more individualized support in living and work environments needs to keep increasing, because opportunities for meaningful social inclusion can be enhanced in more individualized settings. You can read more about some of the policy and legislation that affects the full inclusion of people with IDD in community living in Chapter 1. Several states have also made commitments to address the need for greater social inclusion in their services system (e.g., State of Kentucky, 2014). States and statewide organizations may need to commit to and plan for activities, initiatives, and investments to move inclusive communities to the next phase.

Life Course Expectations and Transitions

Expectations of social life for people with IDD follow the same life course as expectations for those without disabilities. For children in their early years, their strongest relationships are with their family. As children enter preschool and school, relationships develop with same-age peers, including neighborhood friends and playmates. Friendships further develop with those with whom they share interests, such as sports, theater, scouts, etc. In the early teen years, sexual feelings surface and romantic relationships may begin. In the young adult and adult years, employment becomes important and relationships develop with coworkers. More intimate relationships develop as people date, marry, and have children. As people age, the maintenance of social relationships, avoidance of loneliness, and sense of contribution to others become even more important to vitality and longevity.

Such expectations of relationships typical at different ages also apply to people with IDD. Families, allies, and providers can and should model healthy relationships and boundaries for people with IDD as appropriate for each phase of growth. Such modeling should include the development of social skills and finding a broad spectrum of people with whom to relate. Especially if a person with IDD is in a segregated school program, residence, or work environment, they will need support to find other places in which to pursue their interests; find belonging; and experience fun, friendship, and love. If an individual does not use words to communicate or has limited communication ability, they especially will need support to be known by the broader community for their unique talents and personality.

Many families are acutely aware that their child's social inclusion drops once they graduate from school. While a student is still in transition to postsecondary activities, schools and families can support the continuation of relationships after graduation as well as the identification of new employment and recreational opportunities. When students begin their transition to adult programs, it is important to plan for their post-graduation social life. Will relationships with school friends be maintained? Where else will they find people with whom to share interests?

For young adults and adults who continue to live at home, it is important not only to support relationships mediated through the family's social network, but also to support cultivation of the broader interests and personal relationships typical of most adults. Such support will be especially crucial if the family member moves to another living environment. As people transition to their later years, it is necessary to replace work with the maintenance of existing social connections, the development of new ones, and engagement in social activities.

Practical Suggestions and Interventions

This section offers practical suggestions for individuals, families, agencies, and the community at large in cultivating social inclusion, relationships, and friendships for people with IDD.

Environments That Foster Relationships

Places such as faith communities, schools, workplaces, and community organizations can foster either segregated or integrated opportunities for relationship. For example, many human services programs and environments are segregated—the individual with IDD interacts primarily with others with IDD and paid staff. However, there are also segregated community places, such as Sunday school classes for congregation members with disabilities, "special" chapters of community service organizations, and community places where large numbers of people with disabilities congregate during the day (e.g., recycling centers, libraries, and community centers). There is another type of segregation as well, in which people with IDD visit or tour locations on "community outings" or as "community activities," but no real sense of relationship, membership, or belonging is generated.

In contrast are community settings that promote a wider sense of relationship and belonging. In these environments, people with and without disabilities can interact meaningfully and get to know one another; there are places where someone will be missed if they are not present. Integrated school programs, as opposed to segregated classes or schools, can foster such relationships. In integrated workplaces, individuals can be known for their contributions and skills, rather than as just a part of a "special" crew of people with disabilities. Many community service organizations include a member with IDD. Many faith communities have moved beyond the point where members with disabilities simply attend services, to the point of valuing their participation with other congregation members in more meaningful ways, such as in men's groups, women's groups, prayer groups, volunteer projects, etc. (Carter, 2007).

Supporting Relationship Development

Many people with a disability label are capable of developing their own relationships, if provided the environment and opportunity. Parents and teachers play an important role in modeling healthy relationships and boundaries. The desire of some people with IDD for relationship and connection is so strong that they may develop a relationship with any friendly person who comes along and may end up in an undesirable situation as a result. For individuals who are at risk, there are at least two avenues to pursue—ensuring they receive training and support to learn how to watch for potentially abusive people or problematic situations, and pursuing opportunities and efforts to promote safe and healthy relationships.

If it is especially challenging, due to the nature of the disability, for a person with IDD to develop reciprocal relationships, opportunities will only occur if others provide sufficient support. This might require family, staff, and other supporters to seek out opportunities for relationship and make requests of community members.

For people who live with their families, relationships are often mediated by the family. A family can encourage people in the existing network of long-time family friends and relatives to develop their own separate relationship with the family member with IDD. But the family may also need to look outside their network for places and opportunities for the family member with IDD to develop their own social connections.

Staff members providing people with residential, day program, or employment supports need to recognize the key role they play in facilitating relationships. Most individuals receiving support in community programs will only experience greater social inclusion and deeper relationships with others if their support agencies and staff make efforts in this direction. Staff persons need to play a facilitative rather than a hindering role. For example, staff in supported or competitive employment situations need to recognize that they are sometimes a barrier to a worker's relationship with coworkers; if the staff person is constantly with a worker with IDD, coworkers may not want to interfere or may not feel they can get to know their coworker with IDD. Instead, the job coach can play a more facilitative role by guiding coworkers in how to get to know the person with IDD. The same is true in school situations—when a paraprofessional is constantly attending to the student with disabilities, it can interfere with other students getting to know and interact with the student. Staff play a critical role in being facilitators rather than barriers.

Keys to Practical Intervention

The following four keys to supporting increased levels of social inclusion are based on understanding how people make friends:

Key 1: Seeing someone in terms of their gifts. Initial perspectives can be surpassed to identify and see the gifts someone brings so that the focus is on a person's talents, abilities, and contributions instead of his or her disability or deficits. Sobsey (2002) has written about the true joys and benefits that a child with disabilities brings to a family. Most staff and professionals in human services continue working in the field not because of the pay, but because of the benefits and gifts they receive from knowing and supporting the people who receive services. Staff report receiving joy, unconditional love, reminders of what's really important in life, and a sense of accomplishment in supporting someone in achieving something new. When gifts are identified, we can help others see the value in becoming acquainted with or including someone for the sake of their contributions.

Key 2: Looking for places of regular and meaningful interaction. Most people with IDD go to places in the wider community, such as stores, restaurants, and movies. However, people don't typically develop relationships in such places. When people are asked where they have met the people who are now their friends, the answers are usually school, work, church, the neighborhood, and places of mutual interest (e.g., sewing clubs, sports teams, their child's daycare, etc.). Places where most people make friends have two things in common: First, they allow for repeated and regular interactions—not just one-time encounters; they are not simply places of commerce or exchange. Second, they are places where meaningful interaction and shared activities take place, and where people have opportunities to get to know one another over time. These are the types of places to look for when seeking community connection opportunities for someone with IDD.

For example, coworkers in a place of supported or competitive employment can also be supported to have social relationships outside the work environment. Places of regular volunteering are safe places where one can get to know fellow volunteers. Community organizations or clubs based on interests such as gardening, quilting, cribbage, sports, and so on also provide great opportunities for acquaintanceship to develop into friendship.

There are many places in a community to pursue a particular interest, but it is important to consider two questions: Do the same people participate over and over, and is the interaction with these "regulars" meaningful? Someone interested in music may go to regular performances at a local coffee shop, and there may be other "regulars" there. However, if there are not opportunities for meaningful interaction and shared activities with the other attendees, there might be better places for a music lover to make friends. Options might include singing with a community or church choir, volunteering with a high school or college band or orchestra, or joining a fan club that frequently meets face-to-face. Or someone who likes bowling can be supported to join a regular bowling team and league rather than the "special" league.

Key 3: The art and skill of asking. As noted above, most people become friends through meeting at places where they see each other regularly. However, we don't normally become friends with everyone from school or work or other places where we see many people. When we would like to get to know particular people better, we usually ask them to do something outside of that setting, like have coffee or drinks or dinner, or we invite them over or go out to do other things, like going to a movie, shopping, or to a sporting event. The asking is what extends the relationship outside of the initial environment. But because of the great divides between the disability world and the community world, bringing people together across those boundaries often means that families or providers have to ask community members to get involved.

Asking is an extremely important skill, but it also usually requires some "art." Some people are natural at it and unafraid to ask almost anything of anyone. However, many people are either shy or reluctant to ask. Fear of rejection is a common human trait. Identifying ahead of time what to ask and practicing asking the question can be extremely useful. The more one practices and engages in asking, the better one becomes at it. Asking a community member to get to know a person with IDD better might mean everyone—the person with IDD, the community member, and the supporter who is doing the asking—going beyond their comfort zone, but in the end, it can be well worth it for all.

When faced with rejection, it's also important to consider other approaches: Could something different be said? Would someone else be a better person to make the request? Families and staff often find themselves surprised by the positive responses, having had no idea of community members' willingness to befriend someone with IDD until they asked!

Key 4: Reconnecting with previous relationships. During the course of a person's lifetime, one encounters many people, some of whom become very important to us. But sometimes our lives take us in different directions and we lose touch. Thus, another avenue for promoting relationships is to identify important people from a person's past. Were there staff who were significant to the person, or who really loved them? Are there family members or old school friends with whom the person with IDD has lost a connection?

One agency started an "alumni club" and kept former staff connected with the individuals they had cared deeply for. People who currently live in institutions have likely lost some family connections; in such instances, staff can sometimes find relatives willing to reconnect. In some cases, the reconnection is not with parents or siblings of the person who was institutionalized, but rather with nieces, nephews, or others who want to meet and/or reconnect with their family member.

Intimate Relationships

Perhaps the most important thing in life is how much love we experience. When McVilly, Stancliffe, Parmenter, and Burton-Smith (2006) studied the frequency of loneliness reported among people with IDD, they found that it is often related to the lack of an intimate partner—a girlfriend or boyfriend. When a person with IDD wants to have an intimate relationship, they should be supported in doing so. There are many programs to support appropriate dating skills, having safe sex, avoiding abuse, having a satisfying intimate relationship, getting married, and having children. After people are connected, it is often important to keep supporting the relationship, as any romance or marriage has its ups and downs and challenges.

Technology: Barrier and Asset

Although technology is a great asset for many, it can also be a hindrance for supporting relationships. This is the case for people with IDD just as it is for others. For one thing, some people do not have access to computers, email, or accessible technology. For another thing, many "social" relationships among the general public have devolved to texting back and forth, rather than having face-to-face interactions. Having 1,000 "Facebook friends," for example, does not mean one has a rich social life or is loved by many people.

On the other hand, technology can be an asset in promoting relationships. The web is a rich resource for finding others who share similar interests. Websites such as meetup.com and other networking sites can bring people together around mutual interests. In addition, some people find it easier to stay in contact with family and friends more frequently by using email and/or social networking sites.

Supporting Skill Development

As with other skills, social development follows a predictable trajectory that benefits from nurturing and opportunities to interact with those around us. People with IDD gain confidence when taught proper everyday social behavior. Without direct instruction, they are sometimes forced to learn "the hard way," resulting in humiliation, embarrassment, and loss of self-confidence. It is up to family and service providers to offer tools and support for meeting people, keeping friends, and developing respectful relationships with peers.

During the early school years, children learn from peers and begin to test boundaries. Play dates with neurotypical peers, group activities, opportunities to grow in independence, and shared play, including play with kids of different genders, are all important. This is also the time for conversations about what friendship means, about how to approach others to play, about how to have reciprocal conversations, and about gender differences.

As children move closer to adolescence, they learn to depend more on nonverbal cues. Whereas many kids intuitively understand these communications over time, people with IDD depend more on direct instruction from family members and friends (Canney & Byrne, 2006). Playing and coaching through interactive games like charades or engaging with the community in common settings like community gardens, faith-based organizations, or community theater programs, offers a rich environment for practicing crucial skills.

During middle school and high school, young people begin to move away from their families and develop their own identity. Peer groups narrow, and other kids can be silly and curious, but also selfish and rude. This is exceptionally difficult for youth who struggle to see others' perspectives, given that they value friends' and peers' opinions at this stage. Embarrassment, moodiness, heightened frustration, and new behaviors may enter the equation. This is a time for family and allies to talk openly about feelings, and to both reflect on problematic exchanges and rehearse for challenging situations ahead.

Young people moving into adulthood experience a wide range of complex and multifaceted issues. Social factors become much more nuanced as young adults make decisions about their sexuality/reproduction, identity formulation/emotional regulation, career decisions, and intimate/social relationships (Newman, Wagner, Cameto,

& Knokey, 2011). These new social roles must be balanced with the inherent vulnerabilities of many people with IDD as new approaches and supports are sought for their adult years.

Young adults with IDD tend to participate in social and recreational activities designed specifically for people with disabilities, and often limit their social and recreational interactions to their families. But in adulthood, people with IDD whose lives are primarily segregated from mainstream society are limited in their ability to achieve typical social roles (Bigby, Fyffe, & Ozanne, 2007; Crane, 2002; Lemay, 2006). Opportunities to expand their social network beyond friends with disabilities and their immediate families are perhaps more critical than ever during this life stage for the sake of full social inclusion.

Other Supporting Interventions

Supporters (e.g., direct support professionals, friends, allies, parents, social workers) can promote more social inclusion through three broad strategies for meeting others and increasing connections. The following approaches are based on how most people make friends and build their social network.

Connecting through interests and gifts. Many of us become friends with others with whom we share interests. When supporting relationships for a person with disabilities, one should start with a list of the person's interests. What are they most excited about? What do they most respond to?

Second, look for the person's gifts. The first type of gift has to do with things the person does well—their abilities and talents. These can be wide ranging, such as gifts for bowling, quilting, screaming, unique language, getting everyone fired up. Each of these can be a contribution in the right environment. Look for others who would appreciate these gifts, and for places where the gift is valued or would not be a problem. For example, a man who had a gift for screaming but who also loved games with balls (who also had quadriplegia and was categorized as severely impaired) found a valued social role as the number one fan of a senior men's volleyball team. One of the volleyball players said, "He cheers for everybody, not just for who's winning. If you're having a lousy day on the court, he still makes you feel good."

The second type of gift is the benefit one receives from knowing a person. This is reciprocity, which can be so elusive for people with IDD. What do others get from knowing them? As previously noted, paid staff and professionals usually do not continue working in human services because of the compensation they receive, but rather because the people they support bring them intangible gifts, such as joy, humor, love, acceptance, a sense of accomplishment. Additionally, family members are often deeply aware of the gifts the member with disabilities brings to the whole family. One key ingredient to success in supporting relationships is the belief that other community members will also benefit from the same gifts that the staff or family receive in knowing this person.

One-to-one relationships. Many friendships are one-to-one relationships. For individuals who receive services, certain programs are designed around formally establishing one-to-one relationships. In peer or buddy programs at school, for example, a nondisabled student is paired with a special education student as a mentor or buddy. Other one-to-one relationships are established in formal recreation or leisure programs, volunteer opportunities, or programs such as citizen advocacy.

There are also less formal avenues for one-to-one connections. Where might you find a person who would appreciate the opportunity to get to know this individual, or get to know them better? Places to look are community settings where the individual already goes, where people are friendly, and where someone could be invited to get to know them better. What might they be asked to do in order to get to know the person with IDD better? By way of example, a barber who was quite warm toward an individual with a severe disability accepted the invitation to have lunch with the man to get to know him better.

Another example: A young man with autism was interested in drawing in 3-D and to scale, was fascinated with complex underground transportation systems, and had a talent for navigating and memorizing maps. His family found a recent graduate of an architecture program and the two young men met weekly to work on hands-on programs that involved measuring buildings in the real world and entering these measurements into 3-D design software to create miniature models.

Another approach is to think of individuals from the person's past who could be invited back into their life. In some real-life examples, former staff visit a person with IDD regularly for walks and to have coffee. Former school friends reconnect for regular visits. Where might other potential friends be found? Who does someone in the support circle know who might like this person, and also like the opportunity to get to know them better? Such individuals may be found through faith communities, among acquaintances of staff, and by brainstorming with others.

Places of membership and belonging. Another approach is to consider places of membership, where a person with IDD can be part of a group or find a place of belonging. One multifaceted resource to explore is community groups and clubs. Lists of these organizations can be found at a Chamber of Commerce or on a city's website. Newspapers and websites such as meetup.com also list get-togethers. Websites of national organizations such as Jaycees, Rotary, Lions, and other service organizations typically list local contacts. Formal groups almost always include "recruiting new members" as an agenda item at their meetings. Groups form around many different categories beyond just hobbies—men's or women's groups; political, charitable, and cultural interests; and the list goes on.

Other places of membership and belonging are community venues where there are "regulars" and where a person doesn't just visit, but also finds a meaningful role. Some of those are also places where an individual with behavior that seems "challenging" can belong—places where the behavior would not be a problem, or where others engage in the same behavior at least some of the time. For example, a young man with autism who often banged his head practiced regularly with the varsity football team at his high school. A young man whose speech was echolalic and difficult to understand got a job at a family-run laundromat where most of the family did not understand English.

Communitywide Interventions

Approaches on a broader level increase community capacity and build a greater sense of welcome. Communities that take this approach go beyond simply accepting the physical presence of people with disabilities, but seek to be truly welcoming.

The following projects and initiatives exemplify such an approach:

- Involving All Neighbors, in Seattle's Department of Neighborhoods (Carlson, 2000)
- The Community Life Project (O'Connell, 1990) in a Chicago neighborhood
- Community Member Forums (Amado & Victorian-Blaney, 2000) held in different communities in several states
- The Transition to Retirement project (Stancliffe, Wilson, Gambin, Bigby, & Balandin, 2013) in Australia, which assisted individuals to move from sheltered workshops to joining community groups around interests such as cooking, cat rescue, and community gardening

The approaches taken in these examples highlight the power of seeing people with disabilities the same as anyone else. Rather than being cared for, or treated as "special," these programs focused on the interests and contributions of people with IDD, treating them the same as anyone else in the group. This simple yet powerful approach can result in dramatic changes and experiences for everyone involved.

Communities can recognize the importance of developing inclusive programs, as opposed to "special" programs, in their schools, churches, and recreational activities. Community groups and organizations can also make a commitment to include someone with IDD in their group, and to make sure they are fully included. Neighbors can make a commitment to get to know their neighbors with IDD, to support families who have a child with IDD, or to become acquainted with the group home residents on their block or the individuals in their apartment building. They can commit to getting to know them as individuals, finding out their interests, and sharing interests and activities.

Personal Illustration: Todd Lindquist

Todd Lindquist knows cars. As a member of the St. Paul Park–Newport Lions Club for the past 5 years, Todd volunteers every Thursday evening in the summer months for Car Show Thursdays, preparing food and greeting visitors. "I like the classics. I like the old, vintage cars. And I like to serve the people the food and I get to talk to 'em about their cars and I get to hang out and meet people in the community."

Todd can identify the year and make of most cars, and has an uncanny memory for the names of all of their owners. "We did have a contest one day, and he was able to name 60 guys," recalled fellow Lions Club member Andy Fuenffinger. "He had their first names, a couple of their middle names, and most of their last names, so pretty impressive."

Todd was invited to join the Lions Club by Chuck Elliott, a job coach with Lifeworks Services, a nonprofit organization supporting individuals with disabilities and their families in Minnesota. Professionally, Chuck supports Todd with his job at Renewal by Andersen, the replacement-window division of Andersen Windows, where Todd has worked for the past 12 years. Chuck could see that Todd was well liked and valued in his job but did not have deep personal connections outside of work. "He was always busy, but really just followed a routine and went home after work."

"I had a coworker ask me if there was anything I could do for Todd outside of work," said Chuck. "So, I invited him to some events here at the Lions Club." Now, Todd is the guy who remembers everybody's name. "He knows everybody. He's very friendly and likes people. And everybody likes Todd. If they meet him once, they never forget him."

Beyond his passion for vintage cars, Todd finds meaning and satisfaction in being a valued member of a social organization that helps people in his community. "We have a spaghetti dinner that helps raise money for the food shelf," said Todd. "Holidays we do food baskets for the people in need. And we do that for Thanksgiving, Christmas, and Easter." Todd attends almost every club event, though transportation can be an issue as he doesn't drive. Usually there is someone to help out. "I mean, he's just one of the guys in the club," said Andy Fuenffinger, "so whatever he needs we help him out with."

Joining a mission-driven social club has expanded Todd's world, introducing him to dozens of new friends and acquaintances and providing him with a fun, meaningful way to give back to his community. As Chuck sees it, it's been a mutually rewarding relationship. "I think he's done more for the Lions Club than the Lions Club has done for him."

Conclusion

Meaningful, reciprocal, and fun relationships are a key ingredient for a happy life. People with IDD must have sufficient opportunities to develop valued social roles, sustain friendships, and actively give to and receive from their communities. Families, friends, and support staff can nurture social inclusion by assisting people with IDD in finding meaningful involvement in community activities that fit their interests and abilities, being involved in social events, and establishing meaningful relationships. Family members and professionals can cultivate mutually beneficial opportunities for people with disabilities to be seen as valued fellow citizens and friends so that, as a society, we can collectively gain a greater understanding of and appreciation for the many and varied gifts that people with IDD bring whenever they are fully included and welcomed.

In addition, the social experiences of community members can be enhanced by ensuring opportunities for them to meet, befriend, have fun with, and come to love individuals with IDD. Strategies to do this have proven successful, but these have primarily been employed in demonstration projects. Now, such methods need to be embedded in the structures of both human services and the larger society. When the walls between the disability world and the community world are broken down, we will find the critical sense of belonging enhanced for all citizens.

Discussion Questions

- What can providers and professionals do personally and organizationally to support greater social inclusion for people with IDD?
- What practical steps can families, providers, and professionals take to address and overcome barriers, and to promote more authentic relationships and friendships?
- How can families be supported to have expectations of social inclusion in community life, and to support such inclusion for their family member with IDD?
- What system and policy issues and barriers have you encountered that need to be addressed and changed in order to move toward greater social inclusion in community life?
- If you are a staff person or professional who has a personal friendship with someone with IDD, what do both you and your friend gain from the relationship?

Resources

- *Friends: Connecting people with disabilities and community members.* This is a guidebook that addresses skills, tools, and strategies to support relationships. www.umn.edu/friends
- *The Importance of Belonging.* Tools, resources, and information about the power and value of relationships and belonging. http://www.dimagine.com/Belonging.pdf
- Quality Mall includes many tools, resources, and ideas about different topics important to self-advocates and families. www.qualitymall.com
- *Pathfinders: People with developmental disabilities and their allies building communities that work better for everybody.* This book is authored by John O'Brien and Beth Mount and is available through Inclusion Press.

References

Amado, A. N., & Victorian-Blaney, J. (2000, May). Requesting inclusion from the community: The necessity of asking. *TASH Newsletter*, 15–17.

Americans With Disabilities Act of 1990, 42 U.S.C.A. § 12101 et seq. (1993).

Bigby, C., Fyffe, C., & Ozanne, E. (Ed.) (2007). *Planning and support for people with intellectual disabilities: Issues for case managers and other professionals*. Philadelphia, PA: Jessica Kingsly.

Bigby, C., & Knox, M. (2009). "I want to see the queen:" Experiences of service use by ageing people with an intellectual disability. *Australian Social Work, 62*(2) 216–231. http://dx.doi.org/10.1080/03124070902748910

Bogenschutz, M., & Amado, A. N. (2016). Social inclusion for people with IDD: What we know and where we go from here. In *Critical issues in intellectual and developmental disabilities: Contemporary research, practice and policy* (pp. 19–36). Washington, DC: American Association on Intellectual and Developmental Disabilities.

Canny C., & Byrne A. (2006). Evaluating circle time as a support to social skills development—reflections on a journey in school-based research. *British Journal of Special Education, 33*(1), 19–24. http://dx.doi.org/10.1111/j.1467-8578.2006.00407.x

Carlson, C. (2000). *Involving all neighbors: Building inclusive communities in Seattle*. Seattle, WA: Department of Neighborhoods.

Carter, E. W. (2007). *Including people with disabilities in faith communities: A guide for service providers, families, and congregation.* Baltimore, MD: Brookes.

Crane, L. (2002). *Mental retardation: A community integration approach*. Belmont, CA: Wadsworth/Thomson Learning.

Emerson, E., & McVilly, K. (2004). Friendship activities of adults with intellectual disabilities in supported accommodation in Northern England. *Journal of Applied Research in Intellectual Disabilities, 17*(3),191–197. http://dx.doi.org/10.1111/j.1468-3148.2004.00198.x

Friedman, C., & Rizzolo, M. C. (2018). Friendship, quality of life, and people with intellectual and developmental disabilities. *Journal of Developmental and Physical Disabilities, 30*(1), 39–54. http://dx.doi.org/10.1007/s10882-017-9576-7

Gilmore, L., & Cuskelly, M. (2014). Vulnerability to loneliness in people with intellectual disability: An explanatory model. *Journal of Policy and Practice in Intellectual Disabilities, 11*(3), 192–199. http://dx.doi.org/10.1111/jppi.12089

Green, M., Moore, H. & O'Brien, J. (2006). When people care enough to act: Asset based community development. Toronto: Inclusion Press.

Hill, R. A., & Dunbar, R. I. M. (2003). Social network size in humans. *Human Nature, 14*(1), 53–72. http://dx.doi.org/10.1007/s12110-003-1016-y

Kroenke, C. H., Kubzansky, L. D., Schernhammer, E. S., Holmes, M. D., & Kawachi, I. (2006). Social networks, social support and survival after breast cancer diagnosis. *Journal of Clinical Oncology*. Retrieved from http://jco.ascopubs.org/content/24/7/1105.full

Lemay, R. (2006). Social role valorization insights into the social integration conundrum. *Mental Retardation, 44*(1), 1–12. http://dx.doi.org/10.1352/0047-6765(2006)44%5B1:SRVIIT%5D2.0.CO;2

McVilly, K. R., Stancliffe, R. J., Parmenter, T. R., & Burton-Smith, R. M. (2006). "I get by with a little help from my friends:" Adults with intellectual disability discuss loneliness. *Journal of Applied Research in Intellectual Disabilities, 19,* 191–203, http://dx.doi.org/10.1111/j.1468-3148.2005.00261.x.

Newman, L., Wagner, M., Cameto, L., & Knokey, A.M. (2011). *The post-high school outcomes of young adults with disabilities up to 6 years after high school: Key findings from the National Longitudinal Transition Study-2 (NLTS2).* Washington, DC: U.S. Department of Education, National Center for Special Education Research.

O'Brien, J., & O'Brien, C. L. (1987). *Framework for accomplishment.* Atlanta, GA: Responsive Systems Associates.

Green, M., Moore, H. & O'Brien, J. (2006). When People Care Enough to Act: Asset Based Community Development. Toronto: Inclusion Press.

O'Connell, M. (1990). *Community building in Logan Square.* Evanston, IL: Northwestern University Center for Urban Affairs and Policy Research.

Olmstead v. L.C., No. 98–536, 527 581 (1999).

Perry, P. (2014). Loneliness is killing us—We must start treating this disease. *The Guardian.* Retrieved from http://www.theguardian.com/commentisfree/2014/feb/17/loneliness-report-bigger-killer-obesity-lonely-people

Pitonyak, D. (2014, January). *The importance of belonging* [Version 01]. Retrieved from www.dimagine.com

Sobsey, D. (2002, September). The positive effects of children with disabilities on their families. Paper presented at the Early Years Cconference conducted at the meeting of Alberta Early Years, Edmonton, Alberta, Canada.

Solish, A., Perry, A., & Minnes, P. (2010). Participation of children with and without disabilities in social, recreational and leisure activities. *Journal of Applied Research in Intellectual Disabilities, 23*(3), 226–236. http://dx.doi.org/10.1111/j.1468-3148.2009.00525.x

Stancliffe, R. J., Lakin, K. C., Doljanac, R., Byun, S., Taub, S., & Chiri, G. (2007). Loneliness and living arrangements. *Intellectual and Developmental Disabilities, 45*(6), 380–390. http://dx.doi.org/10.1352/1934-9556(2007)45%5B380:LALA%5D2.0.CO;2

Stancliffe, R. J., Wilson, N. J., Gambin, N., Bigby, C., & Balandin, S. (2013). *Transition to retirement: A guide to inclusive practice.* Sydney, Australia: Sydney University Press.

State of Kentucky. (2014). *Community belonging training initiative.* Louisville, KY: Kentucky Department of Developmental and Intellectual Disabilities.

Tay, L., & Diener, E. (2011). Needs and subjective well-being around the world. *Journal of Personality and Social Psychology, 101*(2), 354–365. http://dx.doi.org/10.1037/a0023779

Verdonschot, M. M. L., deWitte, L. P., Reichraft, E., Buntinx, W. H. E., & Curfs, L. M. G. (2009). Community participation of people with an intellectual disability: A review of empirical findings. *Journal of Intellectual Disability Research, 53,* 303–318. http://dx.doi.org/10.1111/j.1365-2788.2008.01144.x

Wolfensberger, W. (2000). A brief overview of social role valorization. *Mental Retardation, 38*(2), 105–123. http://dx.doi.org/10.1352/0047-6765(2000)038%3C0105:ABOOSR%3E2.0.CO;2

Workforce Innovation and Opportunity Act of 2014, Pub. L. No.113-128 (29 U.S.C. Sec. 3101, et. seq.), (2016).

CHAPTER SIX

Self-Determination and Self-Advocacy: It's My Life

Brian H. Abery, Mark R. Olson,
Clifford L. Poetz, and John G. Smith

Advance Organizers

- Self-advocacy and self-determination are not the same thing.
- It is important to teach people with intellectual and developmental disabilities (IDD) the skills they need to advocate for themselves.
- It is important for people with IDD opportunities for self-determination.
- Self-advocacy and self-determination influence quality of life for people with IDD.

The constructs of self-advocacy and self-determination are often used interchangeably. However, *self-advocacy* refers to the ability of an individual to speak on their own behalf—in other words, advocating for themselves—whereas *self-determination* is about an individual taking and having control over their life decisions. In the past, some authors (e.g., Zubal, Shoultz, Walker, & Kennedy, 1997) have considered self-determination a component of self-advocacy. Others (e.g., Abery & Stancliffe, 2003; Algozzine, Browder, Karvonen, Test, & Wood, 2001; Wehmeyer & Abery, 2013) view self-advocacy skills as a necessary element of self-determination. Both self-advocacy and self-determination have provided critical contributions to improvements in the quality of life experienced by people with IDD living in the community.

In this chapter, we explore components and methods of supporting people in determining what they want out of life. We share information on self-determination, and on how people with IDD can become the drivers of their own lives. We also discuss the evolution of self-advocacy and the self-advocacy movement.

People with IDD have not always been supported in making choices, having control, and expressing themselves. Rather, other family members or professionals often make choices and decisions for a person, without including them. As a result, many people with IDD have insisted and demanded that their decisions, choices, and input be respected. Leading a self-determined life is a basic human right for all people.

Since self-determination was first conceptualized, a number of definitions have been offered. In his Functional Model of Self-Determination, Wehmeyer (1992) initially posited that it referred to "the attitudes and abilities required to act as the primary causal agent in one's life and make choices regarding one's actions free from undue external influence or interference" (p. 305). As Wehmeyer and his research group studied the construct, their definition changed to reflect their learnings and to place greater stress on the idea that self-determination involves "the act of making conscious choices that enable one to act as the primary causal agent in one's life and maintain or improve one's quality of life free from undue external influence or interference" (Wehmeyer, Kelchner, and Richards, 1996, p. 632). In their most recent writings, Wehmeyer and his colleagues (Shogren et al., 2015) have extended their Functional Model to incorporate Causal Agency Theory (FM-CAT), and now define self-determination as a "dispositional characteristic manifested as acting as the causal agent in one's life. Self-determined people (i.e., causal agents) act in service to freely chosen goals. Self-determined actions function to enable a person to be the causal agent in his or her life" (p. 258).

Resulting approaches to enhancing outcomes in this area have therefore tended to focus primarily on facilitating learning of the skills, knowledge, and attitudes/beliefs that have been conceptualized to support self-determination. This includes fostering the development of choice and decision making, problem solving, goal setting and attainment, communication, self-advocacy, and self-regulation skills; enhancing self-knowledge, as well as an understanding of the service system and one's rights; and supporting the development of an internal locus of control and sense of self-efficacy (Thoma & Getzel, 2005; Wehmeyer & Abery, 2013; Wehmeyer & Schwartz, 1998).

An alternative approach, focusing on a person-in-environment interactions, has been developed by Abery and colleagues: Tripartite Ecological Theory of Self-Determination (Abery, 1994; Abery & Stancliffe, 1996; 2003). This framework. while acknowledging the importance of individual characteristics, views self-determination as exercised within the context of relationships with other individuals, groups of individuals, or systems and, therefore, stresses the importance of the environment. The resulting operational definition of the construct conceptualizes self-determination as "individuals exercising the degree of personal control they desire within the context of their relationships with other individuals, groups, systems, or cultures, over those areas of life that are important to them" (Abery, Tichá, Smith, & Grad, 2017). The model views self-determination as driven by the intrinsic motivation of all people to be the primary determiner of their thoughts, feelings, and behavior. Self-determination, accordingly, is the product of both the person and the environment—of the person using the skills, knowledge, and beliefs at his or her disposal to act on the environment with the goal of obtaining valued and desired outcomes, including exercising personal control.

This approach to understanding self-determination embraces the idea that a key factor in being self-determined is an individual's ability and freedom to exercise the levels of control they desire. At times the individual may voluntarily share control with or cede it to trusted others either because control over an area of concern is not important to them, or because the area of concern is one in which they believe they would profit from others' support. Self-determination, therefore, involves a "goodness-of-fit" between an individual's desire to exercise personal control and the level of control they actually do exercise in areas of life they consider important.

Self-Determination in Action: The Self-Advocacy Movement

Self-advocacy is a civil and human rights movement led by people with IDD. The Arc of the United States defines self-advocacy as people with disabilities "exercising their rights as citizens by communicating for and representing themselves, with supports in doing so, as necessary. This means they have a say in decision making in all areas of their daily lives and in the public policy decisions that affect them" (The Arc of the United States, 2017). The self-advocacy movement among people with IDD began in Sweden in the 1970s, quickly spread to North America, and is now evident throughout the United States and in countries around the world.

A basic tenet for many in the self-advocacy movement is that members want to be seen as a person first, rather than being defined by a disability label, and many self-advocacy groups still use the term "People First" as their tagline. Another important message of the self-advocacy movement is the call to move away from moral and medical models of disability, which see disabilities as problems that need to be fixed or "overcome" in order for people to fit into society. Instead, the self-advocacy movement is grounded in a civil rights model of disability, which demands that it be the institutions of society that change in order to accommodate the gifts and talents of people with disabilities. Finally, the self-advocacy movement is based on the notion that people with disabilities have things in common and can be helpful to each other. This challenges the stereotype that they need to rely on families or other supports to understand systems and take actions to solve the problems that stand in their way.

People with disabilities participate in the self-advocacy movement in many ways. One is by joining self-advocacy groups. Here, people with disabilities discuss barriers and challenges in their lives, learn from each other about their rights and responsibilities, and become informed about helpful resources available within their communities. An important feature of self-advocacy activities is that people with IDD set the agenda and lead the meetings, though people without such disabilities may act as allies in the process.

Another way people with disabilities work as self-advocates is by serving on advisory bodies or boards of directors that shape how services are delivered to many people with disabilities. They also participate as self-advocates by providing testimony to local, state, and federal policy makers debating laws that will affect people with disabilities. Most people who identify as self-advocates participate in multiple activities as they become more involved and invested in the movement: someone may start by attending local self-advocacy group meetings, then represent the group on a community board, then take on a leadership role in the group, and so forth.

Research has tracked the development of the self-advocacy movement and shown how it has benefited people with disabilities. For example, in a study of self-advocacy group members in the United Kingdom, Clarke, Camilleri, and Goding (2015) found that people with disabilities who were involved in such groups learned about systemic barriers that might be limiting their options. In another study of self-advocacy leaders in the United States, Caldwell (2010) found that being involved in self-advocacy helped people find new role models who had similar disabilities, and learn new ways to resist disability-based oppression by others. Both studies found that the experience of being involved in self-advocacy helped people gain a positive sense of identity around their disability.

Misperceptions and Assumptions

There is a perception among some that self-determination is synonymous with being independent. This view implies that, in order to be self-determined, people should strive to have complete control over all aspects of their lives and that any support from others compromises a person's self-determination. Such a misperception further implies that self-determination is only possible for people with mild impairments.

A related misconception is that building strong communication and self-advocacy skills is the prerequisite to exercising self-determination. Such a view ignores the role of the environment in ensuring that people have opportunities to exercise control over as many choices and decisions as possible given the communication skills they have. It also ignores the role of support persons in becoming attentive to all the ways—verbal and nonverbal—in which a person with disabilities may indicate his or her needs and preferences. Others believe that having control over service dollars is synonymous with feelings of self-determination.

Another misperception is that supporting self-determination of persons with IDD is mostly common sense, and that there are no "best" ways to support its development. In actuality, over the past 3 decades, a great deal of research has identified specific best practices in measuring and supporting the exercise of self-determination among people with all levels of IDD. The most salient of these practices will be reviewed later in this chapter.

There is a misunderstanding that self-advocacy events are mostly social gatherings. More than 400 active self-advocacy groups and organizations for persons with IDD now operate around the United States (Self-Advocacy Online, 2018). Although these groups sometimes hold social events to recruit new members, their primary purpose is to teach people with IDD about their rights, and to plan and carry out advocacy events to change communities and service systems to better accommodate the needs and desires of people with IDD.

A perception also exists among some that the self-advocacy movement is limited to small, community-based groups of people with IDD dependent on support from larger organizations. However, many states have developed independent, nonprofit organizations governed by people with IDD with the express purpose of advocating on their own behalf.

In the past, most efforts at teaching people with IDD about self-determination focused on youth and young adults as they transitioned from school to community living. Current practice in supporting self-determination has moved us beyond such limiting views. We now understand that self-determination is an important issue to consider at every life stage. Research over the past decades has shown that all people, regardless of disability status or support needs, are capable of and interested in exercising control over some aspects of their lives. It is easy to think that people with IDD have more control in their lives than they actually do. Support providers may not realize that the help they provide may actually compromise a person's sense of having the kind of control they want in their day-to-day life. Supporting self-determination is challenging work that requires careful monitoring. Current best practice asks families and support staff to offer people with disabilities many opportunities to make choices and decisions about things they care about and to learn that their preferences matter.

Outcomes Associated With Self-Determination and Self-Advocacy

Although some individuals view self-determination and self-advocacy as an outcome, we prefer to think of both as processes that serve as means to an end. This plays out by considering to what extent people with IDD who are self-determined and good self-advocates experience positive life outcomes.

Over the past 30 years, a substantial number of studies have documented the impact of self-determination. Research findings indicate that self-determination predicts the following:

- greater employment and community access and participation (Shogren & Shaw, 2016; Shogren, Wehmeyer, Palmer, Rifenbark, & Little, 2015; Wehmeyer & Palmer, 2003)
- positive transition outcomes, including higher levels of independent living and the development of positive social relationships (Martorell, Gutierrez-Rechacha, Pereda, & Ayuso-Mateos, 2008; Shogren & Shaw, 2016; Wehmeyer & Palmer, 2003; Wehmeyer & Schwartz, 1997)
- greater access to inclusive residential opportunities (Shogren & Shaw, 2016)
- increased community participation (McGuire & McDonnell, 2008)
- success in postsecondary education (Anctil, Ishikawa, & Tao Scott, 2008; Getzel & Thoma, 2008)
- increased quality of life and life satisfaction (Lachapelle et al., 2005; Nota, Ferrari, Soresi, & Wehmeyer, 2007; Shogren, Lopez, Wehmeyer, Little, & Pressgrove, 2006)
- more positive recreation and leisure outcomes (McGuire & McDonnell, 2008)
- greater stability in outcomes overall (Shogren et al., 2015)

Within the school context, teaching self-determination skills has been associated with increased academic outcomes (Fowler, Konrad, Walker, Test, & Wood, 2007; Konrad, Fowler, Walker, Test, & Wood, 2007; Lee, Wehmeyer, Soukup, & Palmer, 2010; Shogren, Palmer, Wehmeyer, Williams-Diehm, & Little, 2012), greater success in achieving academic and transition goals (Agran, Blanchard, & Wehmeyer, 2000; McGlashing-Johnson, Agran, Sitlington, Cavin, & Wehmeyer, 2003), and greater access to the general education curriculum within inclusive educational environments (Lee, Wehmeyer, Palmer, Soukup, & Little, 2008). Research has also demonstrated that people of all ages with a wide range of disabilities can be taught the skills associated with self-determination (Algozzine et al., 2001; Cobb, Lehmann, Newman-Gonchar, & Alwell, 2009), and that supporting acquisition of these capacities creates opportunities for the exercise of personal control (Algozzine et al., 2001; Wehmeyer et al., 2012).

In spite of the critical role that self-advocacy and the self-advocacy movement have played in improving the lives of persons with IDD of all ages, relatively few outcome studies exist that allow one to connect self-advocacy to personal outcomes. The majority of research in this area focuses primarily on school-age persons with IDD, as opposed to adults. A review of the literature does show that the development of self-advocacy skills is crucial to the successful transition of students with disabilities into adult life (Aune, 1991; Izzo & Lamb, 2002; Test et al., 2009; Wehmeyer, 1992). Yet, research has indicated that the teaching of self-advocacy skills and the provision of opportunities to self-advocate are infrequently included in the education program of students with disabilities (Arnold & Czamanske, 1991; Izzo & Lamb, 2002).

Over the past several decades, the self-advocacy movement, which developed out of the grassroots efforts of persons with IDD and their allies, has played a critical role in creating change at all levels of the ecosystem in the disability field. Through their self-advocacy, persons taking part in this civil rights movement have voiced the need for a shift in how people with IDD are viewed, both among the general public and in disability-related fields. They have successfully advocated at local, state, and national levels for changes in disability law and have facilitated a power shift from professionals and families to persons with disabilities. They have also created the necessary learning and infrastructure for person-centered planning and services, self-directed supports, and a variety of other initiatives that support the exercise of self-determination and have dramatically improved the quality of life of people with IDD of all ages. Federal policy that drives health, education, and home and community-based services (HCBS) now recognizes the basic right of persons with IDD to live self-determined lives, and views both opportunities for and the exercise of self-determination as key elements in judging the quality of services and supports an individual receives (Lachapelle et al., 2005; Schalock, Bonham, & Verdugo, 2008).

In the past 40 years, the number of statewide self-advocacy organizations has increased dramatically, and, as mentioned earlier, in 1994, Self-Advocates Becoming Empowered (SABE) came on board as a national organization directed by people with intellectual disability. As the self-advocacy movement grows, so does its need for resources. On both national and state levels, self-advocacy groups need support to facilitate changes in a service system that still all too often does not support the self-determination of people with IDD.

At the current time, self-advocacy activities, whether they focus on training or advocacy itself, tend to take place separately for people with different forms of disability. If the movement is going to grow in both size and political influence, it needs to focus on drawing together groups of people with a variety of support needs, including persons with different disabilities and of different ages and cultural group membership. This will require a new generation of self-advocate leaders who are skilled facilitators and adept at explaining the system in ways everyone can understand.

Current Controversies and Challenges

Given that high levels of self-determination and effective self-advocacy have been shown to be related to positive outcomes for people with IDD, one might assume that practically all people with disabilities are supported in being self-determined and strong self-advocates. Research, however, indicates that this is not the case. A substantial number of barriers stand in the way of people with IDD acquiring and refining the capacities that support self-determination and self-advocacy, having opportunities to exercise these capacities on an ongoing basis, and having the degree of personal control they desire over the aspects of life most important to them.

Individual Barriers

Person-in-environment (i.e., ecological) approaches to self-determination and self-advocacy actually have the potential to limit self-determination and self-advocacy. Although we believe that the simple ability to effectively communicate "yes" and "no" makes it possible for people to exercise self-determination over their lives, adequate supports are not always provided on a consistent basis. Certain personal capacities, such as effective communication skills, an understanding of rights, and a desire to express wants and needs, although not necessary for the exercise of self-determination and self-advocacy, serve to facilitate these processes when external supports are not available or when barriers are encountered.

Common barriers to self-determination at the individual level include functional limitations with respect to all of the skills associated with these processes: choice and decision making, problem solving, goal setting, communication, self-advocacy, and self-regulation skills. In addition, lack of self-knowledge, along with incomplete understanding of the service system and one's rights as a citizen and a person with a disability, have the potential to limit individuals' ability to speak out for themselves and exercise desired levels of personal control over important life outcomes. Attitudinal and belief systems can also limit outcomes in this area. An external locus of control, a low sense of self-efficacy, and inaccurate attributions for success and failure can all serve to place individuals at a disadvantage as they attempt to assume personal control over their lives (Abery & Stancliffe, 2003).

Environmental and System Barriers

The ecological framework acknowledges the dynamic interplay of the person and their environment. Individuals not only react to their environments but also play a key role in creating them. Put simply, although the environment has an impact on us, our personal capacities, our behaviors, and the social capital we have available all contribute to the risks and opportunities we experience at each level of the ecosystem.

Numerous factors have the potential to limit self-determination and self-advocacy. A family's belief that they need to protect their family member all too often leads to persons with IDD being severely limited with respect to the risks and challenges they are able to take in life. Parents and providers who focus on protection and removing, rather than managing, risk make it difficult for persons with IDD to have opportunities to exercise self-determination, learn from their mistakes, and grow in the process. Low expectations of children, youth, and adults with IDD can also serve as potential barriers to the outcomes of interest at home and school, as well as in the community (Wehmeyer & Abery, 2013). Parents, employers, direct support professionals, and teachers often assume that if a person with IDD is not currently engaging in an activity (e.g., making a choice or decision), they do not have the ability to engage in that activity at a later time or within a different context.

For adults with IDD, the formal supports they receive also can create multiple barriers to self-determination and self-advocacy. Instability of the workforce and frequent turnover of staff lead to persons with disabilities being supported by direct support professionals (DSPs) who are all too often unaware of their preferences and do not have the experience to support them to achieve important personal goals. Inexperienced, undertrained staff who possess minimal knowledge of IDD and/or self-determination may limit social interaction with the persons with IDD whom they support. In addition, provider organizations' need to minimize liability often leads to overprotection and the belief that one must eliminate, rather than manage, risk and challenge in a person's life. As a result, persons with IDD are often not allowed to make mistakes or to experience, within reason, the consequences of less-than-optimal decisions, making it impossible for them to use mistakes as learning experiences. Unfortunately, many of the personal capacities supportive of self-determination are difficult to develop if one is not given sufficient opportunities to exercise desired levels of personal control.

Supporting the development of self-determination and self-advocacy capacities, as well as providing opportunities and support for these processes, requires positive linkages and coordination across systems. System-level connections are critical if capacities developed in one context are to be reinforced and generalized to other microsystems. The provider who creates a residential environment in which the exercise of self-determination and self-advocacy are taught and supported, for example, needs to work with families and employers to ensure that these critical processes are supported across environments. Schools that provide opportunities for self-determination and self-advocacy need to work with families and the community to ensure generalization to those environments too.

A second well-known example is the lack of communication and coordination that often exists between formal supports (residential, school, employment) provided to persons with IDD, which can result in supports found to be successful in one setting not always being fostered in another. In addition, support providers may not agree on what type and level of independence and self-determination a person is capable of. Lack of support for leadership development for people with IDD in the self-advocacy movement is also an issue in the formal support system.

Many barriers to self-determination and self-advocacy for persons with IDD lie in the policies and procedures of agencies that provide formal day-to-day supports, such as schools, community-living settings, or employment organizations. Many agencies providing residential supports still provide DSPs with little to no training related to supporting self-determination. Provider organizations supporting self-advocacy groups often have policies that dictate when the group can meet and for what the group can advocate. The manner in which service planning is undertaken and services are provided can also be a barrier to the exercise of self-determination and self-advocacy. Person-centered approaches to adult service planning and provision, as well as individualized educational plans, continue to be inadequate in most provider organizations and schools. In some cases, the planning process might be considered person-centered, but service delivery is not. In other contexts, the "I" in IEP or ISP (individual support plan or individual services plan) seems to stand more for "institutionalized" than for "individualized."

A final barrier to self-determination and self-advocacy is the relatively few opportunities persons with disabilities receive for direct involvement in setting the agenda for service provision, research, and the implementation and evaluation of supports (Caldwell, 2010; McDonald & Raymaker, 2013). Many provider organizations that support persons with IDD have one or two individuals with disabilities on their advisory committees or boards, but it is rare for those persons to have real decision-making authority or to set the agenda for service provision and/or research efforts.

In the United States and many other countries, societal attitudes with respect to persons with disabilities remain "ableist" in their orientation. According to the Oxford English Dictionary (2018), *ableism* refers to "discrimination in favor of able-bodied people," but, in reality, its impact extends beyond discriminatory acts to the way our culture views people with disabilities. In spite of significant improvements in the lives of people with disabilities over the past 30 years (see Chapter 1), practices and dominant attitudes in society continue to devalue, marginalize, and limit the potential of persons with IDD. Today many of these forms of discrimination are largely normalized and integrated into our culture's very understanding (or, more accurately, disregard) of disabled people's experiences. An ableist attitudinal value system in society limits the opportunities children, youth, and adults with IDD have to experience self-determination in direct and indirect ways, as it reinforces the perspective of many parents, teachers, and other professionals that IDD makes people incapable of effectively exercising control over their own lives.

Practical Suggestions and Interventions

Over the past several decades, a number of formal programs have been developed and field-tested to support the exercise of self-determination. Although a relatively large percentage of these interventions has focused on school-age children and youth, programs aimed at the adult population are available. Based on the existing research literature, a wide variety of informal, nonprogrammatic recommendations can also be made that have the potential to support the development of skills, knowledge, attitudes, and beliefs that foster self-determination in family, school, and community contexts. Regardless of whether supports are formal or informal, current best practices can be summarized with the statement: "Start early and provide as many opportunities as possible."

Individuals and Families

At the individual and microsystem level of practices that families can employ throughout a person's development, research suggests supporting the acquisition and refinement of personal capacities that empower self-determination. Such supports may include fostering in a person with IDD the development of choice and decision making, problem solving, goal setting and attainment, communication, self-advocacy, and self-regulation skills; enhancing the individual's self-knowledge, as well as their understanding of the service system and their rights; and empowering the development of their internal locus of control and sense of self-efficacy (Thoma & Getzel, 2005; Wehmeyer & Abery, 2013; Wehmeyer, Agran, & Hughes, 1998).

Given that self-determination emerges across the lifespan, supporting the development of personal capacities that facilitate self-determination needs to start early in life. During infancy, children begin to engage in intentional behavior and, in a rudimentary way, initiate the process of self-determination. Within the first year of life, infants begin exploring their world. As they mature, the context of this exploration becomes both wider and more varied. Families can facilitate the development of capacities associated with self-determination by supporting their child's interest in exploring their environment and the objects within it (Odom & Wolery, 2003), first by making the environment a safe place in which to explore and, second, by populating it with a wide variety of "high-interest" objects. This experience will naturally lead to children developing preferences for specific activities, games, and toys over others, beginning the process through which they will come to understand their likes and dislikes, what they prefer, and what is of less interest (Shogren & Turnbull, 2006).

A logical next step in the development of self-determination capacities involves simple choice making with a limited number of alternatives (e.g., "Which of these three shirts do you want to wear?"). As early as age two, children display a desire to control their environment, including the food, toys, activities, and other objects to which they have access. Providing children with simple choice-making opportunities consistent with their personal capacities—opportunities that both challenge them to assess the consequences of their choices and support them in the process—will facilitate the development of goal setting, self-regulation, good choice making, and problem-solving capacities. As the verbal skills of a child with IDD develop, families can support their self-determination by providing both the structure and the support they need to express their likes and dislikes. When needed, families can provide accommodations so that those with emerging communication skills can express preferences in alternative ways.

The ability to regulate one's own behavior to achieve personal goals is a critical part of self-determination. Whitman (1990) refers to self-regulation as a capacity that supports persons to take into consideration their situation, their goals, behaviors they can use to address challenges along the way, and both the development and the revision of plans for how to act as they make efforts toward their goals. As children without disabilities develop and mature, personal control gradually shifts from parent to child/young adult. For children and youth with IDD, however, this transfer of decision-making authority often does not occur at all (Stancliffe & Abery, 2003).

An authoritative (not authoritarian) parenting style has been found to predict greater self-reliance, responsibility, independence, and autonomy on the part of children and youth with IDD (Baumrind, 1972; Baumrind & Black, 1967) and to most effectively support the development of their capacities for self-determination (Abery & Zajac, 1996; Booth & Kelly, 2002).

As the child becomes an adolescent and then moves into adulthood, parents must not only provide opportunities for increased decision- and choice-making authority but, within reason, must allow their son/daughter to make decisions in increasingly important areas of life and, on some occasions, to fail—to make bad decisions and have the opportunity to learn from them. Decisions that don't work out the way one intended provide the opportunity to learn more about one's preferences, strengths, and challenges, and about the need to consider long-term as well as short-term consequences. It is also critical at this phase to ensure that an individual's opportunities for choice and decision making are age-appropriate and in areas of life that the young person views as important (Wehmeyer & Abery, 2013), regardless of their support needs.

System- and Program-Level Supports

Developing the capacity to exercise self-determination is a lifelong process. For learners of all ages who live with IDD, various interventions have been designed at the program and system levels, aimed at both increasing opportunities for self-determination and ensuring that people with IDD develop capacities to support this outcome.

The Self-Determined Learning Model of Instruction (SDLMI) is one of the most widely researched models of instruction originally developed to support the self-determination of youth by helping them become self-regulated learners and problem solvers (Wehmeyer, Palmer, Agran, Mithaug, & Martin, 2000). In numerous field tests, students with disabilities including IDD who received SDLMI instruction were found to:

- demonstrate enhanced personal capacities supporting self-determination
- meet or exceed expectations with respect to attainment of their academic and transition goals
- experience greater access to the general education curriculum
- demonstrate significant increases in opportunities for self-determination
- have teachers with higher perceptions of their capacity

Palmer and Wehmeyer (2003) later adapted the SDLMI for K–3 students and found promising results with that age group as well.

During their adult years, people with IDD need access to experiences and opportunities that facilitate the continued development and refinement of the capacities (skills, knowledge, and attitudes/beliefs) that support self-determination. In most cases, this means that personnel within the systems in which the individual functions need to possess the knowledge and resources to support ongoing opportunities for self-determination with respect to the exercise of desired levels of personal control on both a day-to-day and a long-term basis (Wehmeyer & Abery, 2013).

Utilizing person-centered approaches to support planning (O'Brien & Mount, 2005; Pearpoint, O'Brien, & Forest, 1993; Smull, Sanderson, Sweeney, & Skelhorn, 2005) and training direct care staff to deliver services in a person-centered manner are critical aspects of facilitating self-determination. A support planning meeting can be a great opportunity for an individual with IDD to directly exercise self-determination and refine their skills in this arena. The opportunity to determine who attends one's support planning meeting, voice one's preferences and desired life outcomes while others respect and honor them, and ensure that supports strike a balance between what is important *for* oneself and what is important *to* oneself will all serve to strengthen one's sense of personal empowerment.

In recent years, greater opportunities have become available in many states for people with IDD to assume responsibility for directing their own supports. Self-directed support programs make it possible for recipients of services, or their representatives if applicable, to have decision-making authority and take responsibility for managing these supports with the assistance of the system. This alternative to traditionally managed services allows for a person-centered planning process within which recipients determine what services they desire to purchase, how they will be provided, and by whom. States have several options for allowing persons with disabilities to self-direct their supports, including Home and Community Based Services, the Medicaid Community First Choice Self-Directed Personal Assistance Services (CFC-SDPAP), and Home and Community Based Services Waiver Programs 1915(c).

Many people with IDD are currently subject to guardianship and conservatorship. Such substitute decision-making arrangements deprive adults with disabilities of the opportunity to exercise self-determination, make their own decisions, and have these choices legally recognized. Supported decision making (SDM) is a process through which people with disabilities are assisted in making decisions for themselves and effectively communicating these choices to others (Boundy & Fleischner, 2013). It is an approach through which the individual with a disability retains their decision-making authority but is provided support by trusted others (e.g., friends, family members, professionals) who, when needed, are available to explain issues in a manner the individual can understand so he or she can then use that knowledge to make an informed decision (Blanck & Martinis, 2015; Dinerstein, 2012; Quality Trust for Individuals with Disabilities, 2013). SDM is conceptually consistent with Article 12 of the Convention on the Rights of Persons With Disabilities (CRPD), an international human rights treaty adopted by the United Nations in 2006, and supports persons with disabilities to be "causal agents" in their own lives (Wehmeyer, Palmer, Agran, Mithaug, & Martin, 2000). Although SDM is well supported in many countries by persons with disabilities and their families, in the United States, parents and other family members of persons with IDD still tend to support the use of appointed decision makers (Boundy & Fleischner, 2013; Werner & Chabany, 2016). Because SDM is increasingly advocated and used, however, there is a current and critical need for evidence demonstrating the effects of best practices, support structures, and methods, and attesting to the personal outcomes of those who have access to such support (Kohn, Blumenthal, & Campbell, 2012).

Programs designed to support persons with IDD living within the community (e.g., Home and Community Based Service programs) were initially conceptualized to give them greater control over their lives and to provide only the levels of support they needed to live in a self-determined manner. As individuals moved out of institutions and into the community, however, all too often they did not demonstrate increased levels of self-determination (Stancliffe, Abery, & Smith, 2000). This outcome was the result of many factors, including state and county rules and regulations, as well as pushback from parents concerned about the safety of their family member with a disability.

Another great difficulty people with IDD have encountered is when direct support professionals don't understand or have the skills to support self-determination. In an attempt to address this issue, Abery, Tichá, Welshon, Berlin, and Smith (2013) developed an educational program to provide DSPs with the competencies needed to create additional opportunities for self-determination within community-based programs and to provide needed supports to increase the likelihood of this outcome. The 12-module learning curriculum has been field-tested in over 38 community-based residences, with initial results based on behavioral observations and self- and DSP-report suggesting changes in both staff behavior (increased support and opportunities for self-determination) and levels of personal control among residents. A similar educational curriculum for families of adults with IDD living at home, to be delivered via a telehealth format, is currently under development by the same group.

Personal Illustration: Hunter Sargent

Hunter Sargent grew up being told what he couldn't do. "You'll never finish school. You'll never get a job. You'll never get married." Born with fetal alcohol syndrome, he struggled in school and experienced constant bullying. Raised by a loving grandmother and stepmother, he received endless encouragement and developed pride in his American Indian heritage. A member of the White Earth Band of Ojibwe, his Indian name, Eagle Cloud, is tattooed on his arm. In Ojibwe, the name means "messenger."

As a high school student, Hunter found his voice and began speaking up, first about fetal alcohol syndrome and then about the rights of all people with disabilities. Through a local chapter of The Arc, he connected with the self-advocacy group People First. "Self-advocacy means speaking up for your rights and making sure that you are respected and heard," said Hunter, "and treated like a person first, before a person with a disability."

A central belief in the self-advocacy movement is that people with disabilities are the true experts of their own lives. This message resonates with Hunter, who, for more than 20 years, has spoken publicly about his wants and needs and the importance of people with disabilities making their voices heard. "Basically, one thing I've learned in self-advocacy," said Hunter, "is that our lawmakers and politicians are the students and we are the teachers."

Hunter noted that full inclusion requires participation, requiring everyone to make themselves visible in their communities, regardless of their level of disability. "In the disability community, there's a community of voices, but unless we get involved in those communities, we will not know where those voices are, and how impactful they are to our lives."

Even as a community leader, public speaker, and self-advocate, Hunter still continued to hear about what he couldn't do. When he and his girlfriend, Holly, began discussing marriage, they were told by many well-meaning people that it wasn't realistic. "They laid out what couldn't work. We laid out what can work, and what has worked." Hunter and Holly recently celebrated their 8-year anniversary.

Having the right supports in place is one of the reasons for Hunter and Holly's success. "We have somebody come in [to our home] when we need their assistance with something, like shopping, budgeting, and that's great. It's important to have really good staff." As a self-advocate, Hunter is also keenly aware of who should be making the decisions. "We're in the driver seat in our lives, and our staff and the people supporting us are our passengers, you know? They're in the back seat and we're in the front seat."

Hunter urges others to be persistent, confident, and focused when it comes to making your voice heard. His message is forceful and concise: "If you don't do it, nobody else will."

Conclusion

People with IDD can and should be encouraged to make choices about their lives. Formal and informal supports should facilitate self-determination rather than hamper it. Society has come a long way in the past 3 decades in both acknowledging the rights of persons with IDD to live self-determined lives and providing them with the supports to make this vision a reality. Looking to the future, however, it is clear that we still have a long way to go. Counterproductive societal influences still exist and serve as barriers to persons with IDD exercising the degree of control they desire over the aspects of life most important to them. At every level of the system, it is still critical for self-advocates and their supporters to push for the changes at policy, system, and program levels that will enable persons with IDD to enjoy the rights they are due, as spelled out by the Convention on the Rights of Persons With Disabilities (United Nations General Assembly, 2006).

Some of the most critical outcomes associated with self-determination and self-advocacy are improved performance in school, greater success in employment, and a higher quality of life. Barriers to self-determination and self-advocacy exist at the individual level (e.g., functional skill limitations, an external locus of control), the environment level (e.g., lack of DSP workforce skills, stability, and training to support self-determination; federal and state HCBS rules and regulations; guardianship laws), and at the societal/cultural level (e.g., ableism, misperceptions, assumptions).

At the individual and family levels, key strategies include offering opportunities for self-determination early in life at levels commensurate with a child's age and abilities but that still challenge them; managing, rather than trying to eliminate, risks and challenges; allowing for failures and the individual's chance to learn from them; and parenting in an authoritative manner. At the system and provider levels, providing access to person-centered planning, self-directed supports, and self-advocacy training; ensuring a stable, well-trained workforce; and utilizing supportive decision making rather than substitute decision making can all have positive impacts.

Discussion Questions

- How might one work to shift current practices in providing supports to persons with IDD from the medical model toward the civil rights/social justice model? How might this affect the self-determination of individuals with disabilities?
- What are some of the benefits and challenges of supported decision making rather than substitute decision-making arrangements (e.g., guardianship)?
- In what ways do person-centered approaches to service planning and delivery and self-directed supports facilitate the self-determination of persons with IDD?
- What characteristics would you desire in a self-advocacy group if one of its primary focuses was enhancing members' self-determination?
- What are some of the main challenges currently faced by self-advocacy groups? How might these be addressed?

Resources

- Self-Advocacy Online: This website is a one-stop shop for self-advocates and allies and includes resources on self-advocacy, information on local groups, and stories from self-advocates. http://selfadvocacyonline.org
- National Gateway to Self-Determination: National website that provides access for self-advocates, professionals, policy makers, families, and the general public on the current best practices and evidenced-based activities in enhancing self-determination in the lives of people with IDD. http://www.ngsd.org
- National Resource Center for Supported Decision Making: NRC-SDM partners with nationally recognized experts and leaders on SDM, representing the interests of and receiving input from thousands of older adults and people with IDD. They have applied SDM in groundbreaking legal cases; developed evidence-based outcome measures; successfully advocated for changes in law, policy, and practice to increase self-determination; and demonstrated SDM to be a valid, less-restrictive alternative to guardianship. www.supporteddecisionmaking.org
- *What Is Self-Determination and Why Is It Important?* White paper from of the National Gateway to Self-Determination Project, funded by the Administration on Developmental Disabilities. http://buildingalife.ku.edu/sites/default/files/Self-Determination_Wehmeyer.pdf

References

Abery, B. (1994). Self-determination: It's not just for adults. *Impact,6,* 2.

Abery, B., & Stancliffe R. (1996). The ecology of self-determination. In D. J. Sands & M. L. Wehmeyer (Eds.), *Self-Determination across the life span: Independence and choice for people with disabilities* (pp. 111–145). Baltimore, MD: Paul H. Brookes.

Abery, B. H., & Stancliffe, R. J. (2003). A tripartite ecological theory of self-determination. In M. Wehmeyer, B.H. Abery, D.E. Mithaug & R. J. Stancliffe (Eds.), Theory in self-determination:Foundations for educational practice (pp. 43–78). New York: Charles C. Thomas.

Abery, B. H., Tichá, R., Smith, J. G., & Grad, L. (2017). *Assessment of the self-determination of adults with disabilities via behavioral observation: SD-CORES.* Manuscript submitted for publication.

Abery, B. H., Tichá, R., Welshon, K., Berlin, S., & Smith, J .G., (2013). *A self-determination education curriculum for direct support staff.* Minneapolis, MN: University of Minnesota—Institute on Community Integration

Abery, B., & Zajac, R. (1996). Self-determination as a goal of early childhood and elementary education. In D. J. Sands & M. L. Wehmeyer (Eds.), *Self-determination across the lifespan: Independence and choice for people with disabilities* (pp. 169–196). Baltimore, MD: Paul H. Brookes.

Agran, M., Blanchard, C., & Wehmeyer, M. L. (2000). Promoting transition goals and self-determination through student self-directed learning: The self-determined learning model of instruction. *Education and Training in Mental Retardation and Developmental Disabilities, 35*(4), 351–364.

Algozzine, B., Browder, D., Karvonen, M., Test, D. W., & Wood, W. M. (2001). Effects of interventions to promote self-determination for individuals with disabilities. *Review of Educational Research, 71*(2), 219–277. http://dx.doi.org/10.3102/00346543071002219

Anctil, T. M., Ishikawa, M. E., & Tao Scott, A. (2008). Academic identity development through self-determination: Successful college students with learning disabilities. *Career Development for Exceptional Individuals, 31*(3), 164–174. http://dx.doi.org/10.1177/0885728808315331

The Arc of the United States. (2017). *Self-advocacy position statement.* Retrieved from: http://www.thearc.org/who-we-are/position-statements/rights/self-advocacy.

Arnold, E., & Czamanske, J. (1991). *Can I make it? A transition program for college bound learning disabled students and their parents.* Paper presented at the 69th annual convention of Council for Exceptional Children in Atlanta, GA.

Aune, E. (1991). A transitional model for postsecondary-bound students with learning disabilities. *Learning Disabilities Research & Practice, 6*(3), 177–187.

Baumrind, D. (1972). An exploratory study of socialization effects on Black children: Some Black-White comparisons. *Child Development, 43*(1), 261–267. http://dx.doi.org/10.2307/1127891

Baumrind, D., & Black, A. E. (1967). Socialization practices associated with dimensions of competence in preschool boys and girls. *Child Development, 38*(2), 291–327. http://dx.doi.org/10.2307/1127295

Blanck, P., & Martinis, J. G. (2015). The right to make choices: The National Resource Center for Supported Decision-Making. *Inclusion, 3*(1), 24–33. http://dx.doi.org/10.1352/2326-6988-3.1.24

Booth, C. L., & Kelly, J. F. (2002). Child care effects on the development of toddlers with special needs. *Early Childhood Research Quarterly, 17*(2), 171–196. http://dx.doi.org/10.1016/S0885-2006(02)00144-8

Boundy, M., & Fleischner, B. (2013). *Supported decision making instead of guardianship: An international overview* [Fact Sheet]. Northampton, MA: Center for Public Representation.

Caldwell, J. (2010). Leadership development of individuals with developmental disabilities in the self-advocacy movement. *Journal of Intellectual Disability Research, 54*(11), 1004–1014. http://dx.doi.org/10.1111/j.1365-2788.2010.01326.x

Clarke, R., Camilleri, K., & Goding, L. (2015). What's in it for me? The meaning of involvement in a self-advocacy group for six people with intellectual disabilities. *Journal of Intellectual Disabilities, 19*(3), 230–250. http://dx.doi.org/10.1177/1744629515571646

Cobb, B., Lehmann, J., Newman-Gonchar, R., & Alwell, M. (2009). Self-determination for students with disabilities: A narrative metasynthesis. *Career Development for Exceptional Individuals, 32*(2), 108–114. http://dx.doi.org/10.1177/0885728809336654

Dinerstein, R. D. (2012). Implementing legal capacity under Article 12 of the UN Convention on the Rights of Persons With Disabilities: The difficult road from guardianship to supported decision making. *Human Rights Brief, 19*(2), 1–5.

Fowler, C. H., Konrad, M., Walker, A. R., Test, D. W., & Wood, W. M. (2007). Self-determination interventions' effects on the academic performance of students with developmental disabilities. *Education and Training in Developmental Disabilities, 42*(3)270–285.

Getzel, E. E., & Thoma, C. A. (2008). Experiences of college students with disabilities and the importance of self-determination in higher education settings. *Career Development for Exceptional Individuals, 31*(2), 77–84. http://dx.doi.org/10.1177/0885728808317658

Izzo, M., & Lamb, M. (2002). *Self-determination and career development: Skills for successful transitions to postsecondary education and employment* [White paper]. Retrieved from http://www. ncset. hawaii. edu/Publications.

Kohn, N. A., Blumenthal, J. A., & Campbell, A. T. (2012). Supported decision making: A viable alternative to guardianship. *Penn State Law Review, 117*(4), 1111–1158. http://dx.doi.org/10.2139/ssrn.2161115

Konrad, M., Fowler, C. H., Walker, A. R., Test, D. W., & Wood, W. M. (2007). Effects of self-determination interventions on the academic skills of students with learning disabilities. *Learning Disability Quarterly, 30*(2), 89–113. http://dx.doi.org/10.2307/30035545

Lachapelle, Y., Wehmeyer, M. L., Haelewyck, M. C., Courbois, Y., Keith, K. D., Schalock, R. & Walsh, P. N. (2005). The relationship between quality of life and self-determination: an international study. *Journal of Intellectual Disability Research, 49*(10), 740–744. http://dx.doi.org/10.1111/j.1365-2788.2005.00743.x

Lee, S. H., Wehmeyer, M. L., Palmer, S. B., Soukup, J. H., & Little, T. D. (2008). Self-determination and access to the general education curriculum. *The Journal of Special Education, 42*(2), 91–107. http://dx.doi.org/10.1177/0022466907312354

Lee, S. H., Wehmeyer, M. L., Soukup, J. H., & Palmer, S. B. (2010). Impact of curriculum modifications on access to the general education curriculum for students with disabilities. *Exceptional Children, 76*(2), 213–233. http://dx.doi.org/10.1177/001440291007600205

Martorell, A., Gutierrez-Rechacha, P., Pereda, A., & Ayuso-Mateos, J. L. (2008). Identification of personal factors that determine work outcome for adults with intellectual disability. *Journal of Intellectual Disability Research, 52*(12), 1091–1101. http://dx.doi.org/10.1111/j.1365-2788.2008.01098.x

McDonald, K. E., & Raymaker, D. M. (2013). Paradigm shifts in disability and health: Toward more ethical public health research. *American Journal of Public Health, 103*(12), 2165–2173. http://dx.doi.org/10.2105/AJPH.2013.301286

McGlashing-Johnson, J., Agran, M., Sitlington, P., Cavin, M., & Wehmeyer, M. (2003). Enhancing the job performance of youth with moderate to severe cognitive disabilities using the self-determined learning model of instruction. *Research and Practice for Persons With Severe Disabilities, 28*(4), 194–204. http://dx.doi.org/10.2511/rpsd.28.4.194

McGuire, J., & McDonnell, J. (2008). Relationships between recreation and levels of self-determination for adolescents and young adults with disabilities. *Career Development for Exceptional Individuals, 31*(3), 154–163. http://dx.doi.org/10.1177/0885728808315333

Nota, L., Ferrari, L., Soresi, S., & Wehmeyer, M. (2007). Self-determination, social abilities and the quality of life of people with intellectual disability. *Journal of Intellectual Disability Research, 51*(11), 850–865. http://dx.doi.org/10.1111/j.1365-2788.2006.00939.x

O'Brien J., & Mount, B. (2005). *Make A difference: A guidebook for person-centered direct support.* Toronto, Canada: Inclusion Press.

Odom, S. L., & Wolery, M. (2003). A unified theory of practice in early intervention/early childhood special education: Evidence-based practices. *The Journal of Special Education, 37*(3), 164–173. http://dx.doi.org/10.1177/00224669030370030601

Oxford Dictionary (2018). Definition of ableist. https://en.oxforddictionaries.com/definition/ableist

Palmer, S. B., & Wehmeyer, M. L. (2003). Promoting self-determination in early elementary school: Teaching self-regulated problem-solving and goal-setting skills. *Remedial and Special Education, 24*(2), 115–126. http://dx.doi.org/10.1177/07419325030240020601

Pearpoint, J., O'Brien, J., & Forest, M. (1993). *PATH: Planning alternative tomorrows with hope for schools, organizations, business, and families: A workbook for planning positive possible futures.* Toronto, Canada: Inclusion Press.

Quality Trust for Individuals with Disabilities. (2013). *Supported decision making: An agenda for action.* Retrieved from http://jennyhatchjusticeproject.org/node/264

Self-Advocacy Online. (2018). Stories from Self-Advocates. Retrieved from: http://www.selfadvocacyonline.org/stories/

Schalock, R. L., Bonham, G. S., & Verdugo, M. A. (2008). The conceptualization and measurement of quality of life: Implications for program planning and evaluation in the field of intellectual disabilities. *Evaluation and program planning, 31*(2), 181–190. http://dx.doi.org/10.1016/j.evalprogplan.2008.02.001

Shogren, K. A., Lopez, S. J., Wehmeyer, M. L., Little, T. D., & Pressgrove, C. L. (2006). The role of positive psychology constructs in predicting life satisfaction in adolescents with and without cognitive disabilities: An exploratory study. *The Journal of Positive Psychology, 1*(1), 37–52. http://dx.doi.org/10.1080/17439760500373174

Shogren, K. A., Palmer, S. B., Wehmeyer, M. L., Williams-Diehm, K., & Little, T. D. (2012). Effect of intervention with the self-determined learning model of instruction on access and goal attainment. *Remedial and Special Education, 33*(5), 320–330. http://dx.doi.org/10.1177/0741932511410072

Shogren, K. A., & Shaw, L. A. (2016). The role of autonomy, self-realization, and psychological empowerment in predicting outcomes for youth with disabilities. *Remedial and Special Education, 37*(1), 55–62. http://dx.doi.org/10.1177/0741932515585003

Shogren, K. A., & Turnbull, A. P. (2006). Promoting self-determination in young children with disabilities: The critical role of families. *Infants & Young Children, 19*(4), 338–352. http://dx.doi.org/10.1097/00001163-200610000-00006

Shogren, K. A., Wehmeyer, M. L., Palmer, S. B., Forber-Pratt, A. J., Little, T. J., & Clifton, S. L. (2015). Causal agency theory: Reconceptualizing a functional model of self-determination. *Education and Training in Autism and Developmental Disabilities, 50*(3), 251–263. http://dx.doi.org/10.1007/978-94-024-1042-6_5

Shogren, K. A., Wehmeyer, M. L., Palmer, S. B., Rifenbark, G. G., & Little, T. D. (2015). Relationships between self-determination and postschool outcomes for youth with disabilities. *The Journal of Special Education, 48*(4), 256–267. http://dx.doi.org/10.1177/0022466913489733

Smull, M. W., Sanderson, H., Sweeney, C., & Skelhorn, L. (2005). *Essential lifestyle planning for everyone.* Retrieved from https://www.researchgate.net/publication/265179859_Essential_Lifestyle_Planning_for_Everyone

Stancliffe, R. J., & Abery, B. H. (2003). An ecological theory of self. *Theory in self-determination: Foundations for educational practice*, 79–97.

Stancliffe, R. J., Abery, B. H., & Smith, J. (2000). Personal control and the ecology of community living settings: Beyond living-unit size and type. *American Journal on Mental Retardation, 105*(6), 431–454. http://dx.doi.org/10.1352/0895-8017(2000)105%3C0431:PCATEO%3E2.0.CO;2

Test, D. W., Mazzotti, V. L., Mustian, A. L., Fowler, C. H., Kortering, L., & Kohler, P. (2009). Evidence-based secondary transition predictors for improving postschool outcomes for students with disabilities. *Career Development for Exceptional Individuals, 32*(3), 160–181. http://dx.doi.org/10.1177/0885728809346960

Thoma, C. A. & Getzel, E. E. (2005). "Self-determination is what it's all about": What post-secondary students with disabilities tell us are important considerations for success. *Education and Training in Developmental Disabilities, 40*(3), 234–242.

Wehmeyer, M. L. (1992). Self-determination and the education of students with mental retardation. *Education and Training in Mental Retardation, 12*(1), 302–314.

Wehmeyer, M. L., & Abery, B. H. (2013). Self-determination and choice. *Intellectual and Developmental Disabilities, 51*(5), 399–411. http://dx.doi.org/10.1352/1934-9556-51.5.399

Wehmeyer, M. L., Agran, M., & Hughes, C. (1998). *Teaching self-determination to students with disabilities: Basic skills for successful transition.* Baltimore, MD: Paul H. Brookes Publishing.

Wehmeyer, M. L., Kelcher, K., & Richards S. (1996). Essential characteristics of self determined behavior of individuals with mental retardation. *American Journal on Mental Retardation, 100*(6), 632–642.

Wehmeyer, M. L., & Palmer, S. B. (2003). Adult outcomes for students with cognitive disabilities three years after high school: The impact of self-determination. *Education and Training in Developmental Disabilities, 38*(2) 131–144.

Wehmeyer, M. L., Palmer, S. B., Agran, M., Mithaug, D. E., & Martin, J. E. (2000). Promoting causal agency: The Self-Determined Learning Model of Instruction. *Exceptional Children, 66*(4), 439–453. http://dx.doi.org/10.1177/001440290006600401

Wehmeyer, M., & Schwartz, M. (1997). Self-determination and positive adult outcomes: A follow-up study of youth with mental retardation or learning disabilities. *Exceptional Children, 63*(2), 245–255. http://dx.doi.org/10.1177/001440299706300207

Wehmeyer, M. L., & Schwartz, M. (1998). The relationship between self-determination and quality of life for adults with mental retardation. *Education and Training in Mental Retardation and Developmental Disabilities, 33*(1), 3–12.

Wehmeyer, M. L., Shogren, K. A., Palmer, S. B., Williams-Diehm, K. L., Little, T. D., & Boulton, A. (2012). The impact of the self-determined learning model of instruction on student self-determination. *Exceptional Children, 78*(2), 135–153. http://dx.doi.org/10.1177/001440291207800201

Werner, S., & Chabany, R. (2016). Guardianship law versus supported decision making policies: Perceptions of persons with intellectual or psychiatric disabilities and parents. *American Journal of Orthopsychiatry, 86*(5), 486–99. http://dx.doi.org/10.1037/ort0000125

Whitman, T. L. (1990). Development of self-regulation in persons with mental retardation. *American Journal on Mental Retardation, 94*(4), 347–362.

United Nations General Assembly. (2006). *Convention on the Rights of Persons With Disabilities*. Retrieved from https://www.un.org/development/desa/disabilities/convention-on-the-rights-of-persons-with-disabilities.html

Zubal, R., Shoultz, B., Walker, P., & Kennedy, M. (1997). *Materials on self-advocacy.* Syracuse, NY: Center on Human Policy, Syracuse University.

CHAPTER SEVEN

Rights, Choices, and Supported Decision Making

Barbara A. Kleist, Amy S. Hewitt, and Susan N. O'Nell

Advance Organizers

- People with IDD have the right to make their own choices.
- Risk is an inherent function of making choices.
- Best practices in supporting people with IDD to make their own choices and decisions arecontinuing to evolve.
- Supported decision making and some other alternatives can help address the power imbalances in decision making.

For people with IDD, community living has not always been a reality. Historically, this right and opportunity was influenced heavily by others. As the movement to speak up and speak out through advocacy evolved for both people with IDD and their families, their ability to exercise rights and decide where, with whom, and how they wanted to live their lives also evolved. Yet far too often, even now, the capacity of a person with IDD to exercise their rights is assessed, measured, and determined not by themselves but by others.

Human and Civil Rights for All

Adults in the United States have many rights and responsibilities, and much power over their individual choices and decisions. However, adults with IDD are often denied the opportunity to exercise these fundamental and expected rights of adulthood.

Human rights are grounded in the principles of autonomy, freedom, and dignity—the inalienable right to life, liberty, and the pursuit of happiness. Civil rights focus on discrimination, access, and accommodation. As the movement for community living for people with IDD continues, and as what constitutes community is further defined, it is critical that the systems set up to support people with IDD ensure the removal of barriers to the full exercise of human and civil rights.

Today, the right of people with IDD to make their own decisions has evolved from a history fraught with misperceptions, assumptions, and biases. During the era of institutions, people with IDD were subjects of experiments such as the Massachusetts Institute of Technology/Quaker Oats "science club" experiments in the 1940s (Crockett, 2016). Other settings employed Skinnerian approaches (Minnesota Governor's Council on Developmental Disabilities, 2016), including harsh punishments to control or extinguish unwanted behavior. Such practices reinforced societal views that people with IDD were not fully human and were a "burden" on society. Parents were forced, with little or no information to go on, into institutionalizing their child with IDD, and then told to forget about them (Burke, 2016; Kohn, Blumenthal, and Campbell, 2012; Martinis, 2015).

As the atrocities of abuse and neglect within institutions were uncovered (Blatt, 1966) and a movement toward community living and reunification with families evolved, so too did a series of regulations, laws, and policies designed to protect people with IDD from harm. While necessary, they sometimes resulted in emphasizing the need for health, safety, and protection over a person's own choice. The unintended implication of such protections was, and to a great extent still is, that people with IDD are weak, vulnerable, and unable to make their own decisions.

Simultaneously in the United States, other laws, regulations, and policies emerged to vigorously assert the rights of individuals with IDD, including the right to reasonable accommodations (Americans with Disabilities Act (ADA), 1990), to live in the most integrated setting possible, and to express one's own rights (CMS Final Rule, 2014; Olmstead, 1999). Striking a balance between safety and health on the one hand and rights and the dignity of risk on the other is difficult. Often systems and local courts, regulatory bodies, and individual supporters are challenged in finding just the right balance. As such, the practice of assisting people to preserve and express their rights is highly variable across states and communities, and in individual lives.

Progress has been made. However, today states still support nearly 30,000 people with IDD in institutions (Larson et al., 2018), and laws and regulations continue to reinforce the notion that people with IDD are vulnerable and need protection to ensure their health and safety. For many people with IDD, exercising their rights requires support from others. The most common practice in the United States for obtaining this support is to use substitute decision making, in which a guardian or conservator is appointed. In these situations, far too often, the system, providers, and courts turn to the appointed substitute decision makers for all of a person's critical decisions, such as where and with whom they will live, how their resources are spent, what services they receive, and what medical treatments will be used (National Conference of Commissioners on Uniform State Laws, 2017). To maximize the opportunity for people with IDD to make their own choices and exercise their rights, it is important to look at the necessity of guardianship reform and to reconsider how people with IDD are supported to make their own decisions (Burke, 2016; Martinis, 2015).

Supporting people with IDD to exercise their right to make their own decisions has evolved both in policy and in practice since the early 1990s. The passage of the ADA in 1990 provided recognition of the civil rights of people with disabilities. The ADA was the legal basis for the groundbreaking Supreme Court decision, *Olmstead v. L.C.* (1999), often referred to as the Olmstead decision, affirming that people with disabilities had a right to live in the most integrated setting possible. The Olmstead decision also required states to develop plans to ensure that people with disabilities could live in the community, and influenced regulations at the federal level as well. Most notable in this regard was the 2014 implementation of the Home and Community Based Settings Rule (HCBS) (Centers for Medicare and Medicaid Services (CMS, 2014), which requires services funded through certain waivers to be provided in an integrated setting in the community. By affirming the civil rights of people with IDD, these changes in law and policy have also called attention to people's right to make their own decisions, and have directly impacted guardianship laws and regulations (UGPPA, 2007).

While laws, decisions, and regulations provide a legal framework for the rights of people with disabilities, it was a court case involving a young woman who wanted to end her guardianship that put a spotlight on supported decision making (Hatch, 2015; *Ross v. Hatch*, 2013). In its decision, the Court ordered that the guardians were required to use supported decision making with this young woman, and that following the termination of guardianship a year later, she would continue to use supported decision making as an alternative to guardianship. This was the first time a court had ordered supported decision making as an alternative to guardianship for a person with IDD (Martinis, 2015).

Around the same time as the Hatch case, the 2006 United Nations Convention on the Rights of Persons with Disabilities (CRPD) was gaining attention in the United States. The CRPD propelled the disability rights movement forward by providing a human rights framework to promoting the exercise of rights for people with IDD and supporting them to use informed decision making. Despite the fact that the United States has not ratified the CRPD, it provides an international lens of recognition that all people with IDD are presumed competent and are entitled to accommodations and assistance. Specifically, Article 12 of the CRPD spells out a five-principle framework for supported decision making with five key principles that have become the foundation for the case for supported decision making as an alternative to guardianship. Article 12 of the CRPD has also influenced national disability organizations to refine their positions on guardianship. For example, in 2016 the American Association on Intellectual and Developmental Disabilities (AAIDD) and The Arc issued a joint position statement on guardianship and supported decision making. The following excerpt from this statement highlights the national shift in thinking about the rights of people with IDD:

> The personal autonomy, liberty, freedom, and dignity of each individual with IDD must be respected and supported. Legally, each individual adult or emancipated minor is presumed competent to make decisions for himself or herself, and each individual with IDD should receive the preparation, opportunities, and decision-making supports to develop as a decision-maker over the course of his or her lifetime. (Joint Position Statement of AAIDD and The Arc, 2016)

Article 12 of the Convention on the Rights of Persons with Disabilities (2006)

Persons with disabilities have the right to:

1. Be recognized as persons before the law;
2. Enjoy legal capacity on an equal basis with all other people;
3. Access the support they need to exercise their legal capacity;
4. Benefit from appropriate and effective safeguards against abuse; and
5. Own or inherit property, control their own financial affairs, have equal access to financial credit, and not be arbitrarily deprived of their property.

Guardianship and Other Substitute Decision-Making Options

It is not possible to discuss rights, choices, and supported decision making without understanding what guardianship and other substitute decision-making options are, and the profound effect they have had on individuals with IDD. Guardianship is a legal process. The general criteria used in establishing a guardianship are that (1) the person is incapacitated, (2) the person needs the supervision and protection of a guardian, (3) no less-restrictive alternative exists, and (4) the person chosen to act as guardian will do so in the best interests of the person under guardianship. It is difficult to identify the exact number of people with IDD who are under guardianship today in each state, though recent data indicate that, as of 2008, 1.5 million people across the United States were under some form of guardianship (Uekert & Van Duizend, 2011).

While each state has its own laws and regulations on guardianship, there are some common elements, especially in states that have adopted model language from the UGPPA. On paper, state laws governing guardianship require the court to consider, in any given case, whether less restrictive alternatives for substitute decision making exist, including use of appropriate technology such as communication devices or remote monitoring. But even today, in many states, less restrictive alternatives are still not regularly explored. Instead, many people with IDD are put on the fast track to guardianship (Jameson et al., 2015; Martinis, 2015).

Guardians are given decision-making powers over the person they represent (who is often referred to as a ward). How much decision-making power a guardian has depends on what powers he or she has been granted by the court; this varies from state to state. Guardians may have the power to make decisions which can include supervisory authority, which is meant to limit civil rights and restrict personal freedom only to the extent necessary to provide needed care and service that affects:

- where a person lives
- what services and supports a person needs or may need
- care of a person's personal property/belongings
- medical care and treatment
- contracts with others

The guardian becomes the legal representative for the person under guardianship and is expected by the court to make decisions on their behalf that encourage and allow maximum independence. The intent is for decision-making powers to be reasonable and based on clearly established need. While this is the standard, actual application varies widely among guardians. In addition, once the courts have ruled on capacity, it can be difficult for the person under guardianship to reassert their capacity legally, or even informally when there is disagreement with their guardian.

For people with IDD, court-appointed guardians are often parents, siblings, other relatives, or, in some situations, friends. When such individuals are not available or willing to serve as a guardian, a paid professional guardian or a representative from a state or local government agency is appointed to this role. Generally, the standard used by courts is to find and appoint the most suitable and best qualified person among those available and willing to act as guardian.

In addition to full guardianship, in many states other forms of substitute decision making are available. For example, limited guardianship is when courts grant substitute decision-making powers only where needed, such as for medical care or contracts. Another form of substitute decision making is called conservatorship. A conservator, or guardian of the estate, is appointed when a person has property and/or financial assets that need management and protection. These forms of substitute decision making are considered less restrictive, yet they still place decision making in the hands of the court-appointed representative such that, in many cases, the person with IDD is left out of the decision-making process altogether.

Guardianship and other substitute decision-making alternatives can be viable tools for supporting a person with IDD when the person is unable to make decisions for themselves and court oversight of a guardian is necessary. Where reform is needed is in the application of guardianship law as it pertains to people with IDD: it is no longer acceptable to assume a person needs guardianship simply because they have IDD.

From Substitute Decision Making to Supported Decision Making

Over time and as a result of the disability rights movement, advocates, policy makers, and allies have been challenged to support people with IDD in making their own decisions rather than systematically strip them of their rights (Burke, 2016; Campanella, 2015; Jameson et al., 2015; Kohn et al., 2012; Martinis, 2015). This shift involves challenging long-held perceptions and legal standards based on a medical model of disability that have defined and determined the capacity of people with IDD to make their own decisions, in favor of supported decision making, which is based on a civil rights/social model. The Hatch case was the springboard for much of the current activity around supported decision making, including the addition of a definition of the practice in the Uniform Guardianship, Conservatorship, and Other Protective Agreements Act (UGCOPAA) of 2017 (National Conference of Commissioners on Uniform State Laws, 2017). The UGCOPAA defines supported decision making as "assistance from one or more persons of an individual's choosing:

- in understanding the nature and consequences of potential personal and financial decisions which enables the individual to make the decisions; and
- when consistent with the individual's wishes, in communicating a decision once made" (UGCOPAA, 2017).

In other words, supported decision making is a process of seeking carefully crafted guidance from people one trusts to ensure that one is aware of the potential and likely consequences of decisions. Supporters collect and help a person process critical information to make a reasoned decision. It is an alternative to guardianship that has been put in place as a legal agreement. Rather than a court process removing a person's right to decide for him- or herself, supported decision making is grounded in an environment of trust and support that promotes self-determination. A key feature of supported decision making is that it is more responsive and flexible than guardianship in that it allows for changes in decision-making support when needed, resulting in greater autonomy for the person with IDD (Martinis, 2015). It is important to note that supported decision making may not be a viable option for some people with IDD if they need the support of a guardian to ensure protection of their human and civil rights.

While some guardians and substitute decision makers strive always to consult with the person they represent and come to informed decisions together, not all do. A substitute decision maker might not even consult the person under their guardianship on the need to make decisions about spending their money, medical treatment, where to live, or what services they'll receive (Burke, 2016. However, when a person with IDD is able to use supported decision making as an alternative to guardianship, they are presumed competent, are taught about their options, and are provided the support they need to make their own best decisions (Blanck & Martinis, 2015).

Current Controversies and Challenges

New policies, laws, and regulations are pushing practitioners to change their methods, and person-centered planning, practices, and approaches are emerging to understand people's preferences and help them take responsibility for and accept the consequences of their choices. This can lead to struggle, however, because providers, families, and others are sometimes reluctant to support people in making decisions if it seems they might have poor, serious, or risky outcomes.

The Legacy of Presumed Incompetence

For many individuals with IDD, their biggest challenge is overcoming decades of assumptions that they are not competent to make their own decisions, regardless of their legal status (Burke, 2016). Far too often, receiving a diagnosis of IDD sets in motion a trajectory of low expectations, often beginning as early as birth. As a result, very little effort goes into teaching or supporting a person to develop their decision-making capacity.

People with IDD often lack access to support and opportunities to make everyday decisions, or even time alone to make mistakes while no one is looking. Daily decisions are often delegated to others, with little input from the person him- or herself. As a group, people with IDD are encouraged to comply with authority. All of these realities result in a situation where people who generally need more information, experience, and processing time in order to learn and make good decisions actually get far less. The gap in experience and knowledge between a person with IDD and peers without IDD can be quite profound by the time they reach the age of transition to adulthood. This in turn can fuel the image of incompetence.

Yet, supported decision making and changes in guardianship practices are pushing past presumptions of incompetence. As a younger generation of people with IDD comes through inclusive schools and grows up with more progressive expectations on the part of some families and professionals, they challenge the system to understand competence and achievement in a different way. The success of people with IDD in the occupational fields of modeling, acting, and small business is showing a different path and raising the bar for all. When people with IDD are seen as competent today, though they would not have been considered so two decades ago, it holds up a new mirror to societal expectations. It calls into question attitudes and behaviors that used to be generally accepted and gives power to the voice of rights advocacy.

Power Imbalances in Decision Making

The court system maintains a bias when it comes to the process of seeking guardianship and, more often than not, appoints guardians based on a person's diagnosis as opposed to their actual need. People with IDD often use idiosyncratic ways to learn, understand, and decide about things. The court has very little time to get to know a person, understand their uniqueness, and determine whether they are competent. As a result, obtaining guardianship may prove quite easy when a person has a diagnosis of IDD.

Families are often told to seek guardianship for their family member with IDD when they reach age 18. In some situations, this is well intended and serves to protect their loved one from harm, as well as from the "system" making decisions on their behalf. But families are also sometimes discouraged from having high expectations of their family member with IDD (Burke, 2016; Johns, 2012). Thus, they find themselves making decisions for them instead of teaching them decision-making skills and making decisions together. This phenomenon sometimes transfers to provider organizations when staff assume that because a person with IDD has a guardian or substitute decision maker, all decisions must be made by the latter. Unfortunately, inherent in the guardianship/substitute decision maker framework is the perception that the court has granted a guardian sole decision-making power over all aspects of life for the individual with IDD.

Conversely, inherent to supported decision making is the process by which a supporter helps someone with IDD to understand the decision that needs to be made, weigh options and consequences, and make their own choice; the supporter then supports the individual's decision. In this approach, the power to decide rests with the person with IDD and is shared, as he or she desires, with supporters. This process can be formalized in writing or based on informal (often verbal) agreements.

But what happens if a person with IDD and their supporter are faced with a decision with serious or life-threatening consequences? In the emerging area of supported decision making, different strategies are being used to address the ongoing concerns of families, advocates, service providers, policy makers, and others about protections for people with IDD. One example of a formalized approach to supported decision making comes from the state of Texas, where a law was enacted that allows a person and their supporter to complete and sign a supported decision-making agreement that is legally valid and includes a provision for just such a decision-making need. In this type of agreement, the person with IDD can decide whether to delegate decision making under certain circumstances. This agreement is witnessed and notarized as required by law. In addition to the Texas model, the National Resource Center for Supported Decision-Making provides several model agreements. (See additional information on these model agreements later in this chapter.)

It should be noted that using supported decision making as an alternative to guardianship does not mean that a person with IDD has no protection from abuse or harm. The systems set up to report maltreatment of vulnerable adults remain applicable, and in some cases, a supporter is required to report suspected abuse or maltreatment, as if he or she is a mandated reporter.

This shift in decision-making power to people with IDD has been evolving since 1982 as a result of extensive revisions to made to the UGCOPAA, which had not been revised since 1969. The current UGCOPAA, most recently revised in 1997, is a model that many states use to guide changes in guardianship. Additionally, the UGPPA emphasizes the use of less restrictive forms of substitute decision making, such as powers of attorney, health care directives, use of a representative payee, case management, and informal supports such as technology (UGPPA, 1997/1998). The 1997 revisions to the UGPPA continued the momentum toward a system that supports people with IDD in making their own decisions with supports that allow balance between choice and risk.

Fear of Choice and Risk

One way in which the concept of dignity of risk comes up in the lives of people with IDD is when they receive services from a provider agency for help with community living, employment, or in-home support. Providers are often focused on the need to balance risk (which can be seen as bringing about liability/culpability) and choice. Too often the fear of liability and accountability wins out. Dignity of risk is a concept put forth in the 1970s to express the frustration of "eternal childhood" that many people with IDD experience (Perske, 1974). Trying new things, even when those attempts might result in failure, is an important part of learning and results in people having dignity. Dignity of risk is a fundamental argument against protectionism and paternalism toward people with disabilities. It should not be confused with recklessness or lack of caution or adequate planning. However, people must have the opportunity to try, sometimes fail, and then learn from their failures, rather than never getting to try something at all.

Progress is being made on many fronts in terms of supporting people with IDD in making smaller, daily decisions. However, larger decisions that most adults make, or decisions that challenge provider organizations or the service sector, are often not discussed or supported at all. Some people with IDD are systematically cut off from many types of decisions, such as learning to drive, getting a tattoo, having sex, risking a broken heart, and getting married. However, people with IDD can consider and plan for these choices, and succeed at them, with supports from others.

Lack of Training for Supported Decision Making

It is critical to create policy structures and standard models at the provider organization level to support informed choice in balance with risk. Too often, little or inadequate training on these important topics is available for direct support professionals (DSPs), frontline supervisors, care coordinators, and managers. Supporting people with IDD to make their own decisions means figuring out ways to understand what is important to that individual in terms of such things as relationships, places to live, things to do, rhythm and pace of life, status, and control.

The current system of long-term services and supports (LTSS) focuses predominantly on the health and safety of an individual by managing and minimizing risk. Renewed commitments to positive practices that offer people with IDD more choice and control calls for best practices for training in this arena. The Learning Community for Person Centered Practices (TLCPCP) describes supported decision making as balancing what is important *to* a person with IDD and what is important *for* that person (Smull, 2013 TLCPCP, 2017). TLCPCP emphasizes supporting people to have positive control over their lives (TLCPCP, 2017). This brings to light the challenges people with IDD face, as illustrated by the examples in Table 7.1. More about person-centered and positive support practices can be found in Chapter 2.

Practical Suggestions and Interventions

Over the years, practices ensuring that people with IDD enjoy the same rights as others to make everyday decisions have evolved from paternalistic protection and control to where we are today. In this section, we highlight practical examples of programs and practices that are making a difference both at the individual level and in state and federal policies.

Nothing About Me Without Me

Every day we make routine decisions, often on our own without support from others. We also make bigger life decisions in which we seek out advice or support. Most people turn to different individuals for different decision-making situations. For example, if we are trying to decide what to wear to an event, we might consult our fashion-forward friend. If considering whether to move to a new neighborhood, we might consult a realtor. If we are trying to decide about changing jobs, we might talk with someone we know who works where we are thinking about taking a new job. Decisions are as varied as individuals and their circles of support. We should expect and allow this to be the case for people with IDD as much as for anyone else.

The phrase "nothing about me without me" is a powerful mantra that comes out of the self-advocacy movement and captures the essence of supported decision making at the individual level. A number of programs and strategies are being implemented across the United States and around the world that focus on supporting people with IDD to understand their rights and learn how to make informed decisions and, when desired or needed, engage others in supporting their decision making. Common attributes of programs and practices that support people with IDD in making their own decisions include access to peers with shared interests and experiences, and advocacy training and support. Table 7.2 describes organizations and programs that focus on supported decision making.

Table 7.1. *Decision-Making Strategies*

Quality of Life Goal: To feel and be healthy.
What we encourage people without IDD to do: • Work with their provider to weigh risks and benefits of a medication that causes them to suffer a side effect. • Go to a different professional who listens better. • Research other, natural options for managing a condition. • Work on lifestyle changes.
What we have traditionally encouraged people with IDD to do: • Take their medications as ordered. • Think about other things. • Stop complaining.
Person-centered balance: • Spend time teaching the individual about their condition and medication, and the available options. • Help the individual find a professional who will work with them, or help them identify alternatives. • When the consequences of not taking medication are more serious and immediate, ask the person to make a temporary commitment to the medication while learning more about the options and consequences. Develop wellness plan or agreement with clear indicators (e.g., blood pressure under a certain number, number of days without self-harm, etc.) to support informed choices. • Dig deeper to figure out what the issues are. Identify other, more workable ways to manage the side effect.
Quality of Life Goal: To live somewhere that fits with a preferred lifestyle.
What we encourage people without IDD to do: • Set a budget and consider pros and cons of critical aspects of lifestyle, such as transportation, relationships, recreation. • Look until they find a place that is a good match with top criteria. • Accept and learn from the consequences of their choice (high rent, difficulty with roommates).
What we have traditionally encouraged people with IDD to do: • Live where there is an opening and be happy about it. • Stop complaining. • Accept this is "as good as it gets."
Person-centered balance: • Be realistic about support needs as part of the decision. • Be creative. • Expect there to be changes as the person grows and learns. It's not "one and done."

Table 7.2. *Ten Tips for Supporting Choice and Decision Making*

1. Give people lots of opportunities to try things.
2. Support people to expand and develop their communication abilities.
3. Help people consider what they think is important in a situation. Verbalize this and make it explicit.
4. Pay attention to a person's behavior and words to understand what's important to them.
5. Remember that behavior is far more important than words in understanding people and their real preferences.
6. Be enthusiastic and positive with people about their life goals and hopes.
7. Be honest about what you can help people with and what you cannot.
8. Help people start taking steps right away to move toward bigger goals or to resolve concerns.
9. Help people break things down into steps that make sense, and support them in each one. Provide information in ways that are meaningful to them.
10. When people are discouraged or fail, don't let them see *themselves* as failures. Acknowledge that things we want are often difficult to achieve. Let them know you will support them in what's next, based on what they want to do.

Supporting Families

Families are key to building early and ongoing opportunities for decision making and independent thought processes for their child with IDD. At every life stage, families can promote choice and self-determination, but they, like their child, need support along the way. Early access to strategies and interventions is crucial. Early intervention programs that embrace optimism for the future can help families learn to value their child with IDD, and to teach him or her to become an independent thinker and a person with high expectations for his or her life. An early foundation will yield positive first steps toward a child's ability to make decisions. It is also critical to provide training for pediatricians, faith leaders, and other professionals who have regular contact with families of children with IDD in how to best support them. Another essential component to setting the stage early for children with IDD to make decisions as adults is the peer support model of connecting families in similar circumstances so they can learn and obtain information from one another.

The National Resource Center for Supported Decision-Making offers resources for families that focus on ways to nurture and teach decision-making skills to their children across the lifespan, including building decision-making skills into the IEP process. See Table 7.2 for information about how to obtain these resources.

Engaging Communities

Community means different things to different people. For some people, their community is where they live. For others, their community revolves around their spiritual practices or involves being part of a team or sharing an interest such as golf, poker, or reading. In each of these communities, we rely on others to support and guide some of our decision making. It is no different for people with IDD. However, because most services for people with IDD are funded through Medicaid, they have come to focus more on caretaking and "doing for" people, rather than on teaching people skills and connecting them to the community for the help they seek in decision making and in life in general.

Effective strategies and interventions for building community connections are limited in both depth and scope. Much more attention needs to be given to teaching direct support staff within provider organizations about how to facilitate community connection and reliance of people with IDD on community resources for assistance in making decisions, as opposed to letting staff take action and make decisions for them. For example, most staff handle banking for people with IDD; they call the bank and solve problems, instead of supporting the person with IDD to go into the bank (or call their banker), work thorough problems, and find solutions.

Asset-based community development identifies strategies for supporting people's engagement in community life (McKnight & Kretzmann, 1993). This work provides a foundation for person-centered practices such as creating community maps and paths in partnership with people with IDD. Other community initiatives to support decision making by people with IDD involve training first responders and community liaisons to understand the rights of people with IDD, as well as teaching them best practices for supporting a person with IDD who is experiencing a challenge navigating their community or who is in crisis.

Our communities tend to rely on the disability service provider sector to "do for" and meet the needs of people with IDD. We need to create bridges between the community and service providers, using the expertise of the disability network to teach community members and organizations to support people with IDD in making decisions. For instance, church groups that help people in general to find jobs can be trained to help people with IDD to find jobs also. Community organizations that provide affordable housing should support people with IDD in the same endeavor. Youth groups that teach leadership skills to children should teach youth with IDD leadership skills too. One of the best ways to support people with IDD in making decisions is to connect them to people in their communities who have expertise in areas where they need support.

Changing Practices in Criminal and Civil Court Processes

The criminal and civil court system throughout the United States also needs training so court personnel will better understand these issues. Far too often, courts have relied on professionals within the disability services system to tell them what to do, and even what decisions to make. For decades, substitute decision making was used as a matter of routine for persons with IDD. It will take training through law schools, professional trade associations, parent/family organizations, and advocacy organizations to change these practices. As more examples emerge in case law of people with IDD given supported decision-making rights by courts and experiencing positive outcomes, this practice will likely become more common. For now, supported decision making is the exception, not the norm. This must change.

Table 7.3. *Strategies to Support Moving from Guardianship to Supported Decision Making*

1. Identify opportunities early on for people with IDD to make their own decisions; the earlier opportunities are provided, the better the outcomes will be.
2. Ensure that opportunities for decision making are included in educational planning, especially for transition from high school to young adult life.
3. Expect and engage people with IDD to problem-solve. Learn to use person-centered practices to help a person with IDD figure out what they want in life, and support them in attaining it.
4. Watch for barriers and roadblocks in law and policy that get in the way of supported decision making because of concerns about liability, neglect, and vulnerability.
5. Advocate for changes in how the system applies current guardianship laws by educating policy makers, judges, and lawyers about supported decision making.

Educating Providers

Providers are often caught between restrictive state regulations and people's rights to make choices for themselves. Generally, providers want to support people with IDD to have self-determined lives. But often, perceived or real consequences of such self-determination pose challenges for provider organizations related to the health and safety of people for whom they provide long-term services and supports.

Through collaboration with state agencies, policy makers, and peers, providers can be supported to cultivate transparent polices related to supported decision making and informed risk. At all levels within organizations, training must occur on balancing rights protections with restrictions. Most organizations have human rights committees that can be powerful allies in supporting people with IDD to make decisions by balancing risks with choice. Providers can also be important means through which families and guardians get accurate information about alternatives to substitute decision making and how to move toward supported decision making. Often families and individuals are not even aware that other options exist. Once they learn about other options, they may be willing to consider taking steps toward change.

It is key to train staff at all levels within an organization on ways they can empower people with IDD to make decisions. This starts with basic things like when the person eats, what they eat, who their friends are, and what they do for fun. Eventually, the practice expands to supporting people with IDD to understand their rights in making big decisions, such as where and with whom they live and what they do during the day, and balancing the pros and cons of these types of decisions. Staff need to think of themselves as facilitators and teachers who encourage and train the people they support to make everyday decisions first, with the goal of making significant life decisions later.

The following are approaches TLCPCP (2016) offers for training providers who are seeking to change or improve how they support people with IDD to make their own decisions:

- Gather different perspectives by asking the person being supported and their supporters what is working and what is not working, then look for common ground that is helpful in finding solutions. Using this framework helps people to see an issue or situation from multiple perspectives at a particular point in time.
- The 4+1 framework is effective when trying to figure out next steps in response to a need or problem. It starts with a question such as "What can we do to improve communication among _______'s support team?" Team members then identify what they have tried, what they have learned, what they are pleased about, and what they are concerned about. Then they identify next steps, often agreeing to keep doing what seems to be working and identifying one or two new things to try.
- The "donut sort" is both a management skill and a tool to help clarify roles and expectations of staff who are supporting people. Using this tool, staff and supervisors work together to sort their roles and responsibilities into three areas, which allows support staff to use their judgment and creativity in supporting people:
    - » core responsibilities—things a staff person must do or they would be fired
    - » areas where judgment and creativity may or must be used—here, staff can try
    - » different strategies and learn what works and doesn't work
    - » areas of a person's life beyond the role of paid support

Table 7.4. *Examples of Decisions That People With IDD Can Be Supported to Make*

Everyday Decisions
- When to wake up/go to bed
- What to eat and drink
- Who to hang out with or not hang out with
- What to do for fun, and where to do it
- What to wear; freedom to have one's own personal style

Significant Decisions
- Where to live, and who to live with
- Spending money for big purchases like a phone, car, etc.
- Making changes to medication
- Pursuing a romantic or sexual relationship
- What to do after high school: work or postsecondary education

Major Life Decisions
- Consenting to medical decisions or treatment, such as surgery
- Signing a contract for a big purchase, such as a house
- Getting married/divorced
- Having children or not having children
- Planning for retirement and end of life

Transforming Systems Models for Change

State systems are not quick to change and move in new directions. Scaling up new ideas and practices takes time. It is important for the focus to be on emphasizing alternatives to substitute decision making and moving toward supported decision making with a keen focus on upholding the rights of people with IDD. Systems must not only establish expectations of key stakeholders but also support them in becoming actively engaged in developing and refining practices. Several organizations have developed promising practices that can be used by others as examples to follow:

Texas model agreement for supported decision making. The Texas Developmental Disabilities Council (TCDD) developed a model agreement for supported decision making to be used as an alternative to guardianship (TCCD, 2018). This agreement specifies who the person with IDD wants to be a supporter and in what areas of life they want that person to help them make decisions. It clearly states that the designated supporter does not make the decisions *for* the person but provides support in specified ways as identified in the agreement. This document is to be notarized and serves as a legal agreement. The model document can be found here: http://www.tcdd.texas.gov/wp-content/uploads/2015/10/Supported-Decision-Making-Agreement-Oct15.pdf.

Autistic Self Advocacy Network (ASAN) model legislative language. ASAN has developed model legislation for states to consider when developing new statutes concerning guardianship and supported decision making. This model language has been used by many states to guide their changes. It provides definitions of important concepts and terms; gives an overview of the purpose, reason, and scope behind the model legislation; describes conflict of interest and explains the importance of identifying and addressing it; and identifies components of model agreements. This can be found at http://autisticadvocacy.org/wp-content/uploads/2014/07/ASAN-Supported-Decisionmaking-Model-Legislature.pdf (ASAN, 2018).

National Resource Center for Supported Decision-Making. The National Resource Center for Supported Decision-Making works with partners to apply supported decision making in legal cases, create outcome measures related to supported decision making, and advocate for changes in law and practices that increase self-determination and use of supported decision making in the United States. They provide a state-by-state directory of whether and how supported decision making and/or other alternatives to substitute decision making are used in each state. This national center also provides numerous resources on this topic that individuals and states can access. More resources can be found at: http://www.supporteddecisionmaking.org.

Life Course Expectations and Transitions

Supporting people with IDD to make decisions and be prepared for adulthood and community living should happen throughout their life, from birth to death. It is critical that people with IDD be surrounded by people who love and support them, have high expectations of them and the systems that deliver supports to them, and see them as unique individuals with strengths and needs. The types of decisions that people with IDD make vary throughout their lives, so the supports that are needed will vary as well.

Infancy. It is critical to have expectations, beginning at birth, that each person will be competent and able to make decisions that affect their life. When a child is born with a known disability, it is important for families, professionals, and caregivers to make positive assumptions about capacity and opportunity, and to understand the infant as a human being with rights. These expectations will guide how others treat the child as a baby and throughout their lifetime.

Early childhood. Early childhood is a time of rapid development and growth. It is a priority to work with young children to help them learn to communicate verbally, nonverbally, or through alternative or augmentative means. Expressing likes and dislikes and choosing between the two are critical skills that children learn early. Families should work hard to teach choice making during a child's early years and nurture their children in making daily decisions, from which they will learn valuable consequences. Teaching the difference between doing it oneself and learning to ask for support is also valuable during this timeframe.

School age. The school-age years offer many opportunities for learning about others and oneself. Children with disabilities should be encouraged to dream big about their future. They can stretch themselves and take on challenges academically, socially, and in school-related activities, including sports, drama, music, and other extracurricular activities. Children should be active in developing their individualized education plans and/or accommodations. Inclusion ensures that peers with and without disabilities experience a variety of relationships and the decisions that come with them. School environments that proactively practice inclusion and positive social interactions among all members of the school community support all children in developing and building on their strengths.

Transition. Planning for the transition from school to adulthood cannot begin early enough. Youth, along with their families, should consider volunteering in their community, looking for paying work, or taking on leadership roles or tasks that carry responsibility. Families should also emphasize the adult responsibilities that accompany rights and support their young family member with IDD in understanding them. Youth with IDD should be supported in taking concrete steps toward preparing for their individual aspirations for adulthood, whether they are employment, further education, marriage, and/or parenting. Dating, driving, babysitting, and hanging out with friends should be encouraged within a framework that makes sense and is of interest to each individual. While these aspects of life can be stressful for parents, it's important that they remember that adulthood will include sexuality and lifestyle choices without a parental safety net. Supporting youth in learning about and making positive life choices is important. Families should actively plan ahead of time for when the young person turns 18 and should work toward agreements everyone can live with. Formal supported decision-making plans may be viable and preferred over guardianship or other decision-making processes.

Young adulthood. Transition may extend well into young adulthood for anyone with or without disabilities, sometimes more so for people with IDD. However, young adults—even those with disabilities—should not be treated as they were when they were younger. Even if a young adult with disabilities lives at home, new activities and expectations need to emerge to help them continue to develop toward their adult roles. More responsibility around the house and increased social freedoms are important. Career growth, marriage, and parenthood are areas where young adults should be supported to explore, learn, and plan. If they want to live away from home, they should be encouraged to, as an opportunity to learn more about their own strengths, interests, limits, values, and views. Continued discussions should take place about how and when family is best engaged to support decision making, as well as when they are not.

Adulthood. Athough adulthood is often a time of stability, it should not be taken for granted that a person is content with the status quo. Everyone enjoys some aspects of lifelong learning and new self-expression. People with disabilities may still be making up for lost time if they did not have access previously to supported decision-making. If someone is interested in trying new things and considering new options, such as developing hobbies, engaging more closely in faith communities or neighborhood associations, and the like, they should be encouraged and supported in doing so. Community education and volunteer opportunities can provide new perspectives as well. Supported decision-making agreements and the roles of supporters should be revisited periodically to make sure they still meet the needs of the person with the disability.

Aging and retirement. Later adulthood is a period when supported decision-making processes and agreements need to be reconsidered and often restructured. As a person ages, their supporters age as well. If parents have been active, it is time to look at integrating other family members, such as siblings, cousins, the person's own children as they come to maturity, or other younger family members, into support arrangements.

Death and dying. Discussions and pre-planning should take place with people with IDD, as with anyone, before the need is imminent, and results of the conversations should be documented. This allows time to consider options and make arrangements. Before the individual is no longer able to speak or experiences confusion, they can designate someone to communicate their wishes. Choices and options include whether to remain at home or move elsewhere for care, as well as preferences in terms of comfort and life-saving measures. These should be communicated to supporters and documented. Critical supporters and loved ones should be identified, along with how they should or should not be involved.

Personal Illustration: Monty Kempf

"I like my freedom," proclaimed Monty Kempf. "I like it a lot. Knowing that I can do stuff on my own and experience life." Twenty years ago, Monty made the decision to live on his own. Many people in his position, seeking greater independence in young adulthood but wearing a disability label, face obstacles in making and acting on important life decisions. Parents and guardians can become overprotective and unwilling to allow their children to take chances. Fortunately, Monty's parents encouraged him to think about finding his own place. He completed a housing application process on his own, and after 10 persistent years on a waiting list, he moved into an apartment building where a few of his friends lived. "I live in my own apartment. It's got all the amenities. And there's a community room and a commons area."

Monty now lives on his own, but he does not make decisions in isolation. "My parents play a big role. Financial, emotional . . . they're there when I need them. And my sister and brother are a big part of my life, too." For Monty, independence means being in the driver's seat, but not necessarily traveling alone.

At his job with a medical equipment supply company, Monty makes decisions every day. His title of Utility Worker includes duties of cleaning and assembling equipment, emptying trash, cutting the grass, and helping deliver equipment to customers. "I go out on runs with people, you know, when they have a heavy bed because I'm the only one that can lift that stuff." Monty has a good deal of autonomy and flexibility in how he completes his work. When he requires support, his supervisor, Danny Mudge, is there to provide direction. "I watch him and he does do a lot of problem solving. He reads the instructions and goes about his own way of doing it and he gets it done right." Occasionally, Monty has difficulty prioritizing tasks. "Sometimes I'm really not good at making time decisions," said Monty. "Or I get busy and I forget." But for the most part, Monty rises to his employer's expectations. "With the multitude of tasks that he has," said Danny, "it's a huge relief off my shoulders to watch him work as hard as he does and get as many aspects of this warehouse done and in an efficient manner like he does."

Last February, Monty decided he needed a new car. He knew this decision would include a number of complex factors, such as finances and safety features, so he turned to his family for support. "I made that decision with the help of my dad. He's my financial advisor, so he looked into it and tried to find the right one that I could afford." His father provided advice, but Monty was in the driver's seat. "He aided in the process, but I had to make a decision—do I like that car or not? The things that I wanted in the car were a back-up camera and a cross-traffic sensor so

I know not to go in the other lane when there's a car there." Living in Minnesota, Monty also wanted a car with remote start. "That's a luxury," said Monty, "but it comes in handy in the winter when it gets cold." With a better understanding of his options, Monty was able to make an informed choice and purchase a vehicle that met his needs and was within his budget.

Monty is a people person, always ready and willing to share his opinions and offer advice when asked. In his apartment building, he is often the go-to person for help with decision making. "Where I live, people ask me for advice. Sometimes it's about how to program their TV, sometimes it's about who to date. When I give advice to people, I tell them 'do the best you can and think wisely.'"

With persistence and determination, Monty became his own guardian. "This means I make my own decisions. Granted, they're not always the best decisions," joked Monty. "Sometimes when I make decisions, I need a little help." With a large support network, including family, hunting friends, coworkers, and people in his apartment building, support is always at hand.

Conclusion

The expression of the rights of people with IDD to live and participate in the community requires continued strong focus in elevating the civil and human rights for people with IDD. This can be done though self-advocacy, research, training, and policy changes. Practices that confer decision-making power upon surrogates need to be reconstructed. Well-crafted and consistent opportunities must be cultivated for people with IDD to exercise choice, control, and direction at each stage of life. Dignity of risk must be balanced with considerations of best support to ensure that people with IDD have both the experience and the knowledge necessary to understand potential positive and negative outcomes of their choices. Above all, at each step of the way and for each person, a presumption of competence is essential.

Decision-making opportunities must be undergirded by daily support practices that help people express and follow through on both rights and responsibilities as citizen and active participants in their own lives. Advocates, family members, teachers, and providers must be vigilant in pushing for each person's rights and opportunities to have their voice heard and their decisions respected. They must support their loved one with IDD, or the person with IDD to whom they provide services, in dreaming big about life and taking on the responsibilities that go with their rights and dreams. Specific strategies, many of which were described in this chapter, are available and increasingly used to make this happen. Even so, supported decision-making practices must become more deeply embedded in society, ensuring that all components of the community and individual support systems learn these perspectives and person-centered practices.

Discussion Questions

- What are the biggest challenges to people with IDD experiencing rights, choice, control, and direction in their life? What do you recommend to overcome these challenges?
- What concerns do you have about the risks of supported decision making? What might help address these risks without using restrictions or violating rights?
- What are the most effective ways to educate, train, and engage people with IDD, their families, direct support professionals, and others in these discussions and practices?
- How do we move more fully from the prevalent practice of decision making through guardianship, to use of supported decision making instead? What needs to change? What needs to stay the same?
- What role do you need to explore in order to promote supported decision making as an alternative to guardianship for people with disabilities?

Resources

- LifeCourse Tools. The LifeCourse Tools are part of the Charting a LifeCourse framework that was developed for and by families as part of the National Community of Practice for Supporting Families of People with IDD. The LifeCourse Tools are a resource "to support families, with all their complexity and diversity, in ways that maximize their capacity, strengths, and unique abilities so they can best support, nurture, and facilitate the achievement of self-determination, interdependence, productivity, integration, and inclusion in all facets of community life for their family members" (Hecht , Reynolds, Agosta, and McGinley, 2011). http://www.lifecoursetools.com
- "It's My Choice" from the MN Governor's Council on Developmental Disabilities. "It's My Choice" is an easy-to-understand guide that provides a framework for helping people with IDD plan for the life they want. This planning tool supports decision making by helping people with IDD and their supporters look at what the person needs, plan for their future, and figure out what resources are available to support them. Written in plain language that includes activities and checklists to help a person consider all aspects of their life. http://mn.gov/mnddc/extra/publications/Its-My-Choice.pdf
- Self-Advocates Becoming Empowered (SABE). SABE is a national organization whose mission is to ensure that people with disabilities are treated as equals with everyone else and are given the same choices, rights, responsibilities, and chances to speak up to empower themselves, as well as opportunities to make new friends and to learn from their mistakes. One project focuses on ensuring that people under guardianship can exercise their right to vote. http://www.sabeusa.org/
- Self-Advocacy Online (SAO). SAO is a multimedia resource accessible to all, providing information important to people with IDD. The content is translated into plain language and includes videos, interactive lessons, and engaging graphics. One key feature is stories from other self-advocates sharing what they have to say about key topics in self-advocacy, such as self-determination, supports, and person-centeredness. http://selfadvocacyonline.org/

References

American Association on Intellectual and Developmental Disabilities (AAIDD) and The Arc. (2016). *Joint Position Statement on Autonomy, Decision-Making Supports, and Guardianship*. Retrieved from http://aaidd.org/news-policy/policy/position-statements/autonomy-decision-making-supports-and-guardianship#.Wicc1canHIV

American Bar Association's Commission on Disability Rights Supported Decision Making Roundtable. (2012). *Beyond Guardianship: Supported Decision-Making by Individuals with Intellectual Disabilities*. New York. Retrieved from https://www.americanbar.org/content/dam/aba/administrative/mental_physical_disability/Roundtable_brief_10182012.authcheckdam.pdf

Americans with Disabilities Act (ADA) of 1990, 42 U.S.C.A. 12101 et seq. (1993).

Autistic Self Advocacy Network. (2018). Model legislation. Retrieved from: http://autisticadvocacy.org/wp-content/uploads/2014/07/ASAN-Supported-Decisionmaking-Model-Legislature.pdf

Blanck, P., & Martinis, J. G. (2015). "*The right to make choices*": The national resource center for supported decision-making. *Inclusion, 3*(1), 24–33.

Blatt, Burton. (1966). *Christmas in purgatory: A photographic essay on mental retardation.* Boston: Allyn and Bacon.

Boundy, M., and Fleischner, B. (2013). Supported decision making instead of guardianship: An international overview [Fact Sheet]. Washington, D.C.: Center for Public Representation.

Burke, S. (2016). Person-centered guardianship : How the rise of supported decision-making and person-centered services can help Olmstead's promise get here faster. *Mitchell Hamline Law Review, 42*(3). Retrieved from http://open.mitchellhamline.edu/cgi/viewcontent.cgi?article=1030&context=mhlr

Campanella, T. (2015). Supported decision-making in practice. *Inclusion 3*(1), 35–39. https://doi.org/10.1352/2326-6988-3.1.35

Centers for Medicare and Medicaid Services (CMS) Final Rule, 42 C. F.R. 430, 431 et al. (2014).

Crockett, Z. (2016). *The Dark Secret of the MIT Science Club for Children.* PRICEONOMICS. https://priceonomics.com/the-mit-science-club-for-disabled-children/

Hatch, J. (2015). My story. *Inclusion*: *3*(1), 34. https://doi.org/10.1352/2326-6988-3.1.34

Jameson, M. J., Riesen, T., Polychronis, S., Trader, B., Mizner, S., Martinis, J., & Hoyle, D. (2015). Guardianship and the potential of supported decision making with individuals with disabilities. *Research and Practice for Persons with Severe Disabilities, 40*(1), 36–51. doi: 10.1177/1540796915586189

Johns, F. (2012). Person-centered planning in guardianship: A little hope for the future. *Utah Law Review, 1541*(3), 1–33.

Kohn, N., Blumenthal, J., & Campbell, A. (2012). Supported decision-making: A viable alternative to guardianship? *Penn State Law Review*. Retrieved from http://www.pennstatelawreview.org/117/4%20Final/Kohn%20et%20al.%20(final)%20(rev2).pdf

McKnight, J., and Kretzmann, J. P. (1993). *Building communities from the inside out: A path toward finding and mobilizing a community's assets.* Evanston, IL:Asset-Based Community Development Institute, Institute for Policy Research, Northwestern University

Lakin, C., Turnbull, A. (Eds.). (2005). *National goals and research for people with intellectual and developmental disabilities*, Washington, D.C.: American Association on Intellectual and Developmental Disabilities (AAIDD).

Larson, S. A., Eschenbacher, H.J., Anderson, L. L., Taylor, B., Pettingell, S., Hewitt, A., Sowers, M., & Bourne, M.L. (2018). In-home and residential long-term supports and services for persons with intellectual or developmental disabilities: Status and trends through 2016. Minneapolis: University of Minnesota, Research and Training Center on Community Living, Institute on Community Integration.

Martinis, J. (2015). Supported decision-making: Protecting rights, ensuring choices. *BiFocal, 36*(5).

Minnesota Governor's Council on Developmental Disabilities. (2016). *Parallels in time: A history of developmental disabilities.* Retrieved from http://mn.gov/mnddc/parallels/index.html

National Conference of Commissioners on Uniform State Laws. (2017). Uniform Guardianship, Conservatorship, and Other Protective Agreements Act (UGCOPAA) of 2017. Retireved from: http://www.uniformlaws.org/shared/docs/Guardianship%20and%20Protective%20Proceedings/UGCOPAA_Final_2018aug28.pdf

National Guardianship Association. (2016). Position statement on guardianship, surrogate decision making and supported decision making. https://www.guardianship.org/wp-content/uploads/2017/07/SDM-Position-Statement-9-20-17.pdf

National Guardianship Association. (2017). What is guardianship? Retrieved from https://www.guardianship.org/what-is-guardianship/

National Resource Center for Supported Decision-Making. (2016). *Survey on supported decision-making in practice—Final report to administration on intellectual and developmental disabilities.* Retrieved from: http://supporteddecisionmaking.org/sites/default/files/Final%20Report-Survey%20on%20Supported%20Decision-Making.pdf

Olmstead v. L.C., 527 U.S. 581 (1999).

Perske, R. (1974). The dignity of risk and the mentally retarded. *Mental Retardation 10*(1).

Ross v. Hatch, No. CWF120000426P-03, slip op. at 7 (Va. Cir. Ct. Aug. 2, 2013). Retrieved from http://jennyhatchjusticeproject.org/docs/justice_for_jenny_trial/jhjp_trial_final_order.pdf

Smull, M, (2013). Thinking About Risk. Retrieved from http://allenshea.com/wp-content/uploads/2016/10/risk-fiinal.pdf

Texas Developmental Disabilities Council. (2018). Guardianship alternatives. Retrieved from http://www.tcdd.texas.gov/resources/guardianship-alternatives/

The Learning Community for Person Centered Practices. (2014.) Person centered thinking toolkit. Retrieved from http://sdaus.com/toolkit

Uekert, B. K. & Van Duizend, R. (2011). Adult guardianships: A "Best Guess" national estimate and the momentum for reform. In C. Flango, A. McDowell, C. Campbell, & E. Kauder, *Future Trends in State Courts 2011*. Williamsburg, VA: National Center for State Courts. Retrieved from: http://www.eldersandcourts.org/Guardianship/GuardianshipBasics/~/media/Microsites/Files/cec/AdultGuardianships.ashx

United Nations. (2007). *Convention on the rights of persons with disabilities (CRPD).* Geneva, Switzerland: Division for Social Policy and Development. Retrieved fromhttps://www.un.org/development/desa/disabilities/convention-on-the-rights-of-persons-with-disabilities.html

United Nations. (2007*). Handbook for parliamentarians.* Geneva, Switzerland:Division for Social Policy and Development. Retrieved from: https://www.un.org/development/desa/disabilities/resources/handbook-for-parliamentarians-on-the-convention-on-the-rights-of-persons-with-disabilities/chapter-six-from-provisions-to-practice-implementing-the-convention-5.html

World Health Organization (WHO). (2011). World report on disability. Retrieved fromhttp://www.who.int/disabilities/world_report/2011/report.pdf

CHAPTER EIGHT

Wellness Matters: Supporting Health and Wellness for in Adulthood

Lynda Lahti Anderson, Sarah E. MapelLentz, Libby Hallas-Muchow, and Anab A. Gulaid

Advance Organizers

- People with intellectual and developmental disabilities (IDD) live about as long as people without IDD.
- Wellness is not the same thing as health but helps to promote health.
- There are many misperceptions and assumptions about people with IDD and their health and wellness.
- There are health disparities for people with IDD.
- Most people with IDD need support throughout their lives to ensure health and wellness.

Today the longevity of people with IDD is similar to that of people without IDD. Yet health disparities still exist. It is commonly assumed that people with IDD cannot or do not experience wellness or well-being. But everyone can adopt practices that improve their health and well-being. These practices can be supported through physical activity, nutrition, access to mental and emotional health services, social connections, and cultural practices that are incorporated into wellness routines. We use this chapter to highlight some of the factors that lead to health disparities, including misperceptions and assumptions about health and wellness for people with IDD. We also provide practical steps to support health and wellness for adults with IDD.

Wellness is more than the absence of disease. The National Wellness Institute (2017) defines it as "an active process through which people become more aware of, and make choices toward, a more successful existence." This model places importance on the interconnectedness of various aspects of wellness, including physical health, emotional and mental health, meaningful activities, social connections, ability to live according to one's values and beliefs, and opportunities for lifelong learning/creativity (see Figure 8.1). Adopting behaviors that support one's optimal health is an important part of successfully living and participating in the community. While optimal health differs somewhat from person to person, feeling our best allows us to take advantage of more opportunities to live the kind of life we choose. For example, if a person has a job in the community, they have the opportunity for social interactions and friendship. And of course, having income gives them choices about where to live, what food to eat, and what recreation to pursue. It also allows them, at least to some degree, to pay for health care.

Being able to choose what is important is a key part of wellness, but these kinds of choices have not historically been offered to people with IDD. We can support people with IDD to create their own sense of well-being by offering the supports they need to take part in activities that they enjoy and that are meaningful to them.

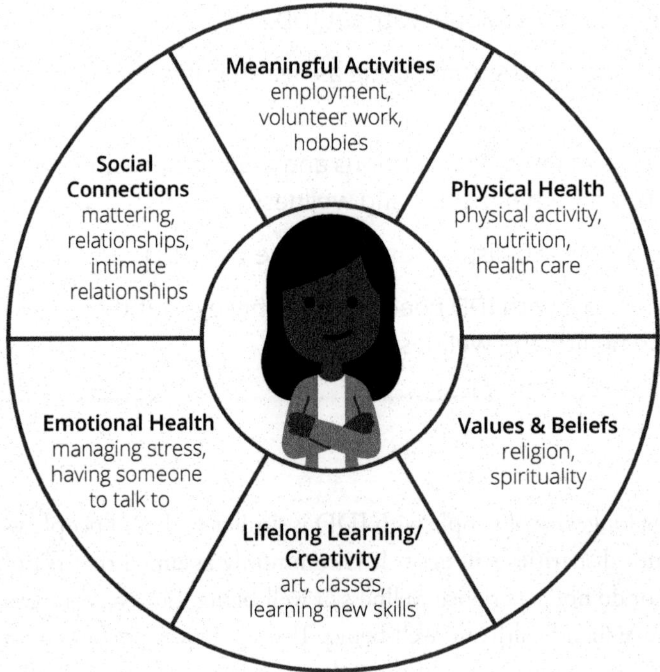

Figure 8.1. Wellness wheel.

Misperceptions and Assumptions

Everyone, regardless of disability, canadopt practices that improve their health and well-being, as there is no single definition of what it means to be well. Wellness has a number of dimensions, each of which influences the others to create an overall sense of well-being. For example, being physically active is beneficial for our bodies, but can also support mental and emotional well-being. Emotional and mental well-being can lead to fewer illnesses and less pain. Wellness is based on what is important to each individual in the various areas of life. One person may want to improve their sense of well-being by spending more time with friends and family. Another person's wellness goal may be increasing physical activity. Many activities address more than one area of wellness. For example, people with strong social connections tend to have better physical and mental health, while exercise plays an important role in maintaining not only physical but also mental health. The aim in wellness is to find a balance across all of the areas that give us a sense of well-being (Holt-Lundstad, Smith, Baker, Harris, & Stephenson, 2015; Stanton, Happell, & Reburn, 2014).

Because many people with IDD do not have full choice or control in their lives over housing, healthcare, employment, etc., others may make decisions about wellness on their behalf. This limits people with IDD in terms of their community participation in aspects of health and wellness. Misperceptions about people with IDD may also limit the resources made available to fully include individuals with IDD (Frey, et al, 2005 and van Schijndel-Speet, et al, 2014). People with IDD frequently have limited choice about their participation in community-centered activities. Rather, they may be provided "opportunities" dictated by others (e.g., parents, direct support professionals, teachers, social workers). In addition, the wellness-activity options they are offered are often in segregated or special disability-only programs (Bannermann, Sheldon, Sherman, & Harichick, 1990). Person-centered decision making allows room for self-determination in community participation and in being an active participant in one's own health.

Historical Views

Historically, understanding the health of people with disabilities used a medical model. In the medical model, healthcare focuses on finding a way to fix what is "wrong" with a person. Health promotion was directed at preventing disability, not at thinking about the health and wellness needs of people with disabilities. Institutions were originally developed to cure or treat people with IDD, which exemplifies the medical model, although their purpose changed over time to that of segregating and isolating people with IDD. In the best cases, institutions provided dental treatment and healthcare on site for residents, but this was often inadequate, leading to shorter life expectancies and high rates of infectious diseases, such as Hepatitis B. Little thought was given to promoting health and well-being for people with IDD.

In the 1960s, the disability rights movement changed the public's view of people with disabilities and their place in society. Society started moving toward a social model of disability. In this model, disability is rooted in the interaction between a person and their environment (Jette, 2006). The social model does not deny that a person has an impairment, but it sees disability as a failure of society to make adaptations for people's differences—which may relate to impairments or to other things. For example, adding curb cuts to sidewalks eliminates a barrier to people using mobility devices such as wheelchairs or walkers. But it also removes a barrier for parents pushing a stroller or for a person walking with a grocery cart. In the social model of disability, the focus of healthcare and wellness is on supporting all individuals to be as healthy as they can be.

In 2002, the Surgeon General of the United States published a report called *Closing the Gap: A National Blueprint to Improve the Health of People with Mental Retardation* (this was accepted terminology at the time). This report notes that people with IDD have more health problems and are less able to see doctors than people without IDD, due to financial and other reasons (U.S. Public Health Service, 2002). A follow-up report in 2005, *The Surgeon General's Call to Action to Improve the Health and Wellness of Persons with Disabilities*, noted that it is possible both to have a disability and to be healthy. The Surgeon General encouraged greater attention to improving access to and the quality of healthcare for people with IDD (USPHS 2005).

These reports identified failures to include people with IDD in public health programs (such as anti-smoking campaigns), lack of access to primary care, inadequate training of medical providers for serving people with IDD, and lack of access to prevention activities (e.g., inaccessible gym facilities) as reasons for poorer health outcomes (USPHS, 2002; USPHS, 2005). The past few decades have seen an increase in efforts to measure the health status of people with IDD, to create health promotions that encourage the adoption of healthy behaviors by people with IDD, and to improve training for healthcare professionals.

Current Controversies and Challenges

Health Disparities

Life expectancy for people with IDD has improved dramatically since the days when institutions were prevalent. Increased attention to the health needs of individuals with IDD means their lifespans are now similar to those of people without IDD. However, people with IDD still experience health disparities—differences in health outcomes across groups. People with IDD are more likely to develop common health conditions such as high cholesterol, high blood pressure, cardiovascular disease, obesity, and diabetes (Krahn, Hammond, & Turner, 2006; Reichard, Stolze, & Fox, 2011). Many of these conditions can be prevented or improved with lifestyle changes such as regular physical activity and a healthy diet.

Individuals with IDD often rely on Medicaid to access dental care. Some state Medicaid programs provide no or insufficient coverage for dental care, and it can be difficult to find a dentist willing to provide care at reduced rates. Difficulty finding proper dental care means that people with IDD are more likely to have periodontal disease, caries, and related dental problems such as decay, missing molars, and dental bridges or artificial teeth (Anders & Davis, 2010; Morgan et al., 2012).

Environmental and Community Barriers

People with IDD encounter barriers to health and wellness because of their environment, ideas others might have about them, and their own knowledge and beliefs about health and wellness. Some individuals with IDD have not had experiences or learning opportunities that support their ability to make decisions about their personal health and wellness (Jobling, 2001). Perhaps they have not had the chance to learn how the body works or to gain the skill of planning a well-balanced meal. Becoming able to make healthy lifestyle choices independently also requires opportunities to practice and further develop health-promoting behaviors. Often, people with IDD are "cared for" rather than empowered and supported to make decisions about their health. Self-determination and health self-advocacy skills are important parts of health and wellness (Shogren, Wehmeyer, Reese, & O'Hara, 2006).

Adults with IDD often have limited financial resources and may live in neighborhoods with fewer resources (Emerson, 2007). It has been shown that living in poorer neighborhoods negatively affects health (Diez Roux & Mair, 2010). These neighborhoods may be "food deserts" with little access to healthy food and may have few safe areas and green spaces for recreational activities. People living in neighborhoods with limited resources have less access to key components of a healthy lifestyle (Jennings, 2015).

Other challenges to health and wellness include community resources that are not accessible, or that do not have staff trained to support people with IDD. For example, many community fitness centers lack accessible fitness equipment. Community programs often do not consider universal design and do not create communication materials that are understandable to people across a wide range of abilities.

System Barriers

Finally, system-level challenges include both provider-patient interactions and policies that create barriers to health and wellness for people with IDD. A high percentage of people with IDD use Medicare and Medicaid for healthcare, both of which have limited reimbursement for healthy lifestyle interventions (Ervin, 2016). Preventive care has proven to be an effective strategy to improve health and well-being, but people with IDD have been largely left out of such initiatives and promotions. Healthcare providers and educators may not see people with IDD as recipients of these important messages; perhaps they assume that other providers or people's families are taking care of them in this regard. Much can be done to improve healthcare messaging so it can be accessed and utilized by people of all abilities.

In addition, healthcare providers are traditionally not trained in how to work with people with IDD (Anderson et al., 2013), and little attention is paid to preventive measures for people with IDD, such as mammograms and other health screenings provided to the general population. People with IDD and their families often report that when they go to a healthcare provider, their disability becomes the focus of the visit and symptoms may be blamed on the disability, even if they are unrelated. This is called "diagnostic overshadowing."

Individuals with IDD experience multiple systemic challenges to access to preventive health care and wellness promotion that can affect long-term health outcomes (Ervin, Hennen, Merrick, & Morad, 2014). It is important for healthcare professionals to be attuned to some of the unique and common needs of people with IDD. In addition, including people with IDD in the conversations that take place at their appointments concerning their own health and well-being is essential so they can be actively involved in decisions and choices that affect them.

Life Course Expectations and Transitions

The life course perspective considers the interconnectedness of all facets of life, and the impact that change or stagnation in one area of life has on other areas. It examines how genetic predispositions, in addition to external factors, affect health and wellness for individuals across the lifespan. External factors include where a person lives, what resources they have access to, and how they spend their time. Regular, age-appropriate health-monitoring activities such as well child checkups, vaccinations, prevention-care checkups (including dental care), and other medical screenings are essential across the lifespan. Yet, it is also important to recognize that needs change based on age, environmental factors, and individual support needs, so it is important to revisit health and well-being activities and supports often. For example, mental health supports may be needed during a stressful transition time, physical therapy must be available after an injury, and more regular lab tests may be needed to monitor medication levels. Other factors that support health and wellness across the lifespan are social inclusion, access to education and/or employment, opportunities for physical activity, safe living environments, and access to basic needs (food, clothing, shelter).

Other types of needs related to health and wellness also change across the lifespan. For example, during the transition from childhood to adulthood, support types change. Children have natural supports in place through school. Once they transition out of school (age 21 at the latest), the school supports disappear. Losing these also results in diminished opportunity for social interaction (both with other children and with adults who are not family members), inclusion in and sense of community, learning, physical activity, and possibly nutrition (if they go from consuming meals prepared by the school to making their own at home). All of these changes affect health and wellness.

Overall, when a person with IDD and their allies engage in life-planning activities, it is important to identify the interconnectedness of all parts of life, and to consider both successes and challenges. Building on an individual's strengths and establishing supports for areas of challenge will ensure the best possible chance for a healthy and happy life.

Practical Suggestions and Interventions

Practical interventions can take place at many levels to support health and wellness for people with IDD. Understanding the various aspects of well-being and their interconnectedness is important in achieving health and wellness goals. All levels of support must take this interconnectedness into account when supporting people with IDD. Small changes done consistently can make a difference in a person's overall health. Promoting activities that support health and wellness should be done with inclusion and community integration in mind.

Introducing Health and Wellness Concepts

Many people with IDD have not been expected to be active healthcare consumers or informed about their health and wellness options. However, people with IDD should be included in information sharing/gathering and supported to make decisions about their health whenever possible. Important aspects of health self-advocacy include:

- communicating about health needs with healthcare professionals and others
- asking questions about health
- being aware of symptoms or changes
- following healthcare orders (such as taking medications)
- practicing self-care through nutrition and physical activity

Families and other caregivers can support these practices by role-modeling, teaching related skills, and providing supports when needed.

Supporting individual wellness practices. Persons with IDD may need intentional support to identify health and wellness goals by exploring activities in each of the areas of wellness. Families and direct support professionals (DSPs) can support people with IDD by helping to identify health-promoting activities and facilities in the community. Examples include city parks and community education systems, which provide opportunities for recreation as well as for social interaction through a wide range of classes: arts, cooking, sports, reading, and more. Many communities also offer recreational opportunities through organizations like the "Y" and other community recreation centers. Additionally, state departments of natural resources offer access to public lands, as well as free or low-cost classes to learn outdoor skills or to learn about nature. When supporting an individual's wellness practices, it is important to offer activities that are fully integrated. While many special or segregated programs exist for people with disabilities, participation in settings that include people without disabilities will lead to fuller integration in the community.

Supporting physical activity. Regular physical activity is one of the most important things we can do for our health. Physical activity should be enjoyable, because people are more likely to do something they enjoy. Helping people choose physical activities includes taking into account physical concerns such as balance or the need for adaptive equipment. Physical activities that also include social opportunities, learning new skills, or sports competitions may encourage movement and exercise (Rimmer, 2016).

Often, supports for people with IDD have consisted of "doing for" rather than supporting an individual's participation in the activities of daily life. Professionals, families, and support staff may wrongly assume that people with significant disabilities cannot benefit from physical activities. However, engaging people in household tasks such as cleaning, walking the dog, or doing yard work, not only helps them increase their physical activity but also promotes their self-confidence, independence, and self-determination as they become better able to make decisions about their day-to-day lives. Being more physically active can be hard for anyone, regardless of disability, but it is equally important for all people for the sake of mobility, health, and well-being.

Supporting nutrition. Making healthful food choices can be challenging for anyone. People with IDD may have food-related sensitivities or intolerances or may have limited cooking skills. Nutritious food may be difficult to obtain because of limited access or financial constraints. While the media is full of messages about what makes a healthy diet, scientific evidence overwhelmingly points to fruits, vegetables, nuts, and seeds as closely related to better health. Families, DSPs, and other allies can support people with IDD in eating well by:

- teaching cost-effective ways to increase fruit and vegetable intake
- buying frozen fruits and vegetables, which are usually cheaper and just as nutritious as fresh (sometimes more so)
- buying in season
- visiting the local farmers' market
- preventing waste by storing food properly and only buying what you can eat
- growing your own food—even a few planters of herbs and vegetables on a patio

Another tip is to focus on vegetables such as carrots or cabbage that are usually inexpensive and still nutritious. And for people with limited cooking skills, simple ways to increase fruit and vegetable intake include adding fruit to cold cereal, adding spinach or tomatoes to scrambled eggs, putting vegetables on pizza (even adding them to frozen pizzas), eating a salad with a microwave dinner, and adding frozen vegetables to canned soup or pasta meals. The journey to eating a healthy, balanced diet is a challenge for many people, but nutrition plays a central role in preserving and promoting health.

Supporting Positive Emotions and Emotional Wellness

Positive emotions contribute to an individual's well-being. Upbeat mental states can improve physical health. Neuroscientists have found that positive emotions can trigger the part of the brain that has been linked to lowering stress hormones. Some simple practices that have been shown to improve emotional health include practicing gratitude (naming what you are thankful for) and volunteering.

Mindfulness can also support emotional and mental wellness, as well as physical health. *Mindfulness* means paying attention to our thoughts without judging them, and focusing on the present rather than the past or future. Some studies have shown that practicing mindfulness can help caregivers better support people with challenging behavior (Singh et al., 2014) and can help people with IDD reduce their instances of challenging behavior (Singh et al., 2011). Mindfulness can be taught using simple techniques such as focusing on breathing, or taking a walk and paying attention to sights and sounds. There are also smartphone apps and online videos available for learning mindfulness.

Supporting social connections. Social connections can reduce stress. See chapter 5 for more information on the importance of love, fun, and friendships. High levels of stress can contribute to heart disease, impair gut function, and harm the immune system (U.S. Department of Health and Human Services, 2017). The caring behaviors that are a part of healthy relationships encourage the body to release hormones that reduce stress (Ozbay et al., 2007). In relationships, both givers and receivers of social support benefit. Many people with IDD do not establish long-lasting relationships with people beyond immediate family and paid caregivers (Amado, Stancliffe, McCarron, & McCallion,2013). It is important to recognize that this lack of friendships can impact other areas of health. The cure for loneliness is not just increasing our social networks, but feeling that we matter to others. Promoting healthy relationships for the people you support is extremely important for their overall health. DSPs and others can be important allies in fostering healthy relationships. Friendships and other relationships can be initiated and maintained through a person's participation, with support as necessary, in activities such as volunteer work, inviting people over for dinner, attending faith events, and participating in self-advocacy organizations or other community groups.

Supporting spiritual wellness. Spirituality is more than a set of religious beliefs, but rather is a feeling of connection to something bigger than ourselves that gives us a sense of belonging (Gaventa & Carter, 2016; Center for Spirituality and Healing,

2017). These feelings can come from association with a religious institution such as a church, temple, mosque, or synagogue. Other people find this sense of connectedness through music, art, the natural world, books, or story-telling. Supporting wellness for persons with IDD includes supporting their interests in connecting with religious communities or finding other means of meeting the human need for a sense of belonging and connectedness to something greater than oneself.

Culture's role in wellness. A number of federal policies now include language around services and supports being delivered in ways that are appropriate for an individual's culture and language (e.g., Olmstead, 1999; IDEA, 2004). These regulations and standards were put in place to ensure that diverse and underrepresented populations with IDD or other disabilities have access to health and wellness resources in a culturally and linguistically appropriate manner. In addition, the National Standards on Culturally and Linguistically Appropriate Services (CLAS) outline professional standards to ensure that services are provided in a way that is culturally and linguistically sensitive. Supporting the role of culture in people's lives includes providing them with access to interpretation and translation services, opportunities to socialize with people of their culture, and the chance to celebrate cultural rituals, customs, and routines. Cultural traditions might include eating certain foods, sharing a home-cooked meal, not eating certain foods, or fasting for a period of time as a religious practice. Being in tune and engaging with one's culture may help one examine the spiritual aspects of wellness, as well as provide opportunities for social participation.

Health self-advocacy. Because wellness is an active process, advocating for one's needs is a key factor in overall well-being. Teaching health self-advocacy skills is one way to promote wellness among people with IDD. Health self-advocacy has two main elements (Feldman et al., 2012): The first is health knowledge. This includes a basic understanding of how one's body works and what one can do to keep it as healthy as possible. The second part involves understanding one's rights and responsibilities, and the importance of respect for others (Feldman et al., 2012). Rights include expecting that healthcare providers will explain terms in plain language. Responsibilities include self-care; for example, a person with hypertension might be asked to regularly check their blood pressure. Finally, health self-advocacy also means respect for others—for example, washing hands before cooking, or not going to work when ill. Expecting people with IDD to be active in their own health and well-being is important. Providing opportunities for them to make choices, explaining ideas in plain language, and seeking input from the individual are all important aspects of supporting health self-advocacy.

Health passports. A Health Passport is a tool that people with IDD and their supporters can prepare to help the individual share information with healthcare and social service providers. Health Passports contain information about how to support an individual with IDD (Perkins, 2011). Health Passports are not medical records, but they include information providers need to know, such as an individual's health conditions;

how they communicate; how a provider would know if the person is in pain; how to position or transfer them if they live with limited mobility; any sensitivities they have to light, touch, or sound; or supports needed for daily activities (Brodrick, Lewis, Worth, & Marland, 2011; Perkins, 2011). Health Passports can include information about a person's cultural or religious needs and beliefs that might affect how care is provided, as well as information related to maintaining health, such as about screenings or lifestyle choices.

Personal Illustration: Emily Prico

Emily Prico is a young, athletic woman who loves to exercise. She became interested in adopting a healthier lifestyle after participating in Partnerships in Wellness, a holistic health promotion curriculum from the Research and Training Center on Community Living at the University of Minnesota that addresses the unique learning needs of adults with IDD.

Emily has a routine she follows to stay in shape. "I'm a member at a fitness club, and there I enjoy the elliptical, and the bike, and the treadmill. I haven't really done a lot of weight training yet, but I'm starting to." Emily tries to go to her gym a couple of times a week, when staff can provide transportation. Fortunately, she has an exercise bike in her apartment building that she uses regularly. She also plays floor hockey and softball.

Beyond the gratification she gets from physical fitness, Emily attributes much of her overall well-being to her close connections with family and friends. "I have a couple girls in this building that I'm really close to." Emily and her friends attend sporting events and book club meetings together. They also participate in walking groups started by Emily's mother. "And then my friend, Jeanne, she's another resident in this building. She's another really good friend." Emily's family lives nearby and visits her frequently. "My family's always been supportive," said Emily. "They keep close watch on what I'm doing."

Even with frequent exercise, Emily feels she needs to do more to stay healthy. "I just want to try to get my weight under control and feel better," said Emily. Her diet used to include fast food and processed snacks. Now she eats a lot of fruits, vegetables, and whole grains. And she recently gave up drinking soda. "I'm trying to drink more water." She's also saving money by no longer frequenting fast-food restaurants. "I recently gave up eating out because I know that's another not-so-healthy choice."

Emily learned from the wellness curriculum that processed sugar is not healthy and is trying to consume only natural sugar. "For a number of years, I've had a really big sweet tooth, so I'm probably going to start eating dark chocolate and fruit at night instead of milk chocolate and brownies and all that because I know that processed sugar is not good for you." But will she ever give up chocolate? "No, that probably won't ever happen," laughed Emily, "because chocolate's a big thing in my life."

It's one thing to adopt a routine of exercise and healthy eating, and quite another to stick with it over time. Emily's supervisor, along with her friends and family, provide encouragement. "He told me that you have to stay consistent in order to stay healthy." She now does more grocery shopping and prepares meals at home. "I like to make new recipes. I enjoy making chili and a lot of pasta dishes, and certain stuff like that."

One Wednesday each month, Emily and friends in her apartment building get together for a meal. "One of the residents' mothers comes in and teaches us how to make a meal and teaches about healthy eating and stuff," said Emily. They all enjoy a good meal together while developing new skills and habits that promote their health and well-being. So far, her exercise and food choices have made a noticeable difference in her quality of life. "I like how it makes my body feel. And I think it really relieves a lot of stress, and it just makes me feel good."

Conclusion

Health and wellness are not simply the absence of disease. Both individual and environmental factors support well-being physically, emotionally, spiritually, and socially. Wellness involves the interplay and balance among multiple aspects of a person's life, including social connections, participation in meaningful activities, physical health, values and beliefs, lifelong learning or creativity, and emotional health. A key component to attainment of a high level of wellness is the opportunity to make personal choices about what to do in one's life. Frequently, people have misconceptions that those with IDD are unable to make personal choices about what is important to them. By focusing on life course expectations and transitions, and acknowledging the interconnectedness of all parts of life, people with IDD and their supporters can develop a long-term plan that builds on their strengths and personal choices to promote successful community living and overall well-being.

People who work with people with IDD can use the practical suggestions and interventions included in this chapter—support of health and wellness goals, physical activity and nutrition, positive emotional health, individualized attention to culture and language, self-advocacy, and Health Passports—to increase the frequency with which individuals with IDD exercise personal choice to increase their own wellness.

Discussion Questions

- Wellness is not just healthy eating and exercise. How do you foster and cultivate wellness beyond physical activity and nutrition?
- What policies, procedures, and resources are in place that enable individuals supported and staff to make better lifestyle choices? Does your organization have a culture of wellness?
- How can you support individuals with IDD to have greater control over their care and to be active participants in managing their health?
- How are resources allocated at the society, agency, and family levels to promote health and wellness? What could be done differently?
- How can you support individuals with IDD to engage/participate in wellness activities in their communities? How do you ensure access to community resources?

Resources

- Health Passports: A communication tool to use with health care providers. http://flfcic.fmhi.usf.edu/docs/FCIC_Health_Passport_Form_Typeable_English.pdf
- Impact: Feature Issue on Supporting Wellness for Adults with Intellectual and Developmental Disabilities. https://ici.umn.edu/products/impact/291/291.pdf
- National Center on Health, Physical Activity, and Disability: Resource for information on physical activity, health promotion, and disability. http://www.nchpad.org/
- Partnerships in Wellness: A Health and Wellness curriculum for people with IDD. https://sites.google.com/umn.edu/piw

References

Amado, A. N., Stancliffe, R. J., McCarron, M., & McCallion, P. (2013). Social inclusion and community participation of individuals with intellectual/developmental disabilities. *Intellectual and Developmental Disabilities, 51*(5), 360–375. https://doi.org/10.1352/1934-9556-51.5.360 https://doi.org/10.1352/1934-9556-51.5.360

Anders, P. L. & Davis, E. L. (2010). Oral health of patients with intellectual disabilities: A systematic review. *Special Care in Dentistry, 30*(3), 110–117. https://doi.org/10.1111/j.1754-4505.2010.00136.x

Anderson, L., Humphries, K., McDermott, S., Marks, B., Sisarak, J., & Larson, S. (2013). The state of the science of health and wellness for adults with intellectual and developmental disabilities. *Intellectual & Developmental Disabilities. 51*(5), 385–398. doi:10.1352/1934-9556-51.5.385.

Bannerman, D. J., Sheldon, J. B., Sherman, J. A., & Harchik, A. E. (1990). Balancing the right to habilitation with the right to personal liberties: The right of people with developmental disabilities to eat too many doughnuts and take a nap. *Journal of Applied Behavior Analysis, 23*(1), 78–79. doi:10.1901/jaba.1990.23-79

Brodrick, D., Lewis, D., Worth, A., & Marland, A. (2011). One-page patient passport for people with learning disabilities. *Nursing Standard, 25*(47), 35–40. doi:10.7748/ns.25.47.35.s49

Center for Spirituality and Healing (2017). What is spirituality? Retrieved from: https://www.takingcharge.csh.umn.edu/what-spirituality.

Diez Roux, A. V., & Mair, C. (2010). Neighborhoods and health. *Annals of the New York Academy of Sciences, 1186*(1), 125–145. https://doi.org/10.1111/j.1749-6632.2009.05333.x

Emerson, E. (2007). Poverty and people with intellectual disabilities. *Mental Retardation and Developmental Disabilities Research Reviews. 13*(2), 107–113. https://doi.org/10.1002/mrdd.20144

Ervin, D. (2016). In Rubin, L., Merrick, J., Greydanus, D., & Patel, D. (Eds.), *Health Care people with intellectual and developmental disabilities across the lifespan* (pp. 177–181). Switzerland: Springer.

Ervin, D., Hennen, B., Merrick, J., & Morad, M. (2014). Health care for persons with intellectual and developmental disabilities in the community. *Frontiers in Public Health. 2*(83), 1–7. https://doi.org/10.3389/fpubh.2014.00083

Feldman, M. A., Owen, F., Andrews, A., Hamelin, J., Barber, R., & Griffiths, D. (2012). Health self-advocacy training for persons with intellectual disabilities. *Journal of Intellectual Disability Research, 56*(11), 1110–1121. https://doi.org/10.1111/j.1365-2788.2012.01626.x

Frey, G. C., Buchanan, A. M., & Rosser Sandt, D. D. (2005). "I'd rather watch TV": An examination of physical activity in adults with mental retardation. Mental retardation, 43(4), 241–254.

Gaventa, B., & Carter, E. W. (2016). Flourishing and spirituality: Healing and wholeness without perfection. *Impact, 29*(1), 6–7. Minneapolis: Institute on Community Integration, University of Minnesota.

Holt-Lunstad, J., Smith, T. B., Baker, M., Harris, T., & Stephenson, D. (2015). Loneliness and social isolation as risk factors for mortality: Ameta-analytic review. *Perspectives on Psychological Science, 10*(2), 227–237.

Individuals with Disabilities Education Act, 20 U.S.C. § 1400 (2004)

Jennings V., & Gaither C. J. (2015). Approaching environmental health disparities and green spaces: An ecosystem services perspective. *International Journal of Environmental Research & Public Health. 12*(2),1952–1968. https://doi.org/10.3390/ijerph120201952

Jette, A. M. (2006). Toward a common language for function, disability, and health. *Physical Therapy, 86*(5), 726–734. https://doi.org/10.1093/ptj/86.5.726

Jobling, A. (2001). Beyond sex and cooking: Health education for individuals with intellectual disability. *Mental Retardation, 39*(4), 310–321.

Krahn, G. L., Hammond, L., & Turner, A. (2006). A cascade of disparities: Health and health care access for people with intellectual disabilities. *Developmental Disabilities Research Reviews, 12*(1), 70–82.

Morgan, J. P., Minihan, P. M., Stark, P. C., Finkelman, M. D., Yantsides, K. E., Park, A., Nobles, C. J., Tao, W., & Must, A. (2012). The oral health status of 4,732 adults with intellectual and developmental disabilities. *The Journal of the American Dental Association, 143*(8), 838–846. https://doi.org/10.14219/jada.archive.2012.0288

National Standards on Culturally and Linguistically Appropriate Services (CLAS) Office of Minority Health. The National CLAS Standards. Retrieved from https://minorityhealth.hhs.gov/omh/browse.aspx?lvl=2&lvlid=53.

National Wellness Institute. (2017). About wellness. Retrieved from http://www.nationalwellness.org/?page=AboutWellness.

Olmstead v. L.C., 527 U.S. 581; 119 S.Ct. 2176 Individuals with Disabilities Education Act, 20 U.S.C. § 1400 (2004)

Ozbay, F., Johnson, D. C., Dimoulas, E., Morgan III, C. A., Charney, D., & Southwick, S. (2007). Social support and resilience to stress: from neurobiology to clinical practice. *Psychiatry (Edgmont), 4*(5), 35.

Perkins, E. A. (2011). My Health Passport for Hospital/Clinic Visits. Florida Center for Inclusive Communities. http://flfcic.fmhi.usf.edu/docs/FCIC_Health_Passport_Form_Typeable_English.pdf

Reichard, A., Stolzle, H., & Fox, M. H. (2011). Health disparities among adults with physical disabilities or cognitive limitations compared to individuals with no disabilities in the United States. *Disability and Health Journal, 4*(2), 59–67. https://doi.org/10.1016/j.dhjo.2010.05.003

Rimmer, J. H. (2016). SELECT a lifetime of physical activity. *Impact, 29*(1), 6–7. Minneapolis: Institute on Community Integration, University of Minnesota.

Rimmer, J. H., Braddock, D., Fujiura, G. (1993) Prevalence of obesity in adults with MR: Implications for health promotion and disease prevention. *Mental Retardation*. 31: 105–10.

Shogren, K. A., Wehmeyer, M. L., Reese, R. M., & O'Hara, D. (2006). Promoting self-determination in health and medical care: A critical component of addressing health disparities in people with intellectual disabilities. *Journal of Policy and Practice in Intellectual Disabilities, 3*(2), 105–113. https://doi.org/10.1111/j.1741-1130.2006.00061.x

Singh, N. N., Lancioni, G. E., Manikam, R., Winton, A. S. W., Singh, A. N. A., Singh, J., Singh, A. D. A. (2011). A mindfulness-based strategy for self-management of aggressive behavior in adolescents with autism. *Research in Autism Spectrum Disorders 5*(3), 1153–1158.

Singh, N. N., Lancioni, G. E., Winton, A. S., Karazsia, B. T., Myers, R. E., Latham, L. L., & Singh, J. (2014). Mindfulness-based positive behavior support (MBPBS) for mothers of adolescents with autism spectrum disorder: Effects on adolescents' behavior and parental stress. *Mindfulness,* 5(6), 646–657.

Singh, N. N., Lancioni, G. E., Winton, A. S., Singh, A. N., Singh, J., & Singh, A. D. (2011). Effects of a mindfulness-based smoking cessation program for an adult with mild intellectual disability. *Research in Developmental Disabilities*, *32*(3), 1180–1185

Stanton, R., Happell, B., & Reaburn, P. (2014). The mental health benefits of regular physical activity, and its role in preveting future depressive illness. *Nursing: Research and Reviews, 4,* 45–53. https://doi.org/10.2147/NRR.S41956

U.S. Department of Health and Human Services. Stress and your health. Retrieved from http://www.womenshealth.gov/publications/our-publications/fact-sheet/stress-your-health.html.

U.S. Public Health Service (USPHS). (2002). Closing the gap: A national blueprint for improving the health of individuals with mental retardation. *Report of the Surgeon General's Conference on Health Disparities and Mental Retardation.* U.S. Department of Health and Human Services, Office of the Surgeon General. Washington, DC: HHS, Office of the Surgeon General.

U.S. Public Health Service (USPHS). (2005). *The Surgeon General's call to action to improve the health and wellness of people with disabilities.* U.S. Department of Health and Human Services, Office of the Surgeon General; Washington, DC.

van Schijndel-Speet, M., Evenhuis, H. M., van Wijck, R., van Empelen, P., & Echteld, M. A. (2014). Facilitators and barriers to physical activity as perceived by older adults with intellectual disability. *Mental Retardation, 52*(3), 175–186.

CHAPTER NINE

Planning for Healthy and Engaged Aging

Julie E.D. Kramme, Roger Stancliffe, Lynda Lahti Anderson, and Merrie Haskins

Advance Organizers

- People with IDD are living longer than at any other time in history.
- Healthy aging includes social, emotional, and environmental factors.
- Active aging can increase quality of life in later years.
- Transitioning into older adulthood and retirement represents a significant life shift.
- People with IDD can benefit from end-of-life planning and supportive discussions about wellbeing, aging, and death.

This chapter explores the physical, mental, and social components of healthy and engaged aging. We describe an active-aging framework that emphasizes quality of life for people with IDD, and we emphasize person-centered practices that promote autonomy and independence as people age.

The chapter also discusses current controversies and challenges to healthy and engaged aging. We identify promising suggestions and interventions known to address these challenges, and we go into detail concerning education, access to health and wellness activities, environmental modifications to promote independence and community inclusion, the importance of maintaining social activities when transitioning from work to retirement, and resources that allow a person to plan for and learn about end-of-life issues. Starting early to plan for healthy aging is important in maximizing a person's quality of life and community inclusion.

Due to advances in medicine, public health, technology, education, and access to community living, more adults with IDD can expect to live into old age. The average life expectancy for a person with IDD is 66 years (Coppus, 2013). Individuals with IDD who have fewer support needs have a life expectancy comparable to that of the general population in the United States. This is decades longer than people with IDD tended to live in recent generations (Stanford Center on Longevity, 2010).

New opportunities and challenges arise as people with IDD live into old age. In this chapter, we provide an overview of the experiences of people with IDD who are aging into retirement and dealing with end-of-life issues. We discuss aging broadly, rather than associating it with a particular age, such as 60 or 75, as some individuals with developmental disabilities may experience premature symptoms of aging. We propose that, rather than emphasizing the absence of disease or disability as a measure of healthy aging, healthy aging and end of life are instead characterized by physical, social, and mental well-being (World Health Organization, 2002; 2000). This definition coincides with a person-centered perspective that emphasizes someone's strengths, needs, and personal goals as a basis for identifying services and supports.

Physical, social, and mental well-being are central to "active aging," a concept proposed by the World Health Organization (2002). "Active aging is the process of optimizing opportunities for health participation and security in order to enhance quality of life as people age" (WHO, 2002, p. 12). This definition aligns with many of the values proposed in chapter 1, "Community Living and Participation: A Comprehensive Framework," such as person-centered practices and community inclusion. Active aging aims to support a high quality of life. This includes the person's perception of his or her life in the context of their culture and values. Goals, concerns, and expectations are also taken into account. Their autonomy and independence are weighty components in influencing quality of life. Self-determination in day-to-day decision making and preserving the right to perform activities of daily living for themselves are seen as important ways that people maintain wellness and combat loss of function as they age.

However, aging as experienced by people with IDD is often quite different from this. People with IDD are prone to potentially avoidable conditions that are associated with less healthy aging, such as obesity and lack of mobility. They often have poorer health and earlier onset of conditions related to aging, compared to aging people in the general population (Bittles, Petterson, Sullivan, Hussain et al., 2002). In fact, many people with IDD do not have a clear understanding of aging or of themselves as growing older (Buys et al., 2008; Cordes & Howard, 2005).

Education and planning may be important components of healthy aging for people with IDD. Person-centered planning provides opportunities for people to experience autonomy and independence throughout the life course and end of life. Importantly, when asked in a recent research study, aging people with IDD said they wanted more out of life, not less, as they aged (Buys et al., 2008). Sometimes this prompts creative thinking and problem solving, as demonstrated in "Robert's Story" on page 199.

This chapter summarizes several major challenges often experienced by aging people with IDD. It presents practical suggestions and interventions related to aging and end of life. Typically, end-of-life care focuses on the last months of a person's life when they have conditions that are progressive and irreversible, but planning for end of life can begin much earlier. Processes that incorporate planning for a person's end-of-life desires are discussed in the sections that follow.

Current Controversies and Challenges

Aging and Health-Related Changes

Most people with IDD experience aging in ways that are similar to those of people without IDD. Across the population, people experience age-related health conditions, but they can maintain good health and an active lifestyle as they age. Important components of maintaining health and wellness include an active lifestyle and eating a nutritious diet. Many people with IDD require supports in doing these things. Lack of knowledgeable and committed support staff may be a barrier to these healthy activities. However, many of the ways to support these practices are similar to methods support staff likely use for their own self-care.

Screenings and regular checks by healthcare providers are intended to identify developing conditions early. Sometimes a health concern related to aging can be overlooked because it is blamed on the person's disability or age rather than the root cause. This bias is called "diagnostic overshadowing." Diagnostic overshadowing can become the source of further health complications. For example, urinary tract infections in the elderly can cause symptoms that resemble dementia, such as confusion. Misattribution of these symptoms can cause the untreated urinary tract infection to get worse.

Some conditions may leave people with IDD at risk of aging earlier than people without the disability. For example, more than half of people with Down Syndrome develop dementia, and many do so at a much younger age than individuals without Down Syndrome (Zigman & Lott, 2007). Cerebral Palsy or other conditions affecting nerves and muscles may increase pain, bone and muscle loss, and the risk of arthritis, which can cause mobility issues (Strax, Luciano, Dunn, & Quevedo, 2010). Treatments for certain conditions may also result in complications as people age. For example, bone loss (osteoporosis) may occur at a younger age as a result of taking certain medications for seizure disorders or depression (Strax et al., 2010). Knowing how conditions often progress, taking into account risk factors associated with particular treatments, and listening to the ways people communicate their symptoms are important factors in supporting someone in planning for healthy and engaged aging.

What's more, continued research on aging with IDD is important because in some cases, such as with autism spectrum disorder, little is known about how the condition progresses in older age (Ladinski-Muaetova, Perry, Baron, & Povery, 2011; Perkins & Berkman, 2012).

Living Arrangements and Family Relationships

Many people with IDD receive support from family members, such as parents or siblings. For example, people with IDD are more likely to live in a family member's home than in any other setting (Larson et al., 2017). When this is the case, the aging of family members can greatly impact living and support arrangements for a person with IDD. Many aging family members experience anxiety about what will happen to their loved one if they are no longer able to provide support. Death of a family member may make it necessary for the person with IDD to move to a new home or receive support from other sources. This is an important reason why person-centered planning must articulate long-term wishes and needs. Documentation of a person's preferences before a crisis supports their involvement so that decision making can reflect their wishes. It can also be beneficial to decouple the shift in care from a death so that the person does not experience grief from losing a family member at the same time that a transition is made to a new support routine.

Employment and Retirement

In comparison to the general population, people with IDD are much less likely to participate in paid employment. For those who do work, employment can be an important tie to friendships and feelings of accomplishment. For these and other reasons, people may choose to work into old age. On the other hand, like anyone else, they may want to retire.

Retirement is defined as the permanent withdrawal from paid work. Retirement can happen at any age, but is often associated with older workers. Workers can retire for many reasons. It is unclear which factors are most likely to lead to retirement for people with IDD, but transitioning from employment can be an intentional process that integrates a person's goals and desires. Unfortunately, this is often not everyone's experience. Many people with IDD see retirement in a negative way, as it involves loss of meaningful activity (work) and social connections at their place of employment. People may fear they will be socially isolated and have too little to do in retirement. Few have a clear idea of available activities and social opportunities in retirement. Sometimes, transitioning from work is necessitated by circumstances such as a health or family crisis rather than through planning or self-determination. The barriers that keep a person from continuing to work as they desire may also keep them from being as active in retirement as they would like.

Given the low participation of people with IDD in the workforce, retirement has received little attention to date from researchers, service providers, or policy makers.

However, as people live longer, many can expect to spend years in retirement. Available research indicates that older workers with IDD are not being supported to make self-determined choices about retirement, if they are even aware that retirement is an option (McDermott & Edwards, 2012). Just as people in the general population plan for and make choices about retirement, it is important to consider the extent to which people with IDD are given the opportunity to do the same.

Transportation

Lack of transportation can be an enormous barrier to community access for people with disabilities across the lifespan. People with IDD are often dependent on public transportation supports, but these may be restricted by funding or accessibility. For example, options may be limited in rural areas or across county lines, as well as to particular times or days. They may ultimately be inaccessible because of mobility challenges. If a person has a driver's license, they may be forced to give it up due to health-related degenerative issues as they age. Supporting an individual in finding accessible transportation can be an important strategy to facilitate their community inclusion, especially in retirement.

Societal Assumptions Surrounding Health, Death, Dying, and Grief

There are sometimes discrepancies between someone's experiences with disabilities and societal assumptions about their capacities and preferences. Sometimes people providing support assume that people with IDD lack the awareness to make health-care decisions for themselves (Gill, 2000). This can complicate decision-making processes when the biases of others are imposed on the person with IDD. However, the majority of adults with mild support needs due to intellectual disability and nearly half of those with moderate support needs as a result of intellectual disability are able to make medical treatment decisions when given information in an accessible form (Cea & Fisher, 2003). Access to information helps people with IDD and those who assist them to make decisions in ways that balance their self-determination with safety.

End-of-life care and participation in memorials and remembrances for others who have died can provide opportunities for self-determination about one's own end of life. Unfortunately, many opportunities are missed because of well-intentioned protection of people with IDD due to concerns about upsetting the person and/or about their capacity to understand what's happening (Kirkendall, Linton, & Farris, 2017; McKenzie, Mirfin-Veitch, Conder, & Bradford, 2017; Wiese, Stancliffe, Read, Jeltes, & Clayton, 2015). It is essential to recognize that almost all people with IDD, like people without IDD, will encounter deaths of family members and friends. Yet, in the spirit of protection, people may not even tell individuals with IDD about the death of someone important to them, and may exclude them from the funeral and other rituals (Wiese et al., 2015). Sadly, such practices are likely to make matters worse.

Alternative approaches to dying and death that help the person with IDD understand and participate are set out in the "Practical Suggestions and Interventions" section at the end of this chapter.

Policy Issues Related to Aging

The Older Americans Act (OAA) was first enacted in 1965, and most recently authorized in 2016 (PL 114-144). The services and protections in the act are for any person age 65 or older, and are intended to help people maintain independence in their home as long as possible. The OAA provides funding through state and local Agencies on Aging. These agencies provide a number of services, such as case management, senior centers, transportation, in-home services (e.g., chore services), nutrition programs (e.g., Meals on Wheels), caregiver support services, and health promotion. While people with IDD are eligible to receive OAA services once they reach 65, limited funding often means long waiting lists. Some local Agencies on Aging have made efforts to also address the needs of aging caregivers of people with IDD, but there has been limited attention to building capacity to better serve the needs of people with long-term disabilities such as IDD (Putnam, 2017).

Home and Community Based Services (HCBS), which include Medicaid waivers (See Chapter 3) were originally authorized in 1981. Since then, all 50 states and the District of Columbia have developed waivers to provide supports and services to individuals with IDD living in the community. In addition, states use waivered services meant to support qualified people age 65 and older to receive long-term services and supports that prevent nursing home placements (Smith et al., 2000). Eligibility and benefits provided through the waivers are determined by each state, therefore services and availability can vary grately. IDD-specific waivers often cover different supports and services than do waivers for the elderly (e.g., the developmental disabilities [DD] waiver may cover employment services while the waiver for the elderly may cover adult day care). Some states also have or are moving towards a universal waiver to serve the support needs of various HCBS population. For some people receiving a DD waiver, it is possible that a waiver for the elderly provides a better match for their support needs when they turn 65. However, limits in waiver availability within a state or lack of service providers may be a barrier to accessing services.

Life Course Expectations

Planning for healthy and engaged aging should be person centered, incorporate significant ongoing relationships, and be revisited often. This chapter emphasizes an active-aging framework. Maintaining physical, social, and mental well-being should be emphasized across the lifespan, especially into older age, to affirm people's right to "participate in society according to their needs, desires, and capacities, while providing them with adequate protection, security and care when they require assistance" (WHO, 2002, p. 12). The aim of well-being in each dimension is to uphold a person's individual perception of their quality of life.

Two key goals are central in providing services and supports for aging people with IDD:

- Autonomy: "the perceived ability to control, cope with and make personal decisions about how one lives on a day-to-day basis, according to one's own rules and preferences" (WHO, 2002, p. 13), and
- Independence: related to the level of supports a person utilizes to perform activities of daily living, including cultural and individual preferences.

Person-centered planning provides the opportunity to document a person's goals, desires, and wishes, and to align those with necessary supports. This planning process should include conversations about employment, retirement, and end-of-life preferences. Important to planning at end of life, living wills can be created to include details about a person's preferences. Planning also presents the opportunity to discuss the person's preferences regarding advance healthcare directives. Established according to the regulations of the state in which a person lives, it documents their preferences for medical interventions and for who is given authority to make healthcare decisions for the person if they are unable to do so on their own. Planning conversations should be revisited and updated from time to time, especially with any major life incidents, such as injury or loss of a major support giver. This ensures that the person's plan continues to accurately represent their goals and wishes.

Practical Suggestions and Interventions

This section presents information on practical steps that can be taken to support a person with IDD who is aging. A number of useful resources are mentioned, many of which have been designed specifically for use by people with IDD and those who provide them support.

Active Aging and Aging in Place

Most people with IDD age much like people without IDD. Across the population, aging need not be viewed as a time to quit participating in activities, employment, or volunteer work simply because one is getting older. Maintaining an active lifestyle that includes regular physical activity, meaningful activities, and social connections is important for the sake of well-being as people age (Bauman, Merom, Bull, Buchner, & Fiatarone Singh, 2016; Rowe & Kahn, 1987). People may participate less or differently, according to their needs and desires, but aging alone need not change a person's routine.

People with IDD may rely on others for support, such as when they live in the home of a family member. Sometimes changing circumstances make different supports necessary. Aging in place is a movement with the aim of providing supports that make it possible for people to remain in their own home rather than move to a more restrictive setting such as a nursing home. Safety is one of the primary reasons people move as they age, but in many cases, simple and cost-effective environmental changes can improve safety and help people remain at home. Examples of useful items that can be installed are better lighting, more stair rails, a hand-held shower and shower chair, non-slip floors, and grab bars (Pynoos, 2001; Pynoos, Caraviello, & Cicero, 2009). Successful aging in place may also include adaptations beyond the physical environment, such as strengthening social networks or promoting community resources. An assessment by an occupational therapist can identify adaptations in a person's daily routine to support aging in place (Chippendale & Bear-Lehman, 2010.

Technology is a growing option for supporting people with IDD to live successfully in their homes as they age. "Smart homes" can monitor a person's health status and welfare. Information can be sent remotely to alert caregivers or healthcare providers about changes in a person's health or behavior (Ojasalo, Suomalainen, Seppälä, & Moonen, 2010). For example, sensors on beds can monitor the number of times someone gets up to use the bathroom at night, prompting a medical examination for a possible urinary tract infection if the number of bathroom visits increases. Homes can also be adapted with technology that assists people with disabilities to control household appliances using switches, touch screens, or voice (Ojasalo et al.,2010; Storey, 2010). Switches are available to control televisions, ceiling fans, or window blinds. Smartphones or personal digital assistants can prompt people to complete routine tasks such as taking medication (Storey, 2010) or locking the doors at night. However, successful use of these technologies necessitates that people have access to the internet, as well as training and support to use these tools.

Supporting Transition to Retirement

Although research and state-level data are sparse, currently the default activity (i.e. service) option for retirees with IDD appears to be to transfer to a disability day program. These programs are typically segregated and/or facilitybased, and may offer inappropriate activities because they mainly serve people who are younger or who have more significant support needs. Instead, the benchmark for retirees with IDD should be the retirement lifestyle of retirees from the general community. This section focuses on supports for transition to retirement with meaningful activity in socially inclusive community settings.

As noted earlier in this chapter, many people with IDD have a limited understanding of retirement and the options available (McDermott & Edwards, 2012). In part, this appears to be due to having few opportunities to learn about retirement. Therefore, one fundamental intervention is for employers to routinely offer information, resources, and planning opportunities about retirement to people with IDD and their families.

A related issue is when to start detailed retirement planning. In keeping with a person-centered approach, this decision should be based on the person's individual preferences, circumstances, and needs. Stancliffe and colleagues (2013) propose a number of "retirement indicators" that may signal the need to develop a plan for retirement:

- Missing a lot of work due to health problems
- Reduced work productivity
- Often being late to work
- Not enjoying work, or avoiding work tasks (e.g., sleeping)
- Social withdrawal at work
- Excessive tiredness

Of course, retirement is not always the best option. Treating health problems, changing jobs or work tasks, or getting more rest may be better responses.

A range of approaches exists for how to promote community-based retirement activities. Some providers offer support to small groups of people with IDD to choose and take part in community activities together (e.g., picnics, movies, fairs, community events). Other people with IDD get together with friends in community settings. One approach to retirement, from an Australian research and service project that focused on supporting older workers with IDD, is to support the individual to volunteer or join a mainstream community group of their choice one day per week instead of working on that day (Stancliffe et al., 2013). Using this approach in the Australian project, people with IDD continued to work part-time on some or all other weekdays so that the transition to eventual retirement was gradual. This enabled them to develop new friendships and activities before losing touch with the world of work and social connections there.

The Australian transition project supported participants to try a community group that met each week at the same time, in the same place, year-round. This meant that they interacted with the same group members each week, which increased opportunities for genuine social relationships to evolve. The type of group was matched to the person's interests as much as possible: one man who liked gardening volunteered at a community plant nursery; a woman who loved animals went to a local cat shelter each week. By design, only one participant with disability attended each group to help maximize social inclusion. Some groups met more than once a week, but project participants initially attended on only one weekday. Over time, some individuals added a second day at the group or joined another group as well.

Types of groups people can join while phasing into retirement are:

- *Volunteering* at a soup kitchen, plant nursery, aviation museum, charity thrift store, animal shelter, frail-aged social group (as a helper)
- *Becoming a member of a community group* such as a seniors' group, exercise and social group, seniors' choir, seniors' bowling league, community garden, walking group, knitting group.

Advantages of mainstream groups. These groups are socially inclusive and usually serve other retirees without long-term disability. They are almost all low-cost and local, and many focus on a specific interest or hobby. As an existing community resource, there is no need to set up a new group.

Age of retirement. People choose to retire at different ages, especially if they are phasing into it. In the Australian project, participants with IDD were age 45 to 72 when they began to transition to retirement. Depending on individual health and other personal circumstances, people retire from paid work at widely differing ages. For example, some people with Down syndrome experience early-onset dementia, which may lead to retirement in their 40s or 50s.

The role of mentors. Day-to-day support at the community group was provided by group members who volunteered to serve as mentors to support the person's participation in activities and social interactions there. Mentors were given some straightforward training and support to take on this role (Stancliffe et al., 2013).

Supporting People Through the Experience of Death and Dying

This section focuses on social support and planning—not medical care or clinical issues—related to death and dying. End-of-life issues are important throughout life, and certainly many years or even decades before death is near. Like other stages of life, end of life offers opportunities for participation and self-determination. Unfortunately, many of these opportunities are missed because of the well-intentioned protection of people with IDD from dying and death due to concerns about upsetting them and/or about their capacity to understand what is happening to their body (Kirkendall et al., 2017; McKenzie et al., 2017; Wiese et al., 2015). Additionally, people with IDD may also be prevented from learning about their own prognosis as a result of disease or injury, or even shielded from learning about the death of a loved one or friend. For everyone, with or without disabilities,, planning and discussing death are parts of the human experience. One aim of this section is to give readers information and resources to help people with IDD learn about and understand dying and death, to participate in rituals such as funerals, and to take part in remembrances, such as anniversaries.

In this section, we discuss the person's own dying and death. However, almost all people with IDD also encounter the deaths of family members, friends, and peers. Intending to protect, people sometimes don't even tell individuals with IDD about the death of someone important to them, and may exclude them from the funeral and other rituals and remembrances (Forrester-Jones, 2013; Wiese et al., 2015). Sadly, such practices are likely to alienate the person and make their grief more complicated (Wiese et al., 2015). This situation is illustrated in "Gina's Story" on page 200.

When asked about going to funerals, many people with ID say they want to go and feel a responsibility to pay their respects (Forrester-Jones, 2013). Some say they would like an active role in the ceremony. However, not all people (with or without IDD) choose to attend funerals. Unless there is a compelling reason not to do so, the default expectation should be that people with IDD are told of and supported to attend the funerals of family and friends, but also that they can choose not to go. Sadly, many people with IDD report not being invited to or even told about funerals (Forrester-Jones, 2013).

Becoming upset is a normal reaction to news that a person has died. Some very helpful tips and resources about breaking bad news to people with IDD are available at *Breaking Bad News* (http://www.breakingbadnews.org) (Tuffrey-Wijne, 2013b) and in the book *How to Break Bad News to People With Intellectual Disabilities* (Tuffrey-Wijne, 2013a). Funerals provide an opportunity to express grief, but also provide comfort through talking about grief, sharing stories, and remembering the person who died. Likewise, remembrances such as pictures, treasured possessions, visits to the grave, or memorial events (e.g., anniversaries, birthdays, holidays) can help people cope with grief.

When asked, almost all people with IDD can identify individuals they know who have died (Stancliffe, Wiese, Read, Jeltes, & Clayton, 2016). This means that the notion of hiding death from people with IDD makes no sense because they already know about it. However, some people with IDD may have an incomplete understanding of death, especially the inevitability of their own death (Stancliffe et al., 2016). One important effect of being informed about the death of others and participating in rituals such as funerals is that it gives the person with IDD a natural opportunity to learn more about end of life. They can share the experience of losing someone and be comforted by the support of others who are also affected. These are important life experiences in their own right, and they contribute to helping the person understand what might happen and what choices could be available when they are dying.

End-of-Life Planning

A person's end-of-life wishes can only be honored if they are known. That means we need to talk to people with IDD about their end-of-life wishes. These conversations should take place many years before the person is faced with death, and should be part of everyday life (Wiese et al., 2015). The death of a celebrity or a funeral on a television soap opera can trigger discussion of what the person with IDD would want for themselves when they are dying. These preferences can involve choosing favorite music for one's funeral, or deciding what should happen to their possessions. There are a number of accessible tools that can be used to help people with IDD think about and plan different aspects of end of life.

People with IDD are beginning to be supported to deal with very challenging issues, such as advance healthcare directives and living wills, when there is clear knowledge that they have a terminal condition (McKenzie et al., 2017). Living wills detail a person's end-of-life preferences, including those related to death and dying. Living wills are an important component of coordinating person-centered supports. However, they need to be carefully distinguished from advance healthcare directives. Advance healthcare directives are legal documents that identify a person's desires for their end-of-life care (Stein, 2007). These directives name an individual who will make healthcare decisions for the person if they are unable to do so. They may also detail a person's preferences for life-sustaining care. States have different requirements for creating an advance healthcare directive, including whether or not a person needs to consult a lawyer and whether the directive must be notarized to be legal. A thorough person-centered planning process can incorporate both a living will and an advance healthcare directive according to a state's requirements. However, like the rest of the community, people with IDD should be free to opt into or out of advance care planning.

There is evidence in the general community that end-of-life planning is associated with a greater feeling of control and reduced distress, both for the dying person and for those around them. It is important for people with IDD to also have the opportunity to experience these benefits. Of course, these issues need to be dealt with sensitively and in a highly individual way. Such plans help ensure that the person is supported in the way they wish, and that they have autonomy throughout their life.

Today, most people's deaths are expected due to a known health condition. This provides the opportunity to plan, to say goodbye to loved ones, and to take part in events that the person has long wanted to experience—the so-called "bucket list." That said, it is still common to withhold news of a terminal diagnosis from people with IDD (McKenzie et al., 2017). The resources mentioned previously about breaking bad news can be helpful in such situations. However, there is not enough evidence to offer clear guidance about disclosure of illness, terminal conditions, and death to people with IDD (Tuffrey-Wijne et al., 2013). In some circumstances, disclosure might cause harm, so each situation must be assessed individually based on available guidelines (Tuffrey-Wijne et al., 2013).

Personal Illustration: Robert's Story

Robert has worked in community employment for the past 37 years. Right now, he works as part of a cleaning crew. His work is meaningful to him, and he has several friends at work. Robert lives in an apartment, and arranges rides to work with a transportation company. Last year, Robert's doctor encouraged him to become more physically active and to lose weight. Robert talked with James, a direct support professional who assists him, about what the doctor had said. James was on Robert's planning team when he created his most recent person-centered plan, so he knows Robert well.

James worked with Robert to help him find an exercise class designed for aging people. It was located within walking distance from Robert's home. James walked the route to the gym with Robert several times until Robert was comfortable enough to walk there and back on his own. At the class, Robert met Pedro, the class instructor. Robert began attending the class twice a week. Over three months participating in the class, Robert lost 10 pounds. He felt good about it and said he would like to lose another 10 pounds.

However, Robert's progress took a hit when he fell at work and broke his leg. He was hospitalized for several days, and then was laid up at home for a few weeks. He was eager to return to work, but his job coach suggested he find another job that was less physically demanding. Robert was un-steady on his feet since his injury, and hadn't regained his strength, but he hoped to return to work over time. His success in his exercise program gave him confidence that he could accomplish this goal.

James visited Pedro and asked if he would make a plan for Robert that would help him get his strength back. Pedro was happy to help. Over several months, Robert worked every day on an exercise plan Pedro had created. Pedro also suggested that Robert work with a dietician to learn more about making nutritious food choices.

Over time, Robert did go back to work part-time, and gradually increased his work hours. When he was ready, he began attending his group exercise class again. He started with once a week and worked back up to twice a week. Robert found that he was not able to work as many hours as he had before his injury, but he often filled that time with walks in the community with James. He also met the people from his exercise class at the gym for tea once a week. Robert is happy about his progress, as well as his new friendships.

Robert experienced some health-related challenges as he aged, but he responded to them in simple but effective ways that maintained his physical, mental, and social well-being. In the course of responding to these challenges, he received support that helped him exercise autonomy and independence. The experiences gave him a higher quality of life. Responding to aging-related challenges in person-centered ways helps to maintain healthy and engaged aging.

Personal Illustration: Not Sharing the News—Gina's Story

Gina is 49 and lives in a supported living program about an hour's drive from her parents. She has regular phone conversations with her mother and enjoys going to her parents' home for the weekend each month. Gina's mother, Joanna, has long-term heart problems. Unfortunately, but not unexpectedly, Joanna has a major heart attack and dies. Gina's father, Wendell, thinks that Gina will not be able to cope with the news of her mother's death. He tells her staff not to mention the death or the funeral. Gina does not attend the funeral and has no keepsakes of her mother apart from a framed photo she has had for years. In the months that follow, Gina asks repeatedly about her mother, but no one will answer her questions. Her father stops inviting Gina to his home because he finds the situation too difficult. Gina begins spending a lot of time in bed. When she does leave her room, she often sits near the phone. If asked why, she says that her mother might call.

Conclusion

People with IDD are living longer lives than in the past; however, they are not necessarily healthier. This is unfortunate, given that lifestyle activities to promote health and wellness for people with IDD are largely similar to those that promote health and wellness for people across the population. An active, healthy lifestyle involving community engagement across the lifespan is entirely possible. Person-centered supports can promote healthy and engaged aging, and planning for healthy aging can start early. Plans can be revisited, particularly as people encounter life events that change their routine. People with IDD should be given the option to transition to retirement and experience a retirement lifestyle if that is their preference. In addition, allowing people to learn about death and dying can be an important way to help them maximize self-determination as they plan for their own death.

Discussion Questions

- Why is planning for healthy and engaged aging important? What are some components of the planning process that are likely to contribute to healthy and engaged aging?
- When a person with IDD receives support from aging family members, what plans need to be in place to ensure that the person receives continued support across the lifespan?
- How is retirement related to self-determination for people with IDD?
- What systems or accommodations can help people with IDD to live healthy lives as they age into retirement?
- What are some opportunities to talk about death and dying with people with IDD? Why is this important?
- How could you support a person with IDD to attend the funeral of a loved one and to understand what is happening?

Resources

- Celebration of Life Checklist. An easy-read document for people with intellectual disability about the end of life and planning for celebrations of life http://www.aging-and-disability.org/documents/celebration_of_life_checklist.pdf
- When I Die. Resources for people with intellectual disability; includes an accessible end-of-life planning form and an example of a completed plan. http://www.pcpld.org/links-and-resources/#resources
- Coalition for Compassionate Care of California. Resources for decision making and thinking ahead to end of life. http://coalitionccc.org/tools-resources/people-with-developmental-disabilities/
- Books Beyond Words. They are designed for people who have difficulty with reading and written words, including some people with intellectual disability. The series has several books on end of life. They contain simple color drawings of typical situations related to illness and death, presenting the issues in a simple and gentle, but concrete and direct, way. Titles include *Am I Going to Die?; Anne Has Dementia; Getting On With Cancer; When Dad Died; When Mum Died;* and *When Somebody Dies.* http://www.booksbeyondwords.co.uk/bookshop/Caring Connections. *Disabilities outreach guide* (2009). National Hospice and Palliative Care Organization. Available from https://www.nhpco.org/sites/default/files/public/Access/Outreach_Disabilities.pdf

References

Bauman, A., Merom, D., Bull, F. C., Buchner, D. M., & Fiatarone Singh, M. A. (2016). Updating the evidence for physical activity: Summative reviews of the epidemiological evidence, prevalence, and interventions to promote "Active Aging." *The Gerontologist, 56*(Suppl_2), S268–S280. https://doi.org/10.1093/geront/gnw031

Bittles, A., Petterson, B., Sullivan, S., Hussain, R., Glasson, E., & Montgomery, P. (2002). The influence of intellectual disability on life expectancy. *Journals of Gerontology Series A, 57A*, 470–472. https://doi.org/10.1093/gerona/57.7.m470

Buys, L., Boulton-Lewis, G., Tedman-Jones, J., Edwards, H., Knox, M., & Bigby, C. (2008). Issues of active ageing: Perceptions of older people with lifelong intellectual disability. *Australasian Journal on Ageing, 27*(2), 67–71. doi: 10.1111/j.1741-6612.2008.00287.x

Cea, C. D., & Fisher, C. B. (2003). Health care decision-making by adults with mental retardation. *Mental Retardation, 41*, 78–87. https://doi.org/10.1352/0047-6765(2003)041%3C0078:hcdmba%3E2.0.co;2

Chippendale, T. L., & Bear-Lehman, J. (2010). Enabling "aging in place" for urban dwelling seniors: An adaptive or remedial approach? *Physical & Occupational Therapy in Geriatrics, 28*(1), 57–62. https://doi.org/10.3109/02703180903381078

Coppus, A. M. W. (2013). People with intellectual disability: What do we know about adulthood and life expectancy? *Developmental Disabilities Research Reviews, 18*, 6–16. https://doi.org/10.1002/ddrr.1123

Cordes, T. L., & Howard, R. W. (2005). Concepts of work, leisure and retirement in adults with an intellectual disability. *Education and Training in Developmental Disabilities, 40*(2), 99–105.

Forrester-Jones R. (2013). The road barely taken: Funerals, and people with intellectual disabilities. *Journal of Applied Research in Intellectual Disabilities, 26*, 243–256. doi: 10.1111/jar.12022

Gill, C. (2000). Health professionals, disability, and assisted suicide: An examination of relevant empirical evidence and reply to Batavia. *Psychology, Public Policy, and Law, 6.*, 526–545. https://doi.org/10.1037//1076-8971.6.2.526

Kirkendall, A., Linton, K., & Farris, S. (2017). Intellectual disabilities and decision making at end of life: A literature review. *Journal of Applied Research in Intellectual Disabilities.* Advance online publication. doi: 10.1111/jar.12270

Ladinski-Muaetova, E. B., Perry, E., Baron, M., & Povery, C. (2011). Ageing in people with autism spectrum disorder. *International Journal of Geriatric Psychiatry, 27*, 109–118. https://doi.org/10.1002/gps.2711

Larson, S. A., Eschenbacher, H. J., Anderson, L. L., Taylor, B., Pettingell, S., Hewitt, A., Sowers, M., & Fay, M. L. (2017). *In-home and residential long-term supports and services for persons with intellectual or developmental disabilities: Status and trends through 2014.* Minneapolis: University of Minnesota, Research and Training Center on Community Living, Institute on Community Integration. Retrieved from https://risp.umn.edu/publications.

McDermott, S., & Edwards, R. (2012). Enabling self-determination for older workers with intellectual disabilities in supported employment in Australia. *Journal of Applied Research in Intellectual Disabilities, 25*, 423–432. doi: 10.1111/j.1468-3148.2012.00683.x

McKenzie, N., Mirfin-Veitch, B., Conder, J., & Brandford, S. (2017). "I'm still here:" Exploring what matters to people with intellectual disability during advance care planning. *Journal of Applied Research in Intellectual Disabilities, 30*(6), 1089–1098, doi: 10.1111/jar.12355

Ojasalo, J., Suomalainen, N., Seppälä, H., & Moonen, R. (2010, October). Better technologies and services for smart homes of disabled people: Empirical findings from an explorative study among intellectually disabled. In *Software Technology and Engineering (ICSTE), 2010 2nd International Conference on* (Vol. 1, pp. V1–251). .

Older Americans Act of 1965 (Pub.L. 89–73, 79 Stat. 218).

Perkins, E. A., & Berkman, K. A. (2012). Into the unknown: Aging with autism spectrum disorders. *American Journal on Intellectual and Developmental Disabilities, 117*(6), 478–496. https://doi.org/10.1352/1944-7558-117.6.478

Putnam, M. (2017). Extending the promise of the Older Americans Act to persons aging with long-term disability. *Research on Aging, 39*(6), 799–820. https://doi.org/10.1177/0164027516681052

Pynoos, J. (2001). Meeting the needs of older persons to age in place: Findings and recommendations for action. *Andrus Gerontology Center: The National Resource Center for Supportive Housing and Home Modification.*

Pynoos, J., Caraviello, R., & Cicero, C. (2009). Lifelong housing: The anchor in aging-friendly communities. *Generations, 33*(2), 26–32.

Rowe, J. W., & Kahn, R. L. (1987). Human aging: Usual and successful. *Science, 237,* 143–150. https://doi.org/10.1126/science.3299702

Smith, G., O'Keeffe, J., Carpenter, L., Doty, P., Burnwell, B., Mollica, R., & Williams, L. (2000). Understanding Medicaid home and community services: A primer. Center for Health Policy Research, Paper 5. Retrieved from http://hsrc.himmelfarb.gwu.edu/sphhs_policy_chpr/5

Stancliffe, R. J., Wiese, M. Y., Read, S., Jeltes, G. & Clayton, J. M. (2016). Knowing, planning for and fearing death: Do adults with intellectual disability and disability staff differ? *Research in Developmental Disabilities, 49-50,* 47–59. doi: 10.1016/j.ridd.2015.11.016

Stancliffe, R. J., Wilson, N. J., Gambin, N., Bigby, C., & Balandin, S. (2013). *Transition to retirement: A guide to inclusive practice.* Sydney: Sydney University Press.

Stanford Center on Longevity. (2010). *New realities of an older America.* Retrieved from http://longevity3.stanford.edu/wp-content/uploads/2014/06/77042_NewRealitiesOfAnOlderAmerica_FINALforPrinting7_16_10REVIS.pdf

Stein, G. L. (2007). *Advance directives and advance care planning for people with intellectual and physical disabilities.* U.S. Department of Health and Human Services. Retrieved from https://aspe.hhs.gov/basic-report/advance-directives-and-advance-care-planning-people-intellectual-and-physical-disabilities

Storey, K. (2010). Smart houses and smart technology: Overview and implications for independent living and supported living services. *Intellectual and Developmental Disabilities, 48,* 464–469. https://doi.org/10.1352/1934-9556-48.6.464

Strax, T. E., Luciano, L., Dunn, A. M., & Quevedo, J. P. (2010). Aging and developmental disability. *Physical Medicine and Rehabilitation Clinics of North America, 21,* 419–427. https://doi.org/10.1016/j.pmr.2009.12.009

Tuffrey-Wijne, I. (2013a). *How to break bad news to people with intellectual disabilities: A guide for careers and professionals*. London: Jessica Kingsley Publishers.

Tuffrey-Wijne, I. (2013b) Ten tips for breaking the bad news. Retrieved from: http://www.breakingbadnews.org/ten-top-tips-for-breaking-bad-news/

Tuffrey-Wijne, I., Giatras, N., Butler, G., Cresswell, A., Manners, P., & Bernal, J. (2013). Developing guidelines for disclosure or non-disclosure of bad news to people with intellectual disabilities. *Journal of Applied Research in Intellectual Disabilities, 26* (3), 231–242. doi: 10.1111/jar.12026

U.S. Centers for Medicare and Medicaid Services [CMS]. (2017). Advance directives & long-term care. Retrieved from https://www.medicare.gov/manage-your-health/advance-directives/advance-directives-and-long-term-care.html

Wiese, M., Stancliffe, R. J., Read, S., Jeltes, G. & Clayton, J. (2015). Learning about dying, death and end-of-life planning: Current issues informing future actions. *Journal of Intellectual & Developmental Disability, 40*(2), 230–235. doi 10.3109/13668250.2014.998183

World Health Organization. (2000). *Ageing and intellectual disabilities- Improving longevity and promoting healthy ageing: Summative report*. Geneva, Switzerland. World Health Organization. Retrieved from http://www.who.int/mental_health/media/en/20.pdf

World Health Organization. (2002). *Active aging: A policy framework*. Geneva, Switzerland: World Health Organization. Retrieved from http://apps.who.int/iris/bitstream/10665/67215/1/WHO_NMH_NPH_02.8.pdf

Zigman, W. B., & Lott, I. T. (2007). Alzheimer's disease in Down syndrome: Neurobiology and risk. *Mental Retardation and Developmental Disabilities Research Reviews, 13*(3), 237–246. https://doi.org/10.1002/mrdd.20163

CHAPTER TEN

Outcomes for Quality of Life: Practices That Promote Quality Outcomes

Renatá Tichá, Bradley Goodnight, Ellie Wilson, and Amy S. Hewitt

Advance Organizers

- Community living outcome measures need to focus on the key dimensions and features of life in the community that are most important to each person.
- Developing good outcome measures involves a comprehensive process that takes time and is important to taxpayers and policy makers to ensure accountability.
- People have different preferences and personal goals. They live in varied communities and contexts and view life through various social cultural and linguistic lenses. Consequently, their desired outcomes vary.
- Effective measurement can ensure that needs are met for people who receive services, enable providers to demonstrate effectiveness of their services, and allow policy makers to justify the need for services and related expenditures.

What Is Outcome Measurement and Why Does It Matter?

One of the key aspects of an outcome measure is to reliably identify "targeted change" in a life area of an individual, group of people, or population that is based on, or can be attributed to, a specific intervention, combination of interventions, plan, process, or program (Ogles, Lambert, & Fields, 2002). Targeted change can be in any number of aspects of life: employment, wages, health, independence in doing specific tasks, activity level, engagement, and others. Person-centered outcome measures are designed to capture targeted change of something that is important to the individual. In thinking about community living and engagement, outcome measures need to focus on the key dimensions and features of community living that are most important to each individual.

In the United States, approximately $42 billion is spent annually on long-term services and supports (LTSS) for people with IDD (Eiken, Sredl, Burwell, & Saucier, 2016). Policy makers and taxpayers want to know whether these resources are being spent on services and supports that yield positive and meaningful outcomes. Increased attention is being paid to outcomes related to community living and engagement for people with disabilities. Thus, to know whether services and supports lead to improved community living and engagement, measures should focus on key outcome areas critical to quality of life, including:

- where and with whom a person **lives**
- whether and where a person **works**
- the **financial resources** available to a person
- what a person does **during the day**
- the quality of **relationships** a person has or desires with others
- what and with whom a person does things of **personal interest**
- a person's **health and well-being**
- whether, where, and with whom a person practices a **faith**
- a person's interest and opportunity to engage in **learning** and personal **growth**
- the opportunities and ability for a person to make **informed decisions** about, and **determine the direction of, their own life**
- the person's **right to assume roles and responsibilities as a citizen,** e.g., neighbor, taxpayer, voter(Schalock at al., 2002; NQF, 2016)

Developing good outcome measures can be challenging, and their development involves a scientific process that takes precision and time. Once the measures are developed, they have to be tested to be sure they measure what they are intended to measure and that, when implemented, different people use the same procedures to find the same responses. Once deemed to be good measures, they have to be implemented to gather enough data to represent enough people to be useful. Furthermore, this data has to be understood, funded, and used by policy makers to create change so that, in the end, many or all people with IDD can get the supports they need to maximize community living and engagement, and therefore their quality of life.

Figure 10.1. Quality outcome measurement model

Important Characteristics of Outcome Measurement in Community Living

Community living and engagement measures should attend to the various outcome areas described in the previous section. For each outcome, measures need to evaluate personal perceptions of current supports and services, changes, and improvements. Each measure must be developed in a way that will identify meaningful change over time. A measure must also be designed in such a way that the preferences of each individual are taken into account. For example, a measure that asks how many times a person goes shopping may not be adequate for measuring community living or engagement because one person may like shopping and another may find it a stressful experience. A good person-centered measure needs to account for personal differences and preferences. When data is collected by organizations at a systems level without accounting for these individual differences, it can affect accuracy related to service delivery and outcomes. Gathering person-centered outcome data at an organizational level is more likely to lead to services that are well matched to the needs of people with disabilities, which in turn is more likely to result in better service outcomes.

There are many challenges to outcome measurement in LTSS for people with IDD. Some people with disabilities and their families are not familiar with the technical processes of developing and evaluating outcome measures. This lack of familiarity can result in mistrust in measurement that can be made worse by poor experiences in which data was gathered without explanation for how it would be used, or feelings of being overburdened with frequent surveys without any visible change from the results. Some service delivery organizations and systems use data collection screening efforts to determine what services a person will get and how many resource will be available for those supports based on the person's support needs. The experience of using assessments to collect data to determine funding allocations to individuals and families may make some people cautious of data collection efforts of any kind.

There is often also a lack of understanding of the benefit that outcome measurement can contribute to people with disabilities when data is collected primarily for developing and updating policies. Often people are misinformed about how and for what purposes the data is being used, especially when they do not see immediate and visible results in terms of services and improved quality of life.

Many measures are poorly constructed and do not account for individual preferences and systems differences. In these situations, people become concerned that the outcome measures are not yielding accurate information. Poor data can certainly lead to incorrect conclusions, as well as to wasted effort and resources. In other words,, some of these concerns are warranted. Measures need to be of good quality, be person centered, and address the community living and engagement area for people served. It is sometimes difficult to find a good existing measure for an outcome of interest. Sometimes states or organizations simply develop a measure without testing it for accuracy and generalizability. When this happens, data can be inaccurate, unclear, or misleading, and can result in policies and practices that are misdirected or ineffective.

Current Controversies and Challenges

Quality Outcomes Difficult to Define

Quality outcomes for people with disabilities, including IDD, are a complex and evolving topic. This complexity is largely a result of the fact that individuals have different preferences and personal goals, live and participate in different community settings and activities, and view life through a variety of social, cultural, and linguistic perspectives. Quality outcomes in community living are also influenced by environmental factors, including the type, setting, availability, and appropriateness of paid and unpaid services and supports, as well as the responsiveness, dependability, and competence of those who provide these services and supports. Medicaid-financed Home and Community Based Services (HCBS) are the largest LTSS investment made in the United States for people with IDD. These services and supports are intended to provide quality community living and engagement options for individuals with disabilities along the dimensions noted above. In addition, the complexities of defining and measuring the quality of LTSS for people who are living in their own home or with family members make measurement more challenging when compared to the conceptualization of quality within congregate care settings.

Another challenge to defining quality outcomes in community living is connected to what constitutes "quality" in this context. Although the Centers for Medicare and Medicaid Services' regulations (CMS, 2017), the newly developed National Quality Forum's framework (NQF, 2016), and an HCBS framework help define the quality of life for people with disabilities, there are no further guidelines about how federal or state governments should and could fulfill their responsibility to quality in HCBS LTSS for its recipients. A key feature of the quality frameworks is the expectation that states will gather and respond to data on "system performance" in outcome areas such as access, person-centered services, participant safeguards, choice and decision making, and participant rights. More nuanced discussion needs to be developed about the differences of measuring quality outcomes at a systems level versus for an individual.

These challenges, however, have created new and exciting opportunities to redefine meaningful outcomes for people with disabilities and ways in which these outcomes are measured. It is important that measures reflect the quality of life not only of people who receive HCBS but also people without disabilities to the extent possible. In this context, this chapter examines the heightened need for quality of outcome measurement for people with disabilities in today's society, barriers that currently exist in this field, and strategies to make this process easier and more useful for all.

Challenges in Person-Centered Outcome Measurement

There is a conceptual difference between assessments developed to measure quality of services at the system level and those developed to measure individual outcomes. Before an assessment instrument is judged, this distinction must be considered. Tools designed to measure quality of services at a state or county level will naturally include more items related to the provision of services (e.g., availability of transportation and support service staff) than personal outcomes (e.g., ways in which a person feels included in their community or is fulfilled by their employment). It is important to build awareness in the community about the different purposes and types of assessments to avoid frustration and misunderstanding of data collection procedures (in-depth interview with someone with a disability versus multiple-choice survey) and use of data (to measure the progress toward person-centered goals versus to make policy decisions).

The level of person centeredness of each item or of a measure is also determined by the data collection method. In assessment tools designed primarily for service quality assurance, a significant proportion of the items are typically collected from existing records (e.g., state databases and case manager files). Tools that have been developed with the goal to obtain personal accounts of different aspects of quality of life, as a result, include more person-centered items. These tools typically use interviews with people with a disability to collect data. For people with limited communication skills, a proxy respondent often fills the role of a data collection participant. The most person-centered approach to identifying proxy respondents is for the individual with a disability to select the person in their life who they think knows them the best (e.g., a parent, sibling, friend, or staff member). Research has found, however, that the reliability of proxy responses varies by the type of proxy and the types of questions (objective versus subjective) asked (Claes et al., 2012).

Person-centered measurement is important for ensuring that the data collected reflects the needs of individuals with disabilities. There is also a place, however, for examining how the system is performing for groups of individuals (e.g., selected by county or type of disability) to be able to make generalizations and improve aspects of the service delivery system that are common to multiple individuals.

Lack of Available Measurements That Are Valid, Reliable, and Sensitive to Change

One of the most important characteristics of good assessments, in addition to usability and feasibility, is their psychometric properties. There is a lack of understanding about psychometric properties of assessment tools, and of why they are so important. Psychometrics focuses on the development of assessments and the evaluation of the assessment characteristics. Development of new assessment tools typically consists of creating new survey or interview questions or observation protocols. The newly developed questions or observation codes need to be evaluated for their measurement properties, including reliability, validity, and sensitivity to change over time.

To adopt an assessment to use for evaluating aspects of the quality of life of people with disabilities and/or the quality of services and service systems, an organization must be confident that they have sufficient time and budget to collect data with this instrument (feasibility). The organization also needs to evaluate whether the data collected by this instrument is usable for the purposes they need. Unfortunately, in the field of services for adults with disabilities, not many assessments have been evaluated for their psychometric properties. There are a few exceptions with respect to widely used instruments and those created as part of development and research grants. Additionally, several initiatives are currently in progress to systematically evaluate widely used instruments and develop new measures of HCBS outcomes in areas where gaps exist across different types of disabilities. For example, the Research and Training Center on Home and Community Based Outcome Measurement was funded (by the National Institute on Disability, Independent Living, and Rehabilitation Research [NIDILRR] within the U.S. Department of Health and Human Services) to improve measurement of HCBS services (rtcom.umn.edu/).

Lack of Understanding That Individual Quality Data Can Drive Systems-Level Policy

Outcome measurement is perceived by some people with disabilities, their families, and direct support staff as an unnecessary activity that is intrusive, takes a lot of time, and does not lead to concrete changes. There are many reasons for these feelings of apprehension: More often than not, individuals and families are concerned with day-to-day living that includes transportation, medications and insurance, service provision, etc. For people with disabilities, daily activities can be much more challenging than for people who do not require supports. The challenges include limited availability of services with respect to timing and area coverage, adhering to schedules of a group residential setting or family, or fluctuating capacities. Adding data collection to the mix might simply feel like too much.

When discussing the importance of good outcome measurement, it is essential that people with disabilities, as participants in data collection, understand the purpose behind the assessment. As discussed earlier in this chapter, there are tools to evaluate the quality of services for groups of people at the county or state level, which can be used to make the necessary changes in policy and service provision in the area. Other types of measures may be more person-centered and designed to evaluate whether a person with a disability is receiving services that meet their needs (e.g., whether the person has the services needed to participate in the community in the way they want to, or to work toward a personal goal such as learning to cook).

Organizations have a responsibility to build awareness of the purpose and benefits of each outcome measurement assessment they conduct among participants with disabilities, their families, and staff members in order to encourage a better understanding of the importance of conducting outcome assessments. This will help to build trust with the people they assess and whose data they use to improve practices and policy.

Practical Suggestions and Interventions

Why Good Measurement Matters

Quality measurement allows providers, health systems, taxpayers, and, most importantly, people with disabilities to track the quality of the services and supports being delivered. For people who receive services, defining and measuring quality outcomes are essential to coordination and communication. Discussion of particular values and desired outcomes can be used as a reliable and consistent basis for person-centered goal and service planning. It can also offer a means for people who use services to hold their providers and states accountable for effective and useful services. For policy makers and advocates who provide oversight, quality measurement provides an essential means to create specific visions and goals around quality assurance and improvement.

One example of how to create a measure of community engagement is to develop a collaborative between a regional organization serving people with disabilities and a think tank or university, because the need is regional or statewide. The think tank or university conducts a pilot study with grant or local funds to evaluate how participants respond to the measure and whether the tool consistently measures characteristics of community engagement. The measure is then refined based on the pilot data. Funding is allocated to fulfill this initiative. The newly developed measure is used to evaluate whether the program/policy implementation is indeed resulting in higher community engagement. If the policy is enforced and supported by high-quality programs, quality of life for people with disabilities improves.

What Outcomes We Should Measure

The quality and effectiveness of services in any setting are inherently important to all people living with disabilities in the United States. The quality of services provided at home, at work, and in the community is closely tied to the quality of life of the people who receive these services. Despite its critical importance, however, quality is a difficult construct to define, especially when considering the evolving personal nature of the elements that compose quality of life for each person with a disability.

It is not only challenging to define quality on a personal level; it has also proven difficult to define for the broad population of people who utilize HCBS. Unlike many other aspects of healthcare and social services, HCBS has historically lacked a construct to define quality outcomes. To address this problem, the U.S. Department of Health and Human Services convened a group of national experts, who worked as consultants for the National Quality Forum (NQF), to develop a framework of the various characteristics of individual and systemic quality outcomes for HCBS.

In 2016, the group published the first National Quality Forum Framework, which organizes characteristics of quality of into 11 categories of outcomes known as domains. Some of the domains include outcomes that are personal and individually measured; others reflect outcomes for the HCBS system at the community, state, or federal level. The NQF domains are included in Figure 10.2.

Each of these domains is defined and further divided into subdomains. In all, the framework defines 11 domains and 40 subdomains that represent quality outcomes that the NQF committee deemed important to measure. By identifying and defining these outcome areas, the NQF provides a structure for research and quality improvement efforts for individuals and communities of people with all types of disabilities. This framework also highlights important areas for progress in measure development. New development will focus on how to measure each quality characteristic accurately and in a way that is meaningful to people who are receiving services to support and enhance their quality of life.

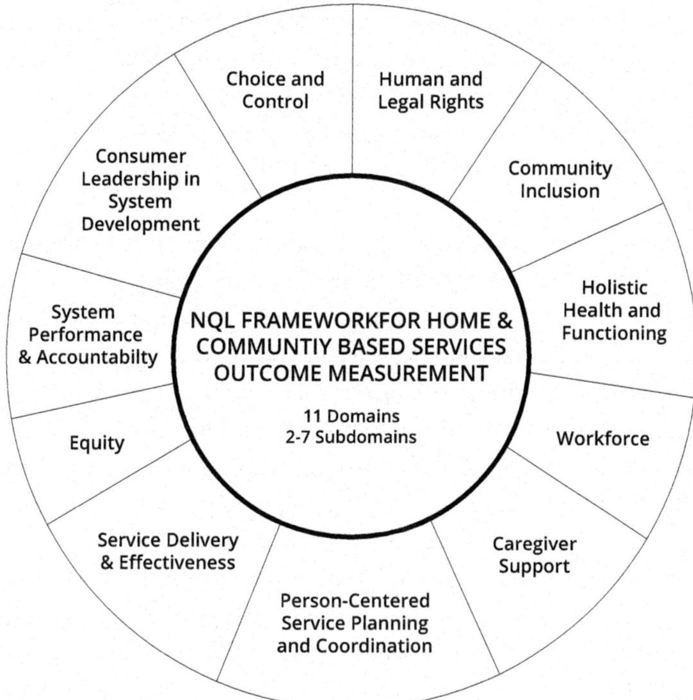

Figure 10.2. National Quality Forum Framework. Source: Adapted from National Quality Framework, http://www.qualityforum.org

How to Measure Person-Centered Outcomes

Methods 101: Reliability and validity. Measurement is a complex subject, and people sometimes consider it intimidating. However, you do not have to be a measurement expert to collect good data. By understanding a few of the ways that measure developers evaluate and compare measures, you can learn how to better select a measure that will provide good data for you, your organization, and the people to whom you provide supports.

A measure is considered reliable when it gives consistent results under similar conditions. If scores are not reproducible, it is difficult to trust or use them. For example, if an IQ test rated you as a genius on Tuesday, and far below average on Thursday, it would be difficult to make decisions based on your score. An untrustworthy instrument cannot provide a good foundation for decision making, which is why reliability is so important.

There are several ways to measure reliability, including test-retest reliability and internal consistency (Furr & Bacharach, 2014). *Test-retest reliability* means that the test provides similar results when given to the same person multiple times. *Internal consistency* means that when people score high on one part of the measure, they also score high on other parts of the same measure. You don't necessarily have to conduct these tests of reliability yourself, but when selecting a measure, you will want to ensure that reliability has been established by the measure developer or consult with a researcher or research institution to see whether the reliability of the tool has been demonstrated.

A measure is considered valid if it assesses what it is intended to assess. For example, a transportation measure is developed to find out whether a person has access to transportation in a way that meets his or her needs. However, if you ask, "Do you have access to appropriate transportation when you need it?" you are also measuring comprehension of the questions and awareness of what it means for transportation to be appropriate. Someone who needs transportation in order to do the activities in the community that they need and want to do on certain days and at certain times may not be aware of all the types and frequencies of transportation that are available to them. As a result, they may answer yes to the question, even if they are not getting the most appropriate transportation option for their needs. The question is therefore invalid because it does not produce an answer that reflects the person's situation.

There are many different forms of validity. One of the most common is *concurrent validity* (Furr & Bacharach, 2014), which indicates that the measure gives similar results to other measures of the same concept. For instance, if a new measure of intelligence was developed, it should provide similar results to the IQ test that is widely used and accepted. If the IQ test identifies someone as a genius and the new test identifies the same person as having below-average intelligence, that result brings the findings into doubt. Concurrent validity can only be established if another measure already exists for the concept being measured, so if you are measuring something specific or novel, there may not be any other measures available. Typically, validity can be established by consulting with experts in the topic area and with measurement experts.

If you use a measure that is not reliable or valid, you may waste time and resources, and come to incorrect conclusions. When selecting a measure, it is important to be certain that the measure developer has taken steps to ensure the reliability and validity of the test. The measure developer should have information that demonstrates the reliability and validity of their instrument available upon request; if they do not, this may indicate that the measure is not trustworthy and should not be used.

Other measurement issues: Sensitivity to change and sampling. A measure must also be *sensitive* enough to detect changes in relevant outcomes over time (Ogles et al., 2002). For example, a measure needs to be able to detect a significant change (or no change) in the type and amount of transportation a person is using across the year, especially if the person had a goal to get to their community activities more effectively. A measure should also be able to detect whether the person sees an improvement in their access to appropriate transportation after some time (e.g., six months). A measure's sensitivity to change is critical when we are evaluating the effectiveness of a person-centered plan, a training program, or a policy. If a measure is not tested for this characteristic, we risk coming to incorrect conclusions about the initiatives we are evaluating, thus misleading the participants and other audiences and potentially investing money inappropriately.

Sampling is the technique of selecting participants for an interview or a survey so as to be able to generalize the results to the right population. Sometimes participants are sampled randomly within an organization or a region. In some cases, however, you want to be more purposeful about whom you select. For example, if you want to make sure you are representing recipients of services within a certain waiver program or with certain types of disabilities, you sample from individuals with those characteristics. If you conduct a survey online, only people who use a computer will be able to access it. People who use computers may be very different from people who do not, and by sampling in this way, you might draw conclusions that only apply to computer users. It is important to ensure that the people whose data is included are representative of the group about which you want to draw conclusions. This means that the people in the sample should be similar to the group you are making decisions about in as many ways as possible. Relatedly, if you use a proxy and get information from a family caregiver or a paid staff as opposed to the individual, they may have their own perspective that influences the answers. Ideally, you should ask the person directly. In summary, you will get different answers depending on whom you ask, so be thoughtful when selecting your sample.

Person-centered measurement. An issue with many measures is that they use a one-size-fits-all approach and do not always account for differences in personal preferences and goals. Measures are often developed from a system-based perspective, meaning that they assess whether services are in line with the system's expectations rather than the individual's. It is important to use a person-centered approach to measurement, where the goals and needs of the person being interviewed take priority. System-based measures ask about things that are important *for* the person, whereas person-centered measures ask about things that are important *to* the person.

Person-centered measures often include open-ended components where the person being interviewed indicates what they value. Only after individual goals are considered can an evaluation of services be conducted. For example, if a measure asks how many times a person sees their family members, it does not take into consideration that some people may not want to spend time with their family. An evaluation of their personal desires must be included first.

How to Use and Interpret Data for IDD Advocacy

Important questions. Before data can be collected or measures can be selected, it is important to clearly understand the goals of your data collection. Unnecessary data collection, without an established plan, is a waste of time and resources that can lead to disillusionment and fatigue and can undermine the measurement process. Before collecting data, therefore, you will want to establish the key question(s) that you want answered. You can start by thinking about a decision you have to make, and then think about what information might make this decision easier. Once you know what you want to know, work backward to develop a question.

Logic modeling. When planning your data collection, it is also often helpful to draw a visualization of the logic of your project, and to familiarize yourself with the relationship between what you are doing and what you are trying to accomplish. A useful tool for this is called "logic modeling," where you start with the things that you are doing (activities) and draw a logical connection between what you produce (outputs) and what you are trying to achieve (outcomes). Once you have laid out the logic of your activities in this way, it is often easier to think about where and how you might want to collect data to ensure that things are happening the way they should. See Figure 10.3.

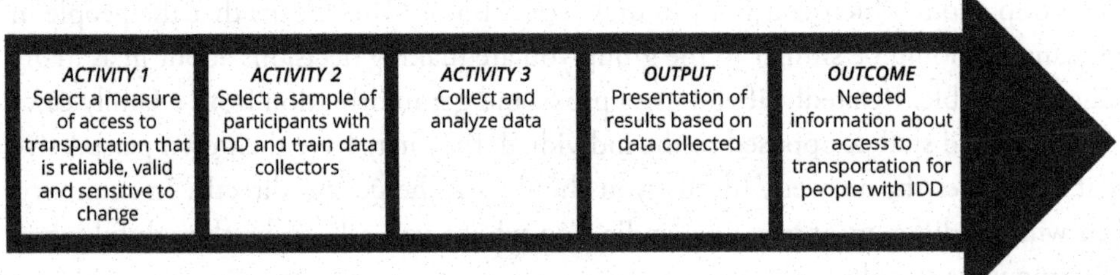

Figure 10.3. Example of a logic model.

Once a logic model is developed, consider how each of the activities, outputs, and outcomes could be measured or otherwise evaluated. The tools you will use to measure or evaluate your activities, outputs, and outcomes are referred to as "indicators." Only after you have identified your activities, outputs, and outcomes can you decide what data you will need to collect to answer your key question(s). Activities and outputs are often easier to measure, as they represent things you are doing and producing. Outcomes, however, are usually the most important, as they represent the purpose and goals of your activities.

There are many important outcomes in community living and engagement for people with IDD, and as you develop your logic model, you will want to think carefully about which outcomes will be addressed effectively by your activities. Once you know what your outcomes are, you should seek high-quality measures and develop a plan for sampling, data collection, and analysis.

Tools for data collection and simple analyses. Before collecting data, you need to plan ahead and decide what software you will use to evaluate the data after collection. Some common choices are Excel, SPSS, SAS, and Tableau. However, in some cases the tools built into your data collection platform, such as SurveyMonkey or Qualtrics, may be enough for your purposes. Complex statistical analyses may not be necessary to meet your needs. Bar graphs may be enough, depending on your question(s). If you do need to conduct more involved analyses to answer your question(s), you may want to partner with a university or another organization. Often, however, the simplest solution is best, especially if your goal is to convey findings to a variety of stakeholders. If you use a type of analysis that is not easily understandable, the results of your work might not be understood and therefore will not be utilized.

Typically, your first steps should be to create a table of descriptive statistics and some data visualizations. Descriptive statistics are the simplest form of statistics available; they only describe your data, and do not demonstrate statistical significance. Common forms of descriptive statistics include frequency scores—a count of how many times something happened, on average, which describes the arithmetic middle of multiple observations—and standard deviation, which is, in essence, how far from average most people are.

With descriptive statistics, you can provide information that allows comparisons between groups and can identify trends. To more clearly illustrate these trends, once they are identified, you can use visualizations such as bar graphs, where averages and frequencies can easily be compared side by side. Data collection software programs such as SurveyMonkey and Qualtrics have some data visualization tools built in, and Excel, SPSS, and most other statistical software programs have the capacity to make visualizations.

Resources for analysis and interpretation help. It could take years to gain the highly specialized technical expertise needed to develop and evaluate measurement tools. However, by establishing collaborations and networking with researchers and academic institutions, you may be able to get help that allows you to improve your data collection and interpretation.

Access to data is often valuable to researchers, and if you have access to a unique population that is of research interest, such as recipients of HCBS services, you may find opportunities for collaboration with universities and research institutions. By reaching out to them, you may be able to receive technical assistance. If the assistance you need is more substantial, you might want to consider paid statistical or measurement consulting.

Personal Illustration: Walter Gill

John F. Kennedy, Jr., wrote: "Quality is defined at the point of interaction between the staff member and the individual with a disability" (Jaskulski & Ebenstein, 1996). In recent years, Walter Gill has found this to be true. After a series of unpleasant experiences with paid staff, Walter hired Sara Stockdale, and by every measure of quality, his life improved. "Sara helps me be more independent," said Walter. "And she helps me live my life the way I want to."

"I take care of his daily needs," said Sara, "but I also see [my job] as so much more." As a direct support professional, her first questions were "How can I help Walter? What can I do to make his life better?"

Walter, a warm, engaging man in his 50s who has Cerebral Palsy, lives in an apartment in Topeka, Kansas. He hires staff to provide supports such as personal care, meal preparation, budgeting, shopping, and assistance with attending community events. The results have not always been positive. "I had people that were supposed to be my friends," said Walter, "but they took advantage of me." Often, people would quit shortly after being hired, or simply stop showing up for work. One employee, while appearing to help Walter pay his bills, was accessing his bank account and stealing money. He endured years of difficult and inconsistent staff, resulting in social isolation and depression. "When I don't have good staff," Walter said, "my quality of life goes down. And I can't do what I want to do and live my life the way I want to."

When Sara began working for Walter, she concentrated on building up his confidence and helping him see that he deserved proper care and support. "He had low confidence, low standards, and low expectations. He had given so much leeway to others." Sara emphasized to Walter that he was the employer, the boss. As Walter grew to trust Sara, he began taking control, making more decisions for himself. "Seeing his confidence and his self-esteem really soar has been just fabulous."

Economic stability is an important indicator of quality for Walter. Sara helped him get his finances in order and reviews his expenses with him monthly. "I feel it's very important that he sits right alongside me and he watches the bank statement," said Sara. "We go through every line." Walter now feels more financially secure. "It makes him feel really good that he can pay all of his bills, that he can still indulge a little bit in what he wants."

Sara prioritizes Walter's wants and needs above the routine tasks of her job. "If he feels that sitting down and having a conversation with me is more important than the dishes getting done right now, or the bed being made right now, we can do that, because it's what Walter wants, and it's his home."

Concerned about Walter's high blood pressure and swollen legs, Sara offered Walter healthier meal choices. Rather than fried or frozen foods, she suggested preparing fresh meals from scratch. "I wanted him to still have the freedom to decide what he likes and what he wants to eat," said Sara. "But we also discussed little changes that we can make." Drinking more water, for instance, and eating fresh fruits and vegetables. Walter's health has improved, and he has more energy. "Now when we go to the doctor," said Sara, "we celebrate because his blood pressure is dropping, and his A1C, which is a diabetes marker, has been lowered."

With the support of a dependable, well-trained DSP, Walter is living the life he desires. "Quality of life means to have more freedom to live how I want to live and do what I want to do."

Conclusion

Quality of life for people with disabilities is closely related to the quality of services they receive. Services differ in quality with respect to their delivery (timeliness, intensity), resources (money, staffing), and appropriateness of fit (setting, equipment). In order to ensure that organizations provide services of the best quality, service evaluation is necessary at various levels. Only high-quality services will lead to the essential outcome of people with disabilities being able to engage in the community as they need and desire.

Quality outcome measurement provides the needed information about whether people with disabilities are successfully working toward and achieving their goals and dreams. Quality outcome measurement involves provider organizations, people with disabilities, and their families. They also require staff who know how to select and administer good measures of the desired outcomes, and how to interpret and apply the results to the question(s) asked in the first place. Important questions are often asked by people with disabilities themselves, their families, provider organizations, and policy makers, including questions about social inclusion, transportation, employment, meaningful activity, service delivery, etc., which are part of the NQF framework presented in this chapter. It is important to examine these questions in line with best practices of outcomes measurement, so that the most helpful answers are discovered that will help to assure that people with intellectual and developmental disabilities have access to services that lead to their full participation in the community.

Discussion Questions

- How does your organization or state measure quality outcomes related to community living and engagement? If they do not measure outcomes, why not? If they do measure outcomes, how are the results used to influence policy and practice?
- Are the measures used in your state or organization person-centered? Why or why not?
- What testing was done in the development process of the measurements used by your state or organization? Are they valid? Reliable? How do you know?

Resources

- National Quality Forum (NQF): The National Quality Forum is a United States-based non-profit organization that seeks to promote quality care and home and community life through measurement and public reporting. http://www.qualityforum.org/HCBS.aspx
- National Core Indicators (NCI): National Core Indicators is a voluntary effort by public developmental disability agencies to measure their own performance. NCI is a collaboration of participating states, the Human Services Research Institute, and the National Association for State Directors of Developmental Disability Services. https://www.nationalcoreindicators.org/
- National Core Indicators – Aging and Disability (NCI-AD) is a voluntary effort by state Medicaid, aging, and disability agencies to measure and track their own performance. The core indicators are standard measures used across states to assess the outcomes of services provided to individuals and families. https://nci-ad.org/
- Council on Quality and Leadership (CQL) assists communities, systems, and organizations to help people discover and define their own quality of life; measure personal quality of life for individuals, organizations, and systems; and improve quality of life for people with disabilities. https://www.c-q-l.org/

References

Claes, C., Vandevelde, S., Van Hove, G., van Loon, J., Verschelden, G., & Schalock, R. (2012). Relationship between self-report and proxy ratings on assessed personal quality of life related outcomes. *Journal of Policy and Practice in Intellectual Disabilities, 9*(3), 159–165. Doi: 10.1111/j.1741-1130.2012.00353.x

Eiken, S., Sredl, K., Burwell, B., & Saucier, P. (2016). *Medicaid expenditures for long-term services and supports (LTSS) in FY 2014: Managed LTSS reached 15 percent of LTSS spending.* Truven Health Analytics. Retrieved from https://www.medicaid.gov/medicaid/ltss/downloads/ltss-expenditures-2014.pdf

Furr, R. M., & Bacharach, V. R. (2014). *Psychometrics: An introduction* (2nd Ed.). Thousand Oaks, CA: Sage Publications.

Health Services Advisory Group (2017). *CMS quality measure development plan: Supporting the transition to the quality payment program 2017.* Baltimore, MD: Centers for Medicare & Medicaid Services. Retrieved from https://www.cms.gov/Medicare/Quality-Initiatives-Patient-Assessment-Instruments/Value-Based-Programs/MACRA-MIPS-and-APMs/2017-CMS-MDP-Annual-Report.pdf

Health Services Advisory Group (2017). *Quality Measure Development Plan Environmental Scan and Gap Analysis Report* (MACRA, Section 102). Baltimore, MD: Centers for Medicare & Medicaid Services. Retrieved from https://www.cms.gov/Medicare/Quality-Initiatives-Patient-Assessment-Instruments/Value-Based-Programs/MACRA-MIPS-and-APMs/MDP_EScan_GapAnalysis_Report.pdf

Jaskulski, T. & Ebenstein, W. (1996). *Opportunities for excellence: Supporting the frontline workforce.* Washington, D.C.: President's Committee on Mental Retardation, U.S. Department of Health and Human Services.

National Quality Forum (2016). *Quality in home and community-based services to support community living: Addressing gaps in performance measurement* (Final Report). Washington, DC: Department of Health and Human Service. Retrieved from http://www.qualityforum.org/Publications/2016/09/Quality_in_Home_and_Community-Based_Services_to_Support_Community_Living__Addressing_Gaps_in_Performance_Measurement.aspx

Ogles, B. M., Lambert, M. J., & Fields, S. A. (2002). *Essentials of outcome assessment.* Hoboken, NJ: John Wiley.

Schalock, R. L., Brown, I., Brown, R., Cummins, R. A., Felce, D., Matikka, L., Keith, K. D., & Parmenter, T. (2002). Conceptualization, measurement, and application of quality of life for persons with intellectual disabilities: Report of an international panel of experts. *Mental Retardation, 40*(6), 457–470. DOI: 10.1352/0047-6765(2002)040<0457:CMAAOQ>2.0.CO;2

CHAPTER ELEVEN

Hiring, Training, and Supporting the Direct Support Workforce

Nancy McCulloh, Claire Benway, Amy S. Hewitt, Barbara A. Kleist, Julie Kramme, and Macdonald Metzger

Advance Organizers

- Direct support professionals (DSPs) provide critical and life enhancing services to people with disabilities.
- Millions of individuals with disabilities, and or their families rely on the services of DSPs.
- Despite expected growth and need in the field, there is a significant shortage of DSPs in the United States.
- Direct support work is often poorly paid and without benefits, training, support, or career pathways.
- Access to the benefits and experiences of community life for people with disabilities is often dependent on the quality of, and access to, well-trained, and competent DSPs.

Direct support professionals (DSPs) play critical roles in supporting community living and participation for people with IDD. DSPs support people to work, develop new and maintain old relationships, have valued roles, practice their faith, learn new skills, and take part in many other aspects of community living and participation. Yet, for over 30 years many issues have made it difficult for people with disabilities, families, and employers to find and keep knowledgeable and skilled DSPs on the job. These challenges can lead to a lack of opportunity for people with IDD to live and participate as they choose in their community.

This chapter provides an overview of the role of the direct support workforce in supporting community living and participation for people with IDD. It provides information on current challenges and promising solutions that will help people with IDD, families, and service providers to find and keep the highly skilled workers needed for community living. Solutions are offered that target both organizations and disability service systems.

Role of the Direct Support Workforce

People with IDD depend on many sources of support to live, learn, and work in the community. An individual may have several different support networks, depending on their strengths and gifts and the kind of support they need. Support networks are made up of people in a variety of roles, includi family, friends, community members, and paid and unpaid workers. DSPs are an important source of support in these networks.

DSPs are known by many job titles, including direct support specialist, habilitation specialist, job coach, residential counselor, family care provider, personal care assistant, and many more. The Congressional Direct Support Professional Recognition Resolution of 2003 (S. Con. Res. 21/H. Con. Res. 94) defines a direct support professional as someone who is employed to "provide a wide range of supportive services to people with IDD on a day-to-day basis. These supportive services include habilitation, health needs, personal care and hygiene, employment, transportation, recreation, and housekeeping and other home management-related supports and services so that their clients can live and work in their communities" and "lead self-directed community and social lives" (Congressional Record, November 4, 2003, p. H10301).

DSPs play a critical role in the long-term services and supports (LTSS) system in the United States as more and more people with IDD are supported through Home and Community Based Services (HCBS) to live, learn, work, and play in their community. More often than not, DSPs work in a family home, individual home, or small supported living program in the community. The change over the years in where people with IDD live has drastically altered the role and expectations of the workforce as well as the settings in which they work.

Person-centered practices are at the forefront of HCBS and, as such, bring a renewed focus on DSPs as community navigators and connectors rather than caregivers. The role of the traditional caregiver has often emphasized job duties focused on health and safety needs, such as medication administration, supervision, activities of daily living (e.g., bathing, dressing, eating), and instrumental activities of daily living (e.g., budgeting, meal planning, shopping). Occupations that fall into the more traditional caregiving roles are personal care attendants, home health aides, and certified nursing assistants. While DSPs do have job duties that require traditional caregiving roles, they are much more than this: their jobs focus on delivering personalized supports that involve what is important to the person they are supporting, including their goals, wishes, preferences, and desires. Sometimes what is important to a person supersedes health or safety needs. DSPs are often faced with situations where they are helping a person with IDD balance what is important *to* them with the risks and consequences of an activity and what is important *for* the person. For example, someone who is fascinated by bees might like to try to learn how to keep bees, though the activity might be understood by some as risky. Given the person's interest in bee keeping, a DSP can support a person to learn about bee keeping and access a hive while balancing risk in this activity.

The varied settings in which DSPs work, and the lack of coworkers and supervisors on site, result in DSPs having significant independence, which requires significant skills in independent problem solving, autonomous decision making, and ethical judgment. Often DSPs are required to fulfill roles similar to many licensed professionals, such as teachers, nurses, psychologists, occupational and physical therapists, counselors, dieticians, chauffeurs, personal trainers, and others. DSPs have unique views of the lives of the people they support because they are around them the most. They provide a wide range of supports on a daily basis in a variety of settings, such as home, residential, employment, recreational, educational, community, and healthcare settings. DSPs may work alone or in teams.

Yet, despite the demands, nature, and autonomy of the work, the DSP workforce has not been valued by community members, policy makers, elected officials, and, in some cases, employers and people with disabilities as highly skilled professionals. Perhaps one of the most obvious ways in which this devaluation of the direct support workforce is shown is by the low wages and limited benefits they are offered. This contributes to a high turnover rate among DSPs, affecting the quality of supports. Constant change in workers creates instability and can result in health and safety issues, as well as a lack of attention to supporting a person to achieve personal goals that require support from a DSP.

Approximately 9 out of 10 direct support workers are women, with the average age being 42 (Paraprofessional Healthcare Institute, 2017). There are a growing number of foreign-born workers entering the field. Education levels vary, with immigrant workers more likely to hold higher educational degrees than non-immigrant workers (Espinoza, 2017). Half of all direct support workers rely on some form of public assistance to make ends meet (Paraprofessional Healthcare Institute, 2017).

It is difficult to estimate precisely the number of DSPs in the United States. The Bureau of Labor Statistics (BLS) does not have a specific occupational title for DSPs; rather, it includes them in the vast cadre of health and human service occupational titles that include personal care assistants, home health aides, and certified nursing assistants. State and agency job titles contribute to the confusion in counting on a national scale. There are nearly 4.5 million direct support workers in these categories, and this sector is among the top five fastest-growing occupations in the nation (BLS, 2015). Nevertheless, the number of workers (particularly women) available to fill current positions is shrinking. These workforce shortages will make it even more difficult in coming years for people with IDD to find the support they need, and will continue to affect the quality of support available to them.

Current Controversies and Challenges

The projected increase in demand for DSPs to support the number of people with IDD, coupled with a current shortage of workers to meet this growing demand, has serious implications for community living and the quality of life for people with IDD. This is a national public health concern and creates challenges for DSPs, families, providers of LTSS, and service delivery systems in assuring people that quality supports are available.

It is estimated that over 5 million workers will be needed by 2020 (Paraprofessional Healthcare Institute, 2017). In addition to the increasing demand for DSPs, the worker pool in the United States is shrinking. The women age 25–54 who make up the majority of the workforce are not entering the workforce at a rate commensurate with the number of those who are aging out (Paraprofessional Healthcare Institute, 2011).

Shortages are also occurring because the direct support workforce experiences high turnover and vacancy rates. Average annual turnover rates are around 45%, and of those who leave their jobs, 35% do so within six months of hire (Hiersteiner, 2016). This figure is striking when compared to the average separation rate of 3.5% across industries in the United States (BLS, 2017). Organizations that deliver LTSS are also operating with a large number of positions they are waiting to fill, while the average vacancy rate across organizations is 9% (Hiersteiner, 2016).

Implications for Direct Support Professionals

High turnover and vacancy rates affect committed DSPs who remain on the job in many ways that make their jobs more difficult. Although many find the profession rewarding, DSPs who are stretched beyond their capacity due to staffing shortages or by working too many hours are more likely to be stressed and experience burnout. DSPs receive minimal training, which is mostly focused on regulatory and mandated topics that do not provide sufficient competency-based training. Often the job expectations placed on DSPs require far more skills than they are trained for.

The national average wage for DSPs is $10.72 per hour (Hiersteiner, 2016), lower than the federal poverty line for a family of four (BLS, 2015). Nearly half of DSPs receive publicly funded benefits, such as medical, food, or housing assistance (Paraprofessional Healthcare Institute, 2017), and most work a second or third job (Test et al., 2003). After adjusting for inflation, DSPs have actually seen a decrease in wages between 2005 and 2015 (Paraprofessional Healthcare Institute, 2017). Many DSPs are also ineligible for employee health and retirement benefits because they either work part-time or are too new to the employing organization to be eligible. Even when they do have access to benefits, they may be unable to afford them. It is estimated that in 2011, about 1.2 million direct care workers worked without any health insurance (Paraprofessional Healthcare Institute, 2013).

Implications for Organizations

The vacancies and constant turnover faced by organizations that employ direct support professionals keep them focused on getting new hires in the door, and as a result, they have less energy and fewer resources to focus on keeping people in their jobs post-hire. This creates significant financial costs. Provider organizations have reported that the cost to recruit and replace a single DSP is between $2,413 and $5,200 (Hewitt & Larson, 2007; ANCOR, 2017 Medisked Connect, 2016). When nearly half of your employees stay for less than a year, replacement costs add up.

Most organizations report that they are not able to grow or serve additional people because they cannot find employees. In a recent study done in New York, 33% of providers say they are forced to delay or deny services to people with IDD because they cannot find staff (Hewitt et al., 2015). Difficulty finding people has also resulted in organizations hiring people who are not a good fit for the job but are willing to take the job regardless. This can lead to poor quality service and additional risk of accidents and abuse/neglect.

Cultural and linguistic diversity among the direct support workforce are strengths in providing supports for diverse populations. People of color, mostly African Americans and Latino immigrants, make up a large portion of the workforce. Of people who provide direct supports, 31% are African Americans and 15% are Hispanic or Latino (Paraprofessional Healthcare Institute, 2013). Between 20% and 42% of all direct care workers were born outside the United States (Paraprofessional Healthcare Institute, 2013). This shift in the demographic makeup of the workforce can present cultural challenges for new immigrants working in this industry, and potentially for the people receiving services and their families. Individuals who do not use speak English fluently, or use the preferred language of the person they support, may struggle to communicate and understand the needs and wishes of people whose cultural background differs from their own. Immigrants may struggle to understand American culture and the service system expectations. Cultural conflicts can also result in DSPs being asked to break or compromise on religious laws from their cultural faith background. Organizations that employ DSPs must be able to respond to these demographic changes by providing intentional training that promotes cultural competence among their staff and the people to whom they provide support.

Implications for Family

The majority of people with disabilities who receive services live in the home of a family member (Larson et al., 2017). DSP workforce shortages have a significant impact on families, which results in family members may be forced to provide support when they were not expecting to do so. This can impact employment for family members if they cannot consistently report to work. Indeed, many family members are unemployed or underemployed due to the need to provide care in the absence of a DSP (Hewitt et al., 2017, Anderson et al., 2011). DSP workforce shortages also can put additional caregiving strain on family members who need to step in on a regular basis to cover for a DSP. In some situations when states allow for self-direction and for family members to be paid, they are paid to provide direct support. But as family caregivers age, many worry about what it will mean for their loved one with IDD if they are no longer able to provide the support needed when DSPs do not show up or cannot be found.

"[T]he greatest challenge to be overcome at this time, before any of the others can be addressed, is the increasing lack of a worker pool, adequate in capacity and skill, to provide the direct support that enables [people with IDD] to survive each day."—Gail Frizzell, Mother (Frizzell, 2015, p. 42)

Implications for the System

Despite the national workforce crisis, policies and procedures continue to be formulated at federal, state, and organizational levels to support community inclusion, choice, and decision making for people with IDD. High expectations for DSPs to be person centered and support community inclusion and engagement at every level are articulated in these policies. Specifically, the Developmental Disabilities Assistance and Bill of Rights Act of 2000 (DD Act—PL 106-402) states that people with developmental disabilities may have access "to opportunities and necessary support to be included in community life, have interdependent relationships . . . [and have] access to and use of recreational, leisure and social opportunities to enrich their participation in community life" (Sec. 101(c)(8)&(12)). Fulfilling these promises is not possible without consistent, competent DSPs. States have also, over recent decades, implemented policies based on the Olmstead Decision that aim to reduce segregation by ensuring people the opportunity to live in the most integrated setting. More recently, the "HCBS Settings Rule" provides concrete definitions for what constitutes a "community setting" and puts forward expectations related to person-centered positive practices. Each of these policies changes the expectations of what LTSS are meant to do and the expected outcomes of such services, which, in turn, has implications for the direct support workforce.

As young adults with IDD transition out of high school, most want to work and live independently and be active members of their communities. Their families and allies want this too. People have higher expectations of services and supports as they move into adult services and supports. Efforts at the federal and state levels to promote community living and participation, use person-centered approaches, implement positive behavior support practices, ensure competitive employment opportunities, and increase supported decision making all require a stable and well-trained workforce. Yet, training requirements have not changed in response to these shifts, nor have systems increased training opportunities. Systems place expectations on providers that rely on a skilled workforce, but these systems have not effectively put in place the means to strengthen, train, and ensure an adequate and well-trained workforce.

Unfortunately, while the landscape of needed services and supports has transformed dramatically over the years, the approach to funding also remains unchanged (Frizzell, 2015), and as such, the workforce challenges remain. States are also faced with increasingly long waiting lists, and their efforts to provide support to all people with IDD who need services will be thwarted if solutions are not found.

Implications for Individuals

Ultimately and most importantly, these chronic and complex workforce issues affect the lives of people in the community who receive services and supports. People receiving services and supports experience a constant revolving door with regard to their staff. This has both a physical and an emotional impact of people with disabilities. Every time there is staff turnover, they experience disruption in routines and services, as well as missed opportunities. Quality community support is based on the relationship established between a direct support worker and the person served. It takes time to build effective relationships, and when as many staff leave within six months as the number who stay, it is difficult to establish trust. Too many DSPs don't even have time to get to know the person they support—and vice versa—before they leave their positions. People with IDD who are supported by DSPs miss out on opportunities for growth, learning, and community participation. The constant vacancies result in unfilled shifts and overworked DSPs, putting people with IDD at greater risk of health and safety issues, as well as neglect and abuse.

Life Course Expectations and Transitions

At each life stage the support needs of people with IDD and their families change. DSPs support people with IDD across the life span: they support children, youth, adults, and older adults. How and what they do are influenced by the person's support needs and preferences, which change over time. The roles and types of support provided by a DSP to someone with IDD and their family will be different at different life stages. Supports provided by the DSP are customized to meet individual needs. A DSP's role across the life course is never one-size-fits-all.

Early in life (birth to age 3). Families with a young child with IDD may be the child's only support, and it may be that no DSP is needed. In other situations, a family may depend on a DSP for significant daily support, which could include medical care or respite. As the child grows, the DSP may need to provide support like feeding and bathing or be responsible to help with occupational and physical therapy routines.

Early childhood (ages 3 to 5). When the child transitions into early childhood, the expectations of the DSP may change to helping follow through on routines that include teaching the child self-care skills, implementing therapy interventions (e.g., behavior, speech, occupational, or physical), and supports designed to promote child development. DSPs might work in a family home, clinical setting, or early childhood setting and support the child with their social-emotional development and educational programming.

School age (5 to 18 or 22, depending on the state). Paraprofessionals or classroom aides may support school-age children in the classroom by providing educational, behavioral, or social supports in integrated and special education settings. During the school-age years, DSPs may work in the child's family home and assist with activities of daily living, community integration, and after-school and other community activities. As the child grows and moves into the transition age (14 to 18), DSPs in schools, provider organizations, and at home support the youth in learning job skills, problem solving, and being a part of their community.

Adulthood (age 18/22+). When the person moves away from home, as most adults do, a DSP may support the person to live independently in their own home, in a shared living situation, or group home. Their role typically includes supporting the person in building relationships with community members and neighbors, maintaining a home, cooking nutritious meals, ensuring health and safety, learning self-advocacy skills, supporting choice and decision making, and participating in lifelong learning. DSPs also serve as job coaches or employment consultants to support people to find and keep employment, including cultivating support networks within their places of work.

Older adults (age 65+). DSPs may find they are supporting older adults to age in place or providing services in long-term healthcare facilities. Often the focus of the DSP turns to supporting the individual to maintain their skills, health, and well-being. DSPs support people with IDD in understanding the life cycle and what dying means, as well as dealing with grief when others around them die.

Practical Suggestions and Interventions

As we have discussed, DSPs play pivotal roles in facilitating community inclusion for people with IDD, but the workforce is plagued with pervasive issues that result in high turnover and vacancy rates, along with unskilled, inconsistent supports. While this problem is large and often feels insurmountable to employers, strategies are available to address the challenges. What follows is an overview of practical suggestions and interventions that can be used to help build and stabilize the DSP workforce.

Recruitment and Selection Strategies

Effective recruitment and selection strategies aim to ensure that candidates are being recruited to apply for positions, understand the duties of the position for which they are applying, and are carefully selected and appropriately matched with people to support. If carefully implemented, these strategies can assist with reducing turnover, particularly early turnover (within the first six months of employment). Many such strategies are identified in the following section and can be utilized in varying combinations based on the needs of the organization.

Targeted recruitment strategies. Targeted recruitment strategies identify characteristics of DSPs who thrive and stay with a given organization and then do targeted marketing toward that audience. Common groups of stayers might be:

- College students
- Empty-nesters
- Retirees
- People from a particular faith
- Single mothers
- Previous volunteers
- People who live within a few miles of their work location
- Displaced workers
- Youth workers (e.g., high school seniors)

Once the target market is identified, job postings are designed for that demographic and placed in locations where they are most likely to engage. For example, if the workforce is primarily empty-nesters, the advertisements can speak to "filling your new time with valued work" or "turning your nurturing and teaching skills into a new profession." Or if the target group is recently displaced workers from a factory, the targeted messages could be "No more line work; bring meaning back into your work" or "Flexible scheduling and fun work environment." To attract high school seniors, you would likely work with school guidance counselors to post job ads. Instead of a one-size-fits-all advertising campaign, targeted marketing encourages organizations to market their open positions with messages that speak to very specific audiences. Depending on that audience, it is also important to vary the location and means through which marketing occurs (e.g., social media and digital platforms, fliers in local agencies or community centers, print media).

Using inside sources for recruitment. Current employees are often the best sources of new referrals. Engaging current employees in the process, and encouraging or rewarding them for their role in filling vacant positions, can be an investment that helps recruit quality employees.

Expanding the pipeline. Conversely, targeting workers by using new marketing strategies or worker pipelines can be an important way of filling vacant positions. Strategies exist to recruit younger workers, such as programs on alternative tracks in high schools that educate students for careers in human services. An example of this is Grove City, Ohio's Community Career Connections Program–Ohio (C3PO). This program gives high school students a pathway to a credential to become a certified DSP. Juniors and seniors in high school gain access to the components of a DSP credentialing program that they can utilize to gain employment in the workforce post-high school. More information on this program is available at http://www.swcsdcareertech.com/c3po.html. Finally, older workers looking to supplement their current income may be another promising population that could be targeted to fill vacancies.

Direct support workforce registries and matching services. Workforce registries and matching services provide a mechanism for linking people who need supports with qualified and appropriate staff. Finding a DSP who is an appropriate match for a person can maximize the quality of person-centered supports. Registries and matching services provide forms that identify and store information regarding likes and dislikes, interests, skills, and DSP competencies. An example of a DSP matching service is MySupport (www.mysupport.com). MySupport may be particularly useful for people who self-direct their services. This means that the person with IDD hires, manages, supervises, and discharges their support staff, instead of utilizing a home care agency. MySupport leads users through a series of questions about their preferences in support-related scenarios. Personality queries and other relevant information are collected to assign a compatibility score between workers and people seeking to employ a DSP.

Realistic Job Previews. Realistic Job Previews (RJPs) provide recruits seeking employment with an opportunity to see, prior to hire, what a day in their work life might look like. Given that over one-third of DSPs hired depart from their position within six months, RJPs provide potential workers with a clear and accurate understanding of the role they will play in a person's life. This can set them up for success in their new position by helping them start with realistic expectations of what the role entails. Conversely, if a person experiences an RJP and then decides they would not be a good fit for the job, the company does not invest in an employee who will not end up staying.

RJPs can take various forms, including fully produced videos, scrapbooks, or photographs with captions of the supports a person needs. Advancements in technology, the use of cell phone cameras, and editing software have made RJPs more common and accessible for people to create quickly and easily.

Retention Strategies

Many organizations report that they have high vacancy rates; the national average is just under 10% (NASDDDS, 2016). The most effective way to avoid vacancies is to keep the staff you do hire. Various strategies can help organizations reduce turnover and increase retention. These include competency-based training, recognition, positive organizational culture, access to fair wages and benefits, and promoting DSP professional identify. Each of these strategies is discussed in the following sections.

DSPs are expected to know and be able to do a lot of concrete things in order to effectively support a person with IDD in the community. Nearly all states have regulations surrounding preservice training for DSPs. For example, a state may require 40 hours of training before the DSP works with a person. Such preservice training is likely to include first aid techniques, cardiopulmonary resuscitation (CPR) certification, medication administration, crisis intervention, and documentation practices. Inservice training or recertification training may also be required annually or at regular intervals after a DSP is hired, based on the number of hours they work. It is difficult for organizations to complete the training of new DSPs because they need people to fill vacancies immediately and often do not have staff to cover open positions while new people are training. As such, training can be rushed and inconsistent in its delivery. While regulatory and mandated training is important, it focuses on topics (vs. skill demonstration) and is not nearly comprehensive enough to develop all of the skills required of effective DSPs.

Competency-based training (CBT) is a method of training designed and used to develop needed skills in DSPs. CBT delineates what a person needs to know, the skills they need to perform, and attitudes and values they should embrace to provide quality support in their work. CBT programs are usually composed of a combination of learning delivery methods, including classroom presentations, on-the-job training, online courses, and assessments (e.g., written tests, skill demonstration, or professional portfolios). Programs are often tiered to offer multiple levels of completion or "step-off points" (e.g., certificates, badges, degrees). The ability to make progress toward completing a program using shorter amounts of time allows DSPs to enjoy greater completion success. These pathways are sometimes called career "ladders" or "lattices," and each step within the credential program is linked to specific needed competencies. CBT programs have been gaining support among DSPs and their employers as a strategy for raising the quality of supports, while reducing turnover and providing benchmarks for wage increases.

National Association of Direct Support Professionals

- DSP Competencies
- Participant Empowerment
- Community Living Skills and Supports
- Communication
- Documentation
- Assessment
- Community and Service Networking
- Facilitation of Services
- Education, Training, and Self-Development
- Advocacy
- Vocational, Educational, and Career Support
- Crisis Prevention, and Intervention
- Organizational Participation
- Building and Maintaining Friendships and Relationships
- Providing Person-Centered Supports
- Supporting Health and Wellness

Note. Source: NADSP (2017). Used with permission.

One study examining CBT programs included (1) online modules aligned with the NADSP competencies and specific desired outcomes for people with IDD (e.g., employment, home living, health and wellness, community inclusion), (2) discussion facilitated by a supervisor or lead DSP of the training content and its application to DSP jobs, and (3) on-the-job skill demonstration. Findings revealed the intervention group had reduced turnover, improved retention, greater DSP satisfaction with supervisors, and improved outcomes for people with IDD (Bogenshutz et al., 2015). Given CBT's targeted focus on DSP competencies and skills, it can be an important tool for raising the quality and consistency of DSP skills. CBT programs may also reduce costs related to injuries or DSPs not adequately prepared for their responsibilities.

No state or national credentialing program is required of DSPs in the United States. However, a few states have efforts underway to implement "portable" DSP credentials, and many organizations have taken it upon themselves to implement such programs. Portable credentials would allow DSPs' training to be recognized by other organizations or across state lines. Such infrastructure could be an important way to incentivize DSPs for their commitment to providing quality support. The National Alliance for Direct Support Professionals (NADSP) is a professional association for DSPs that offers a national credentialing and/or badging program aligned with the nationally validated DSP competencies, but few DSPs have successfully completed this program. NADSP also provides a list of accredited training curricula that are approved and determined to align with the NADSP competencies and accreditation criteria.

Training Programs Accredited by NADSP

- DirectCourse: College of Direct Support
- Relias Learning
- PATHS
- North Dakota Community Staff Training Program
- ARC Broward PATHS Certificate S
- The Academy for Direct Support Professionals
- The Training Collaborative for Innovative Leadership
- Star Services
- Human Services Credentialing Program
- Open Future Learning

Note. NADSP (2017). Used with permission. https://www.nadsp.org/accredited-education-curricula/

Successful completion of credentialing programs provides a way to improve workers' skills, differentiate them from non-credentialed workers, and reward them for their achievements. Incentivizing successful completion of an accredited training program by tying it to wage enhancements can provide a useful policy argument for increased funding to increase wages of credentialed workers. Lack of funding is often cited as a barrier to implementation of credentialing programs. In response to this, the Centers for Medicare and Medicaid Services issued a bulletin to states clarifying that continuing education and training costs for DSPs could be identified by states as an allowable reimbursable cost in Medicaid rate setting (CMS, 2011). A toolkit was developed to help state Medicaid administrators understand strategies and methods that can be used to cover these costs of continuing education (Robbins, Dilla, Sedlezky, & Johnson Sirek, 2013).

Recognition programs. DSPs are often overlooked as professionals, despite the complexity and importance of their jobs. The important work of DSPs was formally recognized in the Congressional Direct Support Professional Resolution of 2003 (S. Con. Res. 21/H. Con. Res. 94). This resolution authorized a week in September that is now also recognized by many state governors and organizations as an opportunity to celebrate and acknowledge DSPs and the direct support profession. National associations have also established awards to recognize outstanding organizations in the field. Moving Mountains is an example of a national award that recognizes organizations that implement outstanding, effective practices. Examples also exist of awards given within local organizations to accomplished and committed DSPs. For instance, some agencies do an annual DSP recognition banquet to thank DSPs for their services.

Yet, awards and designated recognition periods are not enough. Recognition of DSPs has to become a part of everyday interactions between supervisors, management, and DSPs in any organization. Sometimes smaller acts of recognition, such as the following, matter most to DSPs:

- Noticing what DSPs are contributing and doing every day in their work, and saying thank you
- Sending a handwritten note to a DSP on their three-, six-, and 12-month anniversary of employment, and then annually thereafter
- Sending each DSP a birthday card on the date of their birthday
- Having a raffle drawing for a $5 gift card at every staff meeting as a means of saying thank you
- Sharing a story with supervisors and managers about the positive action a DSP took that made a difference in the life of someone they support
- Including staff profiles in every newsletter or email communication that goes to all staff, service users, and families
- Asking the board of directors and families to say thank you to DSPs when they see them

It is also important to ask DSPs, at time of hire, how they like to be recognized. Some prefer formal recognition in front of peers and others; some prefer more humble and individual recognition practices. In order to truly make an employee feel valued, it is important to recognize them in ways that matter and feel comfortable to them.

Creating a positive and respectful organizational culture. Creating an organizational culture that affirms respect and a sense of belonging for employees is an important means of keeping DSPs on the job. When DSPs feel valued by their employer, they are more likely to remain committed to their job, even in the face of challenges. When they feel supported and included by their supervisors, they are also more likely to stay. Organizations can cultivate a culture of respect and professionalism that helps DSPs feel pride and value in their work.

Positive organizational characteristics that support DSP retention

- The organization is a learning organization. Top leadership, managers, and DSPs on the front lines doing the work are all supported to learn. These organizations invest in learning and often strive to improve and make changes based on something they have recently learned. Often the leaders are well versed not only in strategies to support people with disabilities but also in business practices and leadership.
- Leaders of these organizations know who the DSPs are and call them by name.
- Leaders and managers occasionally practice direct support themselves.
- DSPs are afforded purposeful and strategic opportunities to be heard within the organization. Leaders often hold intentional listening sessions, use quick surveys, and/or practice an open-door policy to stay abreast of what DSPs are thinking and doing.
- The organization uses data to drive changes in practices related to the direct support workforce or other areas.
- The organization uses stories as a powerful tool to keep its employees focused on the mission of the organization and on outcomes for people with IDD. Board, leadership, management, and staff meetings often start with a story about how a person who is supported by the organization made a positive connection or contribution to the community or achieved a personal goal. The role the DSP played in such an achievement is also shared.

In addition to these characteristics, it is critical that organizations use culturally relevant practices. The direct support workforce is diverse. Organizations need to be responsive to the different religious, cultural, and linguistic needs and practices of its employees. Having flexible holiday schedules, ensuring that information is shared in languages employees speak, allowing for flexible scheduling to accommodate religious needs, and learning about and recognizing various traditions and aspects of employee cultures are all important actions. It is also essential to teach and train all staff to be culturally competent.

Enhancing the professional image of DSPs. Attracting workers to the direct workforce field and then retaining them can be fostered by enhancing the professional image of DSPs. There are a number of ways to enhance the visibility of the direct support profession as a whole: (1) reaching out into the community to create pipelines for new workers; (2) letting DSPs know that they are part of a larger profession, and offering them opportunities to network with and learn from other DSPs; (3) developing and implementing professional public awareness campaigns.

Most people in the community do not know who DSPs are and what they do. Most children are not taught about human service occupations, such as direct support professionals, as they are about professions like nursing, teaching, and firefighting. Working with primary and secondary schools to help kids become aware of these jobs can increase their likelihood of exploring direct support as a career later on. In schools, this could start with the DSPs and people with IDD the students already see regularly in their halls, lunchroom, and classes. It is also important to offer opportunities within the community for people to learn not only about your organization but also about the jobs it offers and the role of DSPs. Having DSPs co-present at faith communities, service clubs, and other community events can increase awareness of who these workers are and what they do. Participation on workforce boards and other employment- and job-related community organizations is another strategy to increase the community awareness of the direct support profession.

Many states have professional associations for DSPs; most are state chapters affiliated with the National Alliance for Direct Support Professionals (NADSP; www.nadsp.org. NADSP has four priorities: (1) to enhance the status and recognition of DSPs, (2) to provide opportunities for training and education, (3) to support development and implementation of a voluntary credential program for DSPs, and (4) to support public policy initiatives that increase wages and compensation for DSPs, and determine an occupational title that matches the role and responsibilities of DSPs. Organizations can support DSPs by encouraging NADSP membership or purchasing group memberships for their employees.

Various states (e.g., Indiana, Minnesota, New York, Ohio, Oregon) have launched grassroots and public awareness campaigns to increase awareness about the important work performed by DSPs. These campaigns mobilize people to share their stories and advocate for change using various media formats (e.g., billboards, social media, public service announcements, advertisements) and organized political advocacy strategies (e.g., rallies, call-ins, sit-ins, in-person visits, write-ins) to draw attention to the profession and the need to increase wages, benefits, and recognition. Two effective examples of such campaigns are BeFair2DirectCare (https://www.facebook.com/BFair2DirectCare/) and Value the Work, Raise the Wage (www.oregonresource.org/value-the-work.html). Combined, these efforts provide opportunities for engagement, networking, and developing a strong professional identity for DSPs, as well as bringing broader attention to who DSPs are and what they do.

Systems and Policy-level Strategies

Building cost-of-living and wage increases into rate structures. Since the onset of community support for people with IDD, direct support wages have been low and benefits, poor. Over time, DSP wages have not kept up with inflation; thus, wages are lower than they were 15 years ago when adjusted for inflation. Many organizations face the reality that in their communities, they pay lower wages than do grocery stores, fast-food restaurants, and other service industries where employees have far less responsibility and accountability. While most DSPs love their work, many must also consider their financial responsibilities. As a result, good people leave the field.

For many industries funded by the government, cost-of-living increases are a part of the legislation that authorizes the services and funding. One strategy to keep DSP wages from sinking further would be to change policies to make cost-of-living increases a given.

Developing career paths through credentialing programs that lead to various levels of certification can provide a rationale for higher rates paid to providers to, in turn, pay their DSPs who have attained higher levels of training and credentials. Not all DSPs have the same responsibilities. For example, some DSPs pass medications; some do not. Some DSPs implement behavior support strategies for people with IDD who have significant behavior support needs; some do not. Some DSPs provide medical interventions such as tube feeding, wound care, and tracheotomy care; some do not. Credentialing workers for the specific skills they perform might be another way to provide a rationale to policy makers for the need to pay them more.

Self-directed services and natural supports. Self-directed long-term services and supports allow people with IDD to determine their own goals, support needs, and desired services, and to find, choose, and train their own staff. Self-direction promotes independence and allows people to control their own life and the supports they receive. Currently, 41 states offer some type of self-direction as a support option through their Medicaid Home and Community Based Services (DeCarlo, Hall-Lande, Bogenschutz, & Hewitt, 2017). However, availability of such services and the manner in which they are rolled out differ across states. Depending on the state, self-directed services may allow people to pay higher rates to their DSPs; however, this may also make it less likely for DSPs to receive fringe benefits as part of their employment. In some self-directed models, family members can be reimbursed to provide services typically performed by DSPs. This can greatly impact a family's finances when difficulties retaining DSPs have made it hard for family members to maintain their own employment. Extended family and friends can also serve as DSPs, although some people with IDD prefer not to have a relationship with their DSP that crosses into their personal life. On the other hand, allowing friends and family to provide support sometimes leads to quality, consistent support.

In short, self-directed service models solve some issues with the DSP shortage by letting people find their own staff. Even so, only a very small percentage of people with IDD and their families use this type of service. Increasing self-directed options that allow people to use friends, neighbors, and family members as paid support workers, and promoting this as a viable alternative, could be one component of a comprehensive direct support workforce plan.

Independent contractors and cooperatives. Alternatives to the traditional provider organization models exist. In some states and programs, some DSPs are independent contractors. This means they contract directly with the state and are most often paid by the state. In this model, the provider organization has no role or a modified role, which can reduce overhead business costs, increase wages for DSPs, and improve retention. These independent contractors can find work through advertisements, registries, or other methods. Not all states offer this option, but successful models operate in Arizona, California, Oregon, Minnesota, and Washington.

DSP Worker Cooperatives also operate in some states. These are autonomous employment organizations developed and owned jointly by DSPs with the purpose of meeting their common economic, social, and cultural needs. These associations may result in reduced poverty and increased employment opportunities for DPSs as they become business owners and manage aspects of the organization's operation. They also have more control over their wages, benefits, training, and workplace culture. This model is most commonly used in home health services, but it has begun to positively impact the DSP workforce as well.

Natural supports through community inclusion. Perhaps one of the most significant ways to reduce the demand for DSPs is to ensure that people with IDD get connected to their communities through relationships and active participation. The more that people with IDD are engaged in, active in, and supported by their communities, the less they need paid supports. This is sometimes referred to as the use of "natural support" and basically means that people not paid to provide support serve to meet some of a person's support needs. This, in turn, can reduce one's dependency on paid support.

Natural supports are those that are common to most people. They are often based on a relationship connected to an activity or interest a person shares with others. Examples of natural supports for someone with IDD might be friends helping them move, attending sporting events with someone who also wants to go, or meeting up with a buddy at church. Using natural supports can increase the quality of life for a person with IDD while easing demands on the direct support workforce, currently stretched thin, by reducing a person's reliance on paid staff to meet all of their support needs.

Implementing technology-enhanced supports. Advances in technology have been important for increasing accessibility, efficiency, quality, and continuity of supports for people with IDD. Technologies are sometimes used to supplement DSP practices, while other times they are used in the absence of DSPs. Some states now include use of technology as part of what their Medicaid HCBS and State Plan Services provide. Various technologies are used to assist people with transportation and navigating the community. Technologies can also help people do tasks that no one previously recognized that the person was capable of doing (e.g., cooking, using the telephone, cleaning). The use of technology can facilitate greater independence and prevent people from living in more restrictive settings. Following are some technologies currently being used by people with IDD:

Sensors. Sensors can be used to monitor health and safety. A commonly used sensor technology can be worn on a person's wrist or around their neck. The person can push a button to alert a DSP or emergency team if they have fallen. Sensors can also be placed on doorways so that a person's activities can be monitored. Doorway sensors can be installed on entry doors to alert if a person has left their home, or if an unexpected person has entered the home. Sensors can also be placed on beds or in bathrooms to monitor activity or identify health issues. Sensors on beds can identify conditions such as sleep apnea, unusual sleep patterns, and restlessness, or diabetes (unusually high frequency of urination).

Remote monitoring. Use of video monitoring is more controversial than less invasive forms of monitoring and is restricted in many cases. However, remote monitoring can be useful by allowing someone to monitor a person's behavior in the absence of an on-site DSP, or to reduce need for more than one paid staff member in a group home setting during times when people are typically sleeping.

Computer-assisted devices. Computer-assisted devices, such as tablets and smartphones, can support learning and reduce a person's reliance on DSPs. Common uses include applications that utilize Global Positioning Systems (GPS) and voice-activated instructions to support community navigation. Transportation services can be accessed through applications ("apps") like Uber and Lyft. There are also many apps for smart devices that help people communicate when they can't do so verbally. Other apps can be used on job sites to sequence job tasks and reduce dependence on job coaches.

Electronic medication dispensers. Electronic medication dispensers can help people to take medications as prescribed by physicians, which traditionally has been an important role of DSPs. In the absence of adequate or consistent human supports, electronic medication dispensers can reduce the chance of error in taking medicine. Medication dispensers can be programed to offer the correct dosage at a particular time. They can also provide verbal prompts to alert a person to take their medication.

These are just a few of the most commonly used technologies that support independence and community living. Many people with IDD have been able to reduce their dependence on DSPs by using technological support instead of human support. For current information on technology, go to the Coleman Institute website (https://www.colemaninstitute.org/). The Coleman Institute is nationally recognized for its research in technology to promote community living for people with IDD.

Personal Illustration: Hiram Williams

"We had a person we supported who was pretty quiet. Never really said much and just went along with the flow," recalled Hiram Williams, a direct support professional in New York. "I attempted to communicate with him because I felt like there was just something not right." Hiram offered the man a pencil and paper, encouraging him to express himself through drawing. Instead, the man picked up the pencil and began writing words. "This grown man, 50-something years old, could read and write and no one knew." Today he writes letters to his family and uses FaceTime on his iPad. "He can communicate now," said Hiram. "And all it took was for someone to sit him down and understand, instead of going along with the normal routine. That's what did it for me. That's what made me love being a direct support professional." For more than 15 years, Hiram has supported people with IDD in living full, inclusive lives in their communities. The operative word is "support," in a field that has emphasized health and safety through a paternal model of caregiving.

"Today we're focusing on outcomes and personal autonomy and helping people direct the course of their own lives," said Joe Macbeth, Executive Director of the National Association for Direct Support Professionals, an organization committed to advancing the skills and status of the direct support workforce. This is a 180-degree change from the system-centered services that have historically been provided to people with intellectual and developmental disabilities.

"I pretty much try to give people the skills necessary in order to support themselves," said Hiram. As a DSP, Hiram sees his role as facilitating relationships in the broader community, ensuring that the people he supports have the opportunity to participate meaningfully in their neighborhoods—"to make friends, to go out and be able to see a movie, to enjoy everything in life that everyone enjoys."

One person Hiram supports is an older gentleman named John, who uses few words and likes to stay active. "He has an abstract way of communicating, but with spending enough time with him you kind of understand what he's trying to say through his body language, gestures, facial expressions, things of that nature. He's pretty good at articulating his wants and needs." Hiram listens carefully to John and ensures that his wants and needs are met. "At the end of the day, everyone has an opinion on how they feel their life should be. And it's our job to support that and try to make that dream come true for each individual person."

Hiram's work includes a number of routine tasks, such as administering medications, assisting with personal hygiene, planning and preparing healthy meals, and providing transportation. But it is the more nuanced work of actively listening to those he supports and building bridges to the community that defines his role as a successful DSP. "It's a hard job, taking responsibility for other people's lives," stressed Hiram. "And it's not something everyone can do." Hiram embraces his title of direct support professional, but finds that many outside of human services do not have a good understanding or appreciation of the work he does. "Usually I feel like people think that we're like babysitters, and that we're just hanging out, no real work involved."

Joe Macbeth concurs with Hiram's observation. "DSPs are viewed as caregivers, working entry-level jobs, when they are responsible for supporting some of the most vulnerable people in society." There remains a long road ahead before DSPs are as valued and appreciated as teachers and nurses, two related professions. "It is not a babysitting job," said Macbeth, "and we need to do a better job of informing policymakers, elected officials, and the voters of what this workforce actually does."

Before becoming a DSP, Hiram worked in a variety of positions, some more financially rewarding than direct support, but none that offered the level of personal satisfaction he feels today. "The feeling you get for making a difference in someone's life, you get that every day. And that to me is priceless."

Personal Illustration: Michelle Murphy

Michelle Murphy was working for an insurance company in Westchester County, making a long daily commute to a job she didn't love. Her sister, Chrissy, received vocational training supports from an agency closer to Michelle's home and suggested she apply for work as a direct support professional. "Just tell them you know me and they'll probably give you the job."

Michelle now works as a DSP for The Arc of Ulster-Greene, supporting eight individuals in a house, two of whom are married and live in an attached apartment. "It's always been something that's close to my heart and something that I felt that I was good at," said Michelle, who studied social welfare and counseling psychology in college. "Day to day, you're helping people live their best life."

Being challenged to use her education, skills, and experience keeps Michelle fully present in her work supporting a number of individuals with complex medical support needs. "I'm communicating with doctors, insurance companies, and health offices regularly," ensuring people's health concerns are met. Michelle manages schedules, helps with appointments, and facilitates conversations but is careful not to speak for the people she supports. "I really like to encourage them to speak for themselves because they know their health and what they do daily better that I do. I think they should be the first point of contact."

Direct support is not just a job but a career for Michelle. She was eager to expand her horizons and pursued the one-year credentialing course offered by the National Alliance for Direct Support Professionals, a rigorous program that allows DSPs to learn and apply best practices and evidence-based skills and knowledge in the workplace. "In the credentialing program I think I learned more about why I love this work," said Michelle. "I figured out what I needed to do to help a person enhance their life the way that *they* wanted to enhance their life."

Like most DSPs, Michelle struggles to get by on the low wages and works plenty of overtime. But she's found her calling. "This is a wonderful field to work in. And you meet so many different people that make you excited to continue doing the work and encourage you to be the best direct support professional you can be."

Personal Illustration: Nikeeta Smith

"We just get scraps." That's how Nikeeta Smith describes the low wages she and others supporting people with disabilities receive. "People working at Walmart and McDonald's are making more than us, and I think it's a slap in the face to people with disabilities and their families, because to me it's like saying you don't think they're worth it."

But choosing a career path is more than an economic choice. For Nikeeta, supporting others is a deeply held value, and she wanted a career that honored this. At age 19 Nikeeta pursued work leading to becoming a Certified Nursing Assistant. "A lot of friends were doing it," she recalled, though nursing wasn't her passion. And then someone suggested she work in a day program supporting people with developmental disabilities and her career direction changed. "I was fascinated by it. I really liked it."

The variety, complexity, and responsibility of the work were attractive to Nikeeta. "We're wearing so many hats as direct support professionals – counselor, therapist, chef, driver, we're passing medications, doing treatments." Challenging work requiring creative problem-solving has been a good match for Nikeeta, and, most importantly for her, this work makes a difference in the lives of others.

As a mother raising three children by herself, Nikeeta has found that becoming a DSP has made a difference in her life as well. "The work itself has helped me to grow as a person, being more nurturing and person-centered. The work translates; it's not just what we're doing here on the job."

Unfortunately, the pay is not commensurate with the work, and raising children on DSP wages is not easy. Disability associations in many states are fighting for higher wages but the gains have been small. "If you're recognizing [people with intellectual and developmental disabilities] as people," said Nikeeta, "then it should be a no-brainer that the professionals who are working with them daily, and helping them with their goals, and their hygiene, and their medication, and their travel, are treated as and respected as professionals, and compensated for it."

To further her professional development, Nikeeta enrolled in the DSP credentialing program offered by NADSP, an investment in her career that offered not only new knowledge and skills but professional recognition and a pay increase. "I got a $1.50 raise for the first credential, the C1, and another raise after getting a promotion to Assistant Residence Manager."

Nikeeta would like to see all DSPS get opportunities for professional development and advancement, and better pay. "I love what I do. It's very meaningful work and it needs to be recognized."

Conclusion

There is no doubt that DSPs play a critical role in supporting community living and participation for people with IDD. DSPs facilitate and support opportunities for people with IDD so they can live, work, love, and experience community life to the fullest extent possible.

Organizations, families, and people with IDD do often face significant obstacles in finding, hiring, training, and keeping DSPs, due to the shortage of available workers and the difficult working conditions. However, many promising solutions also exist that can be implemented to overcome these challenges and yield a more stable direct support profession and workforce.

Discussion Questions

- How can technology, both high-tech and low-tech, be used as a solution to the workforce crisis? Give some examples of such technologies, and explain how they help solve workforce challenges.
- What are some of the most significant challenges to a stable, professional workforce? What are some of the promising solutions that can help mitigate each challenge?
- What are three strategies an organization can use to recruit qualified direct support professionals? Explain each and how it can help solve the workforce crisis.
- What are some common strategies that organizations can employ to keep and retain high-performing DSPs? How and why do they work to reduce turnover and vacancy rates?
- How do workplace stress and job demands influence turnover intentions among DSPs who support adults with IDD? How do they influence vacancy rates for organizations?

Resources

- Direct Support Professional Workforce Development Toolkit. In response to the growing challenges service providers face in recruiting and retaining direct support professionals, ANCOR, in collaboration with the Research and Training Center (RTC) on Community Living at the University of Minnesota, created a Direct Support Professional Workforce Development Toolkit for ANCOR members. This toolkit includes targeted marketing and recruitment tools such as a realistic job preview, customizable fliers and public service announcements, structured behavioral interview questions, and competency sets for DSPs and frontline supervisors (http://www.nationaladvocacycampaign.org/welcome).
- National Alliance of Direct Support Professionals (NADSP). This national organization is a coalition of organizations that works to improve the quality of human service support by making the direct support workforce stronger. The mission of the NADSP is to promote the development of a highly competent human services workforce which supports people with IDD in achieving their life goals(https://nadsp.org/).
- MySupport. MySupport is an online tool that focuses on matching direct support professionals with people with IDD who are looking for support. This tool is particularly useful for people with IDD who use self-directed supports and services (www.mysupport.com).
- DirectCourse. DirectCourse is a suite of training curricula aimed at direct support professionals (DSPs) and frontline supervisors . It is an online training program based on the latest research in best practices for developing support for people with IDD and other disabilities. It comes with a powerful learning management system that helps track training records. It is designed to develop the skills and competencies of DSPs and frontline supervisors. (http://directcourseonline.com/).
- Paraprofessional Healthcare Institute (PHI) Workforce Data Center. PHI's data center is a place to find direct support workforce wage and employment statistics, across states and nationwide. PHI provides customized, up-to-date snapshots on this quickly growing workforce (https://phinational.org/policy-research/workforce-data-center/).
- The ARC DSP Toolkit. The Direct Support Professional Workforce Development (DSP) Toolkit addresses several resources that chapters of The Arc and people with disabilities and their families served by chapters can use to improve their workforce development practices (www.thearc.org/for-chapters/dsp-toolkit).

References

Administration on Community Living (2017) History of the DD Act. Administration on Community Living. Retrieved from https://www.acl.gov/node/105

ANCOR. (2017). Addressing the Disability Services Workforce Crisis of the 21st Century Retrieved from: https://cqrcengage.com/ancor/file/ZuL1zlyZ3mE/Workforce%20White%20Paper%20-%20Final%20-%20hyperlinked%20version.pdf

Anderson, L. L., Larson, S. A., & Wuorio, A. (2011). 2010 FINDS National Survey Technical Report Part 1: Family Caregiver Survey. Minneapolis: University of Minnesota, Research and Training Center on Community Living.

Application of the Fair Labor Standards Act to Domestic Service. (2013). Federal Register (National Archives & Records Service, Office of the Federal Register), 78(190), 60454-60557.

The Arc DSP Toolkit. Retrieved from www.thearc.org/for-chapters/dsp-toolkit

Bureau of Labor Statistics, U.S. Department of Labor (2017). Economic new release: Table 3. Total separations levels and rates by industry and region, seasonally adjusted. Retrieved from: https://www.bls.gov/news.release/jolts.t03.htm

Bureau of Labor Statistics , U.S. Department of Labor Occupational Outlook Handbook 2012–13.

Bureau of Labor Statistics , U.S. Department of Labor. (2015r). Fastest growing occupations. Occupational Outlook Handbook. Retrieved from https://www.bls.gov/ooh/fastest-growing.htm

Bogenschutz, M., Hewitt, A., Nord, D., & Hepperlen, R. (2014). Direct support workforce supporting individuals with IDD: Current wages, benefits, and stability. *Intellectual and Developmental Disabilities, 52,* 317–329.

Bogenschutz, M., Nord, D., & Hewitt, A. (2015). Competency-based training and worker turnover in community supports for people with IDD: Results rrom a group randomized controlled study. *Intellectual & Developmental Disabilities, 53*, 182–195. doi:10.1352/1934-9556-53.3.182

Centers for Medicare and Medicaid Services (2017) What is LTSS? Long-Term Services and Supports Technical Assistance Center.

Centers for Medicare and Medicaid Services. Retrieved from https://www.cms.gov/Outreach-and-Education/American-Indian-Alaska-Native/AIAN/ltss-ta-center/

Churilla, A., Smith, K., Potter, S. J., & Duncan, C. (2005). Is this a sustainable occupation? A profile of the direct dare giver workforce in the United States. Conference Papers-American Sociological Association, 1–7.

Congressional Budget Office(2013) The 2013 long term budget outlook. Congressional Budget Office. Retrieved from https://www.cbo.gov/publication/44521

DeCarlo, M., Hall-Lande, J. Bogenschutz, M. & Hewitt, A. (2017). State of the states in self-direction for individuals with intellectual and developmental disabilities. *Policy Research Brief, 26,* 1, Research and Training Center on Community Living at the University of Minnesota.

Department of Health and Human Services. Annual update of the HHS poverty guidelines. 80 Fed. Reg. 3236. (2015).

Developmental Disabilities Assistance and Bill of Rights Act of 2000. Pub. L. No. 106-402. (2000).

Frizzell, G. (2015).The direct support workforce crisis: A parent's perspective.

Espinoza, R. (2017) Immigrants and the direct care workforce. New York: Paraprofessional Healthcare Institute. Retrieved from https://phinational.org/sites/default/files/research-report/immigrants_and_the_direct_care_workforce_-_phi_-_june_2017.pdf

GAO (2016) Long-term care workforce. Better information needed on nursing assistants, home health aides, and other direct care workers. United States Government Accountability Office. Retrieved from http://www.gao.gov/assets/680/679100.pdf

Graham, J., (2017) Severe shortage of direct care workers triggering crisis.

Kaiser Health News, Disability Scoop. Retrieved from https://www.disabilityscoop.com/2017/05/09/severe-shortage-care-crisis/23679/

Gray, J. A., & Muramatsu, N. (2013). When the job has lost its appeal: Intentions to quit among direct care workers. *Journal of Intellectual & Developmental Disability, 38,* 124–133. doi:10.3109/13668250.2012.760728

Green, A. E., Miller, E. A., & Aarons, G. A. (2013). Transformational leadership moderates the relationship between emotional exhaustion and turnover intention among community mental health providers. *Community Mental Health Journal, 49,* 373–9. doi:http://dx.doi.org.library.capella.edu/10.1007/s10597-011-9463-0

Hetzler, L (2016) Minimum wage and the revolving door: Poor pay and high turnover rates of direct support professionals. Retrieved from https://www.reliaslearning.com/blog/minimum-wage-and-the-revolving-door-poor-pay-and-high-turnover-rates-of-direct-support-professionals

Hewitt, A. (1998). Community residential core competencies: Necessary competencies for direct support staff working in community residential services for people with developmental disabilities. Minneapolis: University of Minnesota, Institute on Community Integration, Research and Training Center on Community Living.

Hewitt, A., Keiling, K., Sauer, J., McCulloh, N., & McBride, M. (2006). Find, choose, and keep great DSPs: A toolkit for individuals with disabilities and families. Minneapolis, MN: Research and Training Center on Community Living, University of Minnesota.

Hewitt, A., & Larson, S. (2007). The direct support workforce in community supports to individuals with developmental disabilities: Issues, implications, and promising practices. Developmental Disabilities Research Reviews, 13, 178–187. doi:10.1002/mrdd.20151

Hewitt, A., Larson, S., Edelstein, S., Seavey, D., Hoge, M.A., & Morris, J. (2008). A synthesis of direct service workforce demographics and challenges across intellectual/developmental disabilities, aging, physical disabilities, and behavioral health. Minneapolis: University of Minnesota, Institute on Community Integration, Research and Training Center on Community Living.

Hewitt, A., Nord, D., Larson, S., & Lakin, C. K. (2008). Building careers, supporting lives: Outcomes of a competency based national training program. *Journal of Intellectual Disability Research, 52,* p. 763.

Hewitt, A., Lakin, C., Macbeth, J., Kramme, J., & Benway, C. (2017). *President's Committee for People with Intellectual Disabilities Report to the President 2017: America's direct support workforce crisis: Effects on people with intellectual disabilities, families, communities and the U.S. Economy*. Washington D.C.: President's Committee for People with Intellectual Disabilities. Retrieved from: https://www.acl.gov/sites/default/files/programs/2018-02/2017%20PCPID%20Full%20Report_0.PDF

Hewitt, A., Taylor, M., Kramme, J., Pettingel, S., & Sedlezky, L. (2015). Implementing direct support professional credentialing in New York: Technical report. Minneapolis: University of Minnesota, Research and Training Center on Community Living. Retrieved from https://www.opwdd.ny.gov/opwdd_about/commissioners_page/DSP-CredentialingReport

Hiersteiner, D. (2016). National Core Indicators: 2015 Staff Stability Survey Report. Cambridge: Human Services Research Institute and The National Association of State Directors of Developmental Disabilities Services, Inc.

Larson, S. A., & Hewitt, A. S. (Eds.). (2005). Staff recruitment, retention, and training strategies for community human services organizations. Paul H Brookes Publishing Company.

Larson, S., Nord, D., Salmi, P., Doljanac, R., & Hewitt, A. (2008). Critical competencies and priority training needs for frontline supervisors. *Journal of Intellectual Disability Research, 52,* p. 763.

Larson, S. A., Eschenbacher, H. J., Anderson, L. L., Taylor, B., Pettingell, S., Hewitt, A., Sowers, M., & Bourne, M.L. (2017). In-home and residential long-term supports and services for persons with intellectual or developmental disabilities: Status and trends through 2015. Minneapolis: University of Minnesota, Research and Training Center on Community Living, Institute on Community Integration.

Leadership Council of Aging Organizations (2012) The direct care workforce: A report on practices to promote quality long term care. Leadership Council of Aging Organizations. Retrieved from http://www.lcao.org/files/2012/12/LCAO-LTSS-REPORT.pdf

MediSked. (2016). The Staffing Struggle is Real. Retrieved online from http://www.medisked.com/resources/the-staffing-struggle-is-real/

Marquand, A., & York, A. (2016). Squaring to the challenge: Who will bBe tomorrow's caregivers?. *Generations, 40*(1), 10–7.

National Alliance of Direct Support Professionals. (2018). Accredited education curricula. Retrieved from: https://www.nadsp.org/accredited-education-curricula/

National Association of State Developmental Disabilities Directors. (2016). 2015 Staff Stability Survey Report. Retrieved from https://www.hsri.org/files/uploads/publications/2015_Staff_Stability_Survey_Report_V2.pdf

National Association of Direct Support Professionals (NADSP). 15 NADSP competency areas (2017). Retrieved from https://nadsp.org/15-competency-areas/.

National Association of Direct Support Professionals (NADSP). List of accredited curricula (2017). Retrieved from https://nadsp.org/list-of-accredited-curricula/.

Ng, S. M., Ke, G. N., & Raymond, W. (2014). The mediating role of work locus of control on the relationship among emotional intelligence, organisational citizenship behaviours, and mental health among nurses. *Australian Journal of Psychology, 66*, 207–215. doi:10.1111/ajpy.12049

Olmstead v. L.C., No. 98–536, 527 581 (1999).

Paraprofessional Healthcare Institute (2017). Workforce Data Center. Retrieved from https://phinational.org/policy-research/workforce-data-center/

Paraprofessional Healthcare Institute. (2001). Direct-care health workers: The unnecessary crisis in long-term care. Retrieved from https://www.phinational.org/sites/phinational.org/files/clearinghouse/Aspen.pdf

Paraprofessional Healthcare Institute. (2011). Who are direct-care workers? *PHI Facts.* Washington, D.C.: Author. Retrieved from https://www.phinational.org/sites/phinational.org/files/clearinghouse/PHI%20Facts%203.pdf

Paraprofessional Healthcare Institute (2013). Fact #3, America's Direct-Care Workforce. New York: Paraprofessional Healthcare Institute. Retrieved from https://phinational.org/sites/phinational.org/files/phi-facts-3.pdf

Paraprofessional Healthcare Institute (2015). Paying the price: How poverty wages undermine home care in America. Washington, D.C.: Author. Retrieved from https://phinational.org/sites/phinational.org/files/research-report/paying-the-price.pdf

Rehabilitation Act of 1973. 29 U.S.C. § 701 et seq. (1973)

Robbins, E., Dilla, B., Sedlezky,L., & Johnson Sirek A. (2013). Coverage of direct service workforce continuing education and training within Medicaid policy and rate setting: A toolkit for state Medicaid agencies. Retrieved from https://www.medicaid.gov/medicaid/ltss/downloads/workforce/dsw-training-rates-toolkit.pdf

Taylor, M., Bradley, V., & Warren Jr., R. (1996). The community support skill standards: Tools for managing change and achieving outcome. Human Services Research Institute: Cambridge, MA.

U.S. Government Publishing Office (2003). Proceedings of Congress and General Congressional Publications. Congressional Direct Support Professional Recognition Resolution in 2003 S. Con. Res. 21/H. Con. Res. 94. 108 Congressional record Volume 148, Issue 158. H10297-10300